investing in residential income property

investing in residential income property

Douglas M. Temple

HENRY REGNERY COMPANY · CHICAGO

Library of Congress Cataloging in Publication Data

Temple, Douglas M.
    Investing in residential income property.

    1. Real estate investment.   2. Real estate investment—United States.
    I. Title.
HD1379.T285   332.6'324'0973   74-6917
ISBN 0-8092-8404-9

Published by Henry Regnery Company
114 West Illinois Street, Chicago, Illinois 60610
Manufactured in the United States of America
Library of Congress Catalog Card Number: 74-6917
International Standard Book Number: 0-8092-8404-9

To my wife
Hazel

Contents

Introduction

In the search for financial security the individual is faced with a multitude of alternatives. The problem of finding a way to build an estate to provide that security is probably more difficult now than it ever has been in the past. Inflation is the villain!

Many informed investment advisers have concluded that the owner of real estate probably has a somewhat better than average chance to beat inflation. But the problem is not solved simply by purchasing the first piece of real estate you come across. Many people have achieved substantial wealth through real estate but they have worked hard at it. It is important to know how to determine value and hence the maximum price to pay. You must be familiar with how to arrange the best financing and how to maximize the benefits of income tax regulation. You have to have an investment strategy geared to your objectives. You then must be prepared to search for, buy, and manage the property that will be the most suitable for *you*.

This book has been written to provide a guide to the amateur investor—the person who wants to try to find his financial security through real estate investing. There are many ways to invest in real estate, and they are explained, discussed, and compared. The information and ideas will make it easier for you not only to decide what you want to do but also give you step-by-step guidance in making an investment in residential income property, the type of real estate investment considered to be extremely suitable for the investor wishing to be active in handling his own affairs. It is also a type having a very favorable chance of making it possible to achieve investment objectives.

There are two basic investment objectives: to maximize current income to replace or supplement employment income, and to maximize long-term capital appreciation, particularly for retirement. Here are some of the reasons why an investment in residential income property may appeal to you as you try to achieve these objectives.

Maximum income from your investment in an apartment building will be generated by skillfully managing the property to minimize operating expense, obtain maximum rents, and use as little borrowed funds as possible. A well situated and managed property can return an after-tax rate in excess of that obtainable from investments with comparable risk. Because income tax rules permit charging not only all cash expenditures but also depreciation against income, the ultimate income tax payable on the return is much less than on, say, bonds, business profits, or other income-producing investments. And because depreciation is a non-cash expense, the actual cash return is greater than the after-tax income. Even for owners who buy an apartment to provide current income, there also is the possibility of long-term capital appreciation to be "cashed in" when the property is sold.

Many types of investments can be made with partly borrowed funds, thus employing leverage—the technique of using someone else's money to earn a return greater than the cost of the borrowing. The advantage of the real estate investment is the relatively lower cost of using leverage. The property is used as security for the loan—and mortgage rates are lower than for loans for many other types of investments.

And back to inflation. What investment can offer the greatest hedge against the future reduced purchasing power of the dollar?

The investor needs a vehicle that will increase in value at at least the inflation rate or else he is losing ground. At least in the past, much real estate has tended to increase in value over time and so to the extent that that will continue in the future, it has the necessary characteristic. In fact, the factors that cause increased prices for goods and services act on real estate values in the same manner. Long-term capital gains are taxed on a favorable basis.

Many people have discovered that it is desirable to shelter their current income from income taxes and thus there are many investment opportunities offered as "tax shelters." Real estate—and in particular, residential income property—is highly suitable for the investor seeking to minimize income to be shared with Uncle Sam. A unique characteristic of residential income property is the investor's ability to have an operating loss for tax purposes, largely because of depreciation expense, yet have enough cash from rents to cover the cash expenses. Under these conditions the loss can be charged against other income, thus reducing the total amount of income taxes payable. For certain types of residential income property accelerated depreciation is permitted, thus increasing the tax-sheltering benefits.

Just how do you measure the return from an investment? With a savings account the interest earnings, when left to compound, give an illusion of growth—your ending balance is greater than the beginning. Realize, of course, that as long as the inflation rate exceeds the after-tax interest rate, you are actually losing money by using a savings account as an investment. As a shelter for emergency use funds, OK. As an investment, probably very poor. Typical well-managed apartment houses return for their owners a current income rate in excess of interest rates even on savings certificates.

There may be some opportunities to buy corporate bonds at a discount. If you hold them to maturity and they are redeemed at face or par you may have achieved what is thought of as a capital gain. The problem is that the reason for the discount is the relatively low annual yield rate and the "appreciation" in part offsets it. And there is the possibility of default. Certainly no opportunity for appreciation beyond the redemption value.

In real estate your investment return may come from as many as three sources: current income (net of rents and operating expenses), long-term appreciation in value, and mortgage reduction (equity build-up) if you have used borrowed funds and the debt is repaid out of income. The tenants truly may buy the property for you!

So you see, when it comes to computing yields, just what are you including? It is not practical to make any statement of overall yield from an investment in real estate that can be compared directly with alternative opportunities. The matter is too complex. But the various yields for a specific property can be calculated. To show how is a major purpose of this book.

A possible disadvantage to investing in real estate is its relative lack of liquidity. Residential real estate in particular is most suitable for long-term investing. It is difficult and expensive to get your money out of this type of real estate on short notice and soon after you have invested. For the long term, however, the demand for multiple-unit housing appears strong and recovering an original investment plus realizing the capital gain should be relatively easy. There is an effective market mechanism for buying and selling—thousands of real estate brokers—thus providing the investor with ample assistance in making and liquidating investments.

Now that you are convinced (you are, aren't you?) that an investment in residential income property is for you, you'll want to know more about how to make such an investment. Read on.

Here are some of the things you will learn from the following pages:

How to analyze an investment opportunity to calculate the maximum price to pay, and what your before-and-after-income tax yield will be both for the first year and for the long term

How to arrange financing, negotiate the purchase, and close the deal

How to manage the property to obtain the greatest return and how to prepare for liquidating the investment

How to maintain adequate accounting records with a minimum of effort—and to do it yourself if you wish.

You will find a complete example of a typical investment in a fourplex, illustrated by the use of a specially devised fact sheet and analysis forms. You can use these in analyzing your own opportunities. The investment tables in the back of the book will be of particular help in making some of the calculations.

There are no guarantees of success offered here. By following the ideas and suggestions presented, however, you should have a better than otherwise chance of success in achieving financial security through investing in residential income property. Others have already, why not you?

1

Investing in Real Estate

U<small>NDERNEATH</small> everything is the land. There is a finite supply of land, and for all practical purposes no more is being created. Yet there is a continuing increase in the population and the demand for land. With that built-in advantage, real estate obviously has something "extra" going for it that most other investment vehicles do not. But not all kinds of real estate investment are right for all people all of the time. How do you choose?

In this chapter we will look at several kinds of real estate investment vehicles: owning your own home, vacant and raw land, industrial and commercial property, condominiums, syndication, real estate investment trusts, and residential income property.

After considering the special features of each real estate investment vehicle from an investment point of view, including income tax considerations, the conclusion will become inescapable: for the "small" private investor, residential income property—the small apartment building—is the best real estate investment vehicle.

What is Real Estate?

A piece of land defined and designated by a description of

boundaries or other form of "legal description" is known as real estate or real property. When a structure is placed on the land, it becomes a part of the "realty." It is possible legally to treat land and structure separately, but most of the time the term real estate means land and any and all things attached to it.

Because real estate is an asset, title to which can be transferred, modified, and so on, there needs to be an orderly way to describe a particular piece of real property. There are two basic systems of describing land and its improvements: by "metes and bounds" and by lot and block number in a subdivision.

In colonial times tracts of land were described in writing by using topographical features such as rivers, trees, rocks, fences, and structures as points of reference. Even today in many states, land descriptions may include such things. This is the "metes and bounds" method. One should be able to follow such a description on the ground, so to speak.

As towns were developed, land was divided into blocks, then into smaller units on which houses and commercial buildings were built. In the process surveyors prepared maps showing the area divided into uniform-sized segments. Each segment was numbered for ease of reference, and a copy of the map was filed as a public record. Today it is customary legally to describe a piece of real estate by its lot and block number in a subdivision of a particular name. This system is further tied into a federal system of land identification, and it is from this federal system, the so-called Government Survey, established in 1785, that we get such terms as "principal meridian," "township," and "range."

The legal description of a piece of property is a matter of public record, and all changes and transfers of title are recorded by a County Recorder or Registrar of Deeds or similarly titled public official. We will discuss additional aspects of this later when we cover escrows and title insurance.

Under ordinary circumstances no mention whatever is made of buildings or lots. *Title* to the property is transferred, and that, unless stated to the contrary, automatically includes anything that is a part of the realty—not only buildings, but mineral rights and right to the airspace above the land, though this latter right, of course, does not mean you can charge United Airlines with trespassing when its plane flies over your property.*

To summarize: customarily to obtain title to a piece of real estate we arrange for a deed, the title document, to be filed and recorded, thus showing to the world at large who is the title-holder of, say, Lot 4, Block 3, Wistful Vista Estates, Shangri-La County, State of Paradise, U.S.A.

Advantages to Real Estate Investment

There are, of course, several ways in which real property can be used for investment purposes, but the following characteristics apply across the board. First, there is utility. A building can serve as housing for people, for a commercial activity, or for government service. Land by itself can be used just to look at (as a park), to grow agricultural products, or to be held for conversion to another purpose. In short, land and buildings can always be *used* (and the use will dictate the economic value).

When land is used for an economic activity, the owner will either gain the return represented by the value of the use or will be paid a rent geared to the utility value. The owner's goal should be to put his land to the "highest and best use" in order to command the maximum return. If you own land, you can use it yourself or you can realize an income from it (an owner/user must not forget that there is a use-value to the property even though a rental payment is not received).

If you own land and change its use to increase its utility, you increase its economic value. But the opposite may also occur. Thus the sound management of property requires that it be put to the highest and best use. We will discuss later the prospects for investment gain by, for example, remodeling a building to increase the

---

*In theory the owner of the land could erect a building without limit of height, as the ownership is limited only by the horizontal boundaries of the parcel. The use of property is, however, subject to building codes and zoning ordinances as well as potential court action by neighbors objecting to a structure that would infringe on their rights to a view or for esthetic considerations. An owner may grant permission to, say, a governmental agency to construct an elevated road or railway over his land, thus through his "airspace."

number of rental units; at this point we need simply to realize that many types of real estate lend themselves to the making of changes that may lead to increased value both currently and in the future.

In general over the past forty years, the money value of real estate has been increasing—and at a rate greater than the rate at which the value of money has been decreasing. In other words, there has been a *real* gain. The increased demand for real estate by a burgeoning population, the increased cost of construction, and inflation have all caused the value of much real property to appreciate. Moreover, although all physical assets, including buildings, have a tendency to wear out—to depreciate—in the case of buildings in the recent past such depreciation has been more than offset by appreciation; a 2-bedroom home bought in 1946 for $5,000 now may sell for $20,000. Not every piece of property has increased in value in this way or to this extent, of course, but enough have to support the generalization that in the past appreciation has exceeded depreciation and there has been a long-term gain for the owner of real estate.

This gain is *not* automatic and depends on many factors, some of which are quite beyond the control of the owner-investor. Other kinds of assets—shares of stock, for example—at various times in the past have also appreciated in value (the converse has also occurred). The difference, however, is that the owner of real estate may be in a position to *influence* the change in value of his asset, whereas a stockholder who does not hold a controlling interest in the ownership of the corporation is essentially powerless to do anything about the changes in the value of his investment.

Thus the second advantage to real estate investment is its *potential for long-term capital appreciation.*

Real estate investments also can produce significant *income*, from lease or rental income that exceeds expenses or from interest income from making loans secured by real estate.

Real estate, in short, can provide means to the realization of both basic investment objectives—income *and* long-term gain.

Investment in other vehicles may also produce current income and/or long-term gain, of course. But only real estate provides massive *tax advantages*. Thanks to Congress's recognition of the need to provide tax benefit incentives to achieve socially desirable goals, income and gain from certain types of real estate investments are treated beneficially under the income tax laws. This generally holds true also for state income tax regulations.

By the use of the options granted, depreciation expense can be charged against rental income, for example, and thus serve to convert current income to long-term capital gain. And why is that important? Because long-term capital gains are taxed generally at 50 percent of the rate applicable to current income.*

Real estate investment qualifies for these tax breaks because it is designed to contribute to the social good (as well as to make money for the investor). There is a clear need for new housing in virtually all parts of the country. In some cases, government has built it. In the overall, however, it has been government policy to leave the job to the private sector. But the private sector works best under maximum profit incentives, the mainstay of our free enterprise system. By allowing depreciation to be charged against current income, thus reducing income tax payable on earnings, and minimizing the tax payable on long-term gains, government has made real estate projects attractive to investors, thus providing a continuing supply of housing, particularly in the form of apartment buildings. Thus the "loopholes" are not really loopholes at all. The rules were deliberately devised to achieve specific objectives. Those capable of creating housing, for example, are in fact encouraged to utilize the tax regulations to their full advantage.

Real estate investors consider this factor very carefully; it is of major concern. But it is equally important to realize that even if the tax advantages currently available to investors are eliminated, the fundamental advantages of a real estate investment will still apply.

---

*This has been true in the past and is currently so. Proposals have been made to Congress to change these favorable tax "loopholes" to reduce or eliminate the benefits to real estate investors. A prudent investor will keep current on these developments and act appropriately. You might even let your Congressman know how you feel about such proposals.

The conclusion then must be that there probably is some form of real estate that is the "right" investment for you. Note that we have not said anything yet about how much money you need; that comes later. So do not be inhibited at this point by worrying about whether your investment nest egg is adequate. You will probably be pleasantly surprised. In the meantime, let us look at the real estate investment choices available to you.

Owning Your Own Home

We have said there are two ways in which to invest in real estate: to buy it and to lend money on it. We will discuss the latter choice later. The first choice involves your personal living accommodation. The great American dream is to own your own home; nonetheless, it is a real estate investment.

The single-family home you own and occupy does not produce rental income, but your cost for housing is reduced from what you would pay if you did not own a home by the amount you can deduct on your income tax return for property taxes, uninsured physical property damage or loss over a minimum, and mortgage interest, if any. Too, if you own the property long enough, keep it in reasonable repair and the neighborhood doesn't go to pot, you stand a good chance of selling the property for more than you paid for it, thus realizing a long-term gain. Moreover, you may have an additional advantage because of the favorable income tax treatment of that gain. Indeed, the income tax advantage to home ownership is one of the prime reasons for the widespread development of condominiums (reputed to be an invention of the Romans), because you do not have to own and occupy a single-family dwelling to qualify for these benefits. You can buy an apartment created with condominium ownership features and treat it, for income tax purposes, as a single-family home.*

---

*When you own a condominium unit, your ownership boundaries stop at the underside of the paint on the interior walls. You also have an undivided interest in all the common ways of the structures and the outside areas. All other condominium unit owners share this ownership with you. In effect you have bought the airspace in your unit. As a consequence you share in the property taxes and can make the appropriate income tax deduction. If you have a mortgage, the interest is likewise deductible. The purchase of condominium units is financed in the same way as single-family dwellings as far as individual unit buyers are concerned.

A co-operative apartment provides much the same benefits, except that there is less flexibility in disposing of your apartment investment than in the case of the condominium. With the latter you can sell the unit virtually as you can a single-family home. In a co-op your ownership interest is in the form of shares in the co-op association and the purchaser must meet the membership requirements of the association. In effect the purchaser must be passed on by other members. This does not necessarily pose a problem, but it may. Investment in a co-op, in short, has less liquidity.

If you live in a portion of a multiple-family dwelling that you own, such as a duplex, the tenant is helping to buy the building for you. Here again the tax laws help. To reduce your taxable income, you can deduct all of the property taxes, the mortgage interest, and, with respect to the portion rented out, depreciation and operating expenses. You declare the rents as income, of course. When you dispose of the property, your taxable long-term gain will be determined by the amount of depreciation charged against income during the time you owned it. (How this is handled will be discussed in great detail later.)

Closely related to an investment in your home is that of a vacation or "second" home property. Here too you have the opportunity for long-term gain if the property appreciates. If you choose to rent it out for the time you do not wish to use it, you have the potential for rental income. The accounting becomes slightly more complex in such cases because you have to separate the time you use it for yourself from the time it is used by others for a charge. Thus you must prorate the depreciation and perhaps some of the operating expenses to arrive at the amounts to be deducted from your taxable income.

There has been recently a fascinating development in how second-home or vacation-type property ownership involves partnership. Let's assume you would like to have the use of a house or apartment at a resort but do not want to own the property completely. Rent is too expensive. Further assume that your need would be met if you could use the property for one month in the year. Well, find eleven others with the same idea, form a partnership, buy the property, and agree as to which month each partner will have the use of the building. In this way, each partner can charge against his other income one-twelfth of the property taxes and mortgage interest. No depreciation could be charged unless you rented out your month. Then you would report the rental income received and charge expenses, including your share of the depreciation. The net result is to minimize the cost of using the vacation accommodation. There would also be the potential for long-term gain on the resale. We have described here the basics of a limited partnership or syndicate; much more on that later.

Some creative real estate and title insurance people have come up with another way of doing what has just been described. Instead of forming a partnership to own real estate, they have found a way to write a deed so that during a stated *period of time* each calendar year the titleholder owns the property. He is free to sell his ownership interest, arrange financing, and so on. This provides more flexibility than the partnership-syndicate plan. The technique is referred to as "Interval Ownership" and its development is credited to Interval Incorporated, Coral Gables, Florida. The staff of the Lawyers Title Insurance Corporation assisted in setting up this imaginative plan.

Speaking further of real estate you might own, we should look at mobile homes. It is now a long time since "trailer" was the designation of less than desirable living accommodations. Today there are luxurious mobile home parks where you can have all the benefits of the latest in housing comforts at relatively low cost. You can spend large amounts, too.

How is this an investment in real estate? In many mobile home communities you rent the space and buy the mobile home. From a tax point of view the only deduction you may have is interest expense and a motor vehicle tax. The owner of the land has rental income and property tax and other operating expense. But it is also possible to set things up so you can have the advantages a non-mobile home owner has. Buy the lot and finance the mobile home much the way you would obtain a home mortgage. Some mobile home parks are simply land subdivisions where lots are for sale subject to rules concerning the installation of mobile homes. Lenders now will make loans for terms up to fifteen years and there is even federal mortgage insurance available. Then, when you want to take a trip, rent the mobile home to someone and charge depreciation in addition to property taxes and loan interest against your taxable income. Now you're a landlord (in a mobile home park).

Finally, let's look at the advantages of buying a homesite for a second home. There has been substantial development of vacation areas to make small plots of land available to those who, while they may use it at first simply to camp on, ultimately build a cabin or year-round second home. There is more to say later about buying raw land as a speculation; for the present we are concerned with those planning to use and build for themselves. Once you take title, or enter into a sales contract under which you are to pay the property taxes, you can charge as a deductible expense the amount of those taxes. Any financing expense is also deductible. Here again, you have a real estate investment even though you may think of it as simply a small plot of the good earth high in the mountains. There is also a potential for long-term gain, and certainly the land salesman wants you to believe that. Regrettably, in every part of the country there have been abuses and purchasers have been disappointed, though some, of course, have in fact done quite well. In some cases the potential is clearly there.

To summarize: in terms of future financial security, you should seriously consider *owning* the place where you live. Even for situations where in the past it has been normal only to be able to rent, arrangements now can be made to be an owner-occupant. But now that it is clear your first investment in real estate should be for your own personal living accommodation, we are ready to look at some additional opportunities to build future values.

Investing in Land

Why not go out into the country, find some acreage for sale at a few dollars an acre, hold it for a few years, and sell it to a subdivider at thousands an acre and thus become rich? It can be done. It has been done. It will be done again in the future. What are your chances of making a success of it?

Development Potential

Here are some of the problems to overcome. Will there be an opportunity to develop the property? This land we are discussing is referred to as "pre-development" land and the expectation is that there will be development in the future; that is, the property will be subdivided, built on, or put to some use that will increase its economic value. *Guessing where development will come is a risky business.*

It is possible, if you are going to get involved on a big scale, to have feasibility studies made by experts in the field. Such experts are not always correct in their projections, and all you really have for your money is an educated guess as to the possible future of your land. If you are involved on a small scale, you will have to trust your own judgment. And that is a risky business. In short, while there are large profits to be made in speculating in raw pre-development land, commensurate with such profits is considerable risk.

Along with the risk are expenses. During the time you hold the raw land, you will have to pay property taxes. If the land is such that you can rent it for agricultural or storage purposes, that income might offset the expense. But never forget that when it comes to investing, your funds can *always* earn, as a minimum, the interest rate on a risk-free savings account. Unless you can be reasonably assured that your land investment is growing in value at at least the savings account rate, think more than twice about getting involved. There are other, better places for your money.

On the other hand, all presently developed property was once pre-development land. Timing of your investment is most important. Buying acreage shortly before there is a need for it to be sub-divided is what you are aiming to do.

You may even find it exhilarating, and profitable, to sub-divide it yourself. But be careful: subdividing is no longer an activity for amateurs. Most states have laws that govern the subdividing of land and sale of the parcels to the public. The basic requirement applicable to most situations is that a subdivision report, disclosing all pertinent facts about the property, be prepared, approved by the state real estate department or commission, and made available to prospective purchasers. There are also local zoning and land use laws to consider and comply with before subdivided land can be offered. As a subdivider you will incur expense for land surveying, legal advice, and probably financial assistance. In most areas it is almost as complicated to divide a large lot into two or three smaller pieces as it is to create a thousand homesites from acreage.

But there is substantial profit potential, and you should not be discouraged from at least investigating what would be required in a particular instance. Note that if you are a prospective purchaser of a plot in a new subdivision, you must insist that the seller give you all of the information required by the local subdivision regulation.

Is the purchase of a vacant city lot a sound real estate investment? Perhaps. The owner will receive a property tax bill and that expense must be considered as an additional investment in the project even though there may be some income tax benefit. Having a tax-deductible expense does not *automatically* mean you are making money. No matter what tax bracket you are in, the expense is reduced only by the income tax saved; you still will have paid out some money. For example, you buy a lot for $10,000 and plan to hold it for resale at a higher price because you see that property of this type is scarce and you have good reason to expect that because of changes taking place in the neighborhood the lot will be very attractive a few years hence. You get a property tax bill of $250 for a year, and you are in a 40-percent tax bracket. Your actual out-of-pocket expense for property taxes on the lot is $150. Thus to determine whether the lot was a good investment, add the net tax expense each year you owned it to the original cost and then deduct that total from the net proceeds.

Another factor to consider when investing in vacant land is

zoning. Virtually all communities today have master plans and zoning and building ordinances. Property will be zoned or approved for specified uses; that means that some uses are forbidden. It may be possible to have the zoning changed, but it would be unwise always to count on being able to persuade a planning commission and, perhaps, the adjacent property owners to approve the changes. One hedge in such circumstances is to offer to buy *subject to* obtaining appropriate zoning modifications, thus sharing the risk with the seller.

An important characteristic of residential income property, as will be emphasized later, is the fact that a multiple-dwelling unit —say, a fourplex—often can be erected on land otherwise used for a single-family dwelling, actually quadrupling the land use. That is one of the major reasons for the attractiveness of a small apartment as a real estate investment. The cost of the land is spread over several units. As a prospective investor in vacant city lots, watch for opportunities to buy land that is or can be zoned for multiple-family use. *Aim to purchase land that is not being used for its highest and best use and for a price that does not reflect such use.* Be sure, of course, that you can obtain the necessary approval to put it to the highest and best use and thus realize a return commensurate with your risk and ingenuity (and good fortune).

A final word about vacant land. Up to this point we have talked mostly in terms of land being subdivided and used for dwelling purposes. There are other uses. In days gone by, much industrial and commerical activity was located according to considerations that did not include much land planning. In recent times, land planners have applied some of the basic principles of residential subdividing to the creation of industrial parks and shopping centers.

If you are aware of a community that is underdeveloped as far as shopping centers are concerned, that might mean an investment opportunity for you. Industrial parks often receive preferential local tax concessions in order to attract jobs and payrolls. It might just be that your talent and resources are needed right where you are to create such a project.

Investing in Commercial Property

Some prospective investors in real estate are attracted to store and office property where, they feel, getting tenants who would always pay their rent would not be too difficult. For many situations this observation is quite sound, but what frequently happens is that the tenant becomes successful in his business, decides to retain for himself the benefits of owning property, and thus becomes an ex-tenant. On the other hand, businessmen are often better off retaining their capital in the business and charging rent expense on a fully tax-deductible basis. There *is* a role for a landlord.

How would you like to have a large nationwide food chain ask you to build a building to their specifications and agree to sign a long-term lease, particularly when you found that your bank would lend you money on the strength of the lease? No apparent risk in getting a tenant and certainly no rent-collection problems. The tenant will even offer to pay for the insurance and property taxes. Large corporations often erect buildings, sell them to investors, and lease them in order to minimize their investment in real estate because they can make more on those funds in their business. (This is known as "lease-back.")

So what's the catch? Although the companies will want an option to renew the lease, they are not under any obligation to do so. If at that time the property is no longer suitable for their use, perhaps because of neighborhood deterioration, they simply walk away. The owner-investor is then faced with finding a new tenant, and that might be difficult—and expensive.

In the meanwhile, of course, he will have experienced a relatively trouble-free investment in real estate. Indeed, the technique of "sale and lease-back" is widely used in many different situations, including federal, state, and local government projects. Many post office buildings, for example, are rented from private investors, who have had buildings constructed to government specifications.

The areas of real estate investment discussed thus far generally have involved the owner-operator. That is to say, you have done the investing and managing yourself. And there are some distinct advantages to that: you can exercise control and your own judgment and take action you think will be in your best interest. Later, we are going to go into great detail as to how you can do just that with a small apartment house. At this point, however, so that you can evaluate all the alternatives you face, we need to look at how you can become involved in a real estate investment without personal activity and active participation in the managing of the investment.

Non-Participative Investing

Here, by definition, we mean that it is solely your money that is put to work, not yourself. The most passive role is that of the person who lends money on property by way of mortgages and trust deeds. In addition, as we have seen, there are opportunities to own real estate and rent it to others. But in such cases someone has to obtain tenants, collect the rent, pay the expenses, and generally tend to the business. The person who puts up the money does not have to do that work himself; he can hire a manager to take care of the bulk of such activity, and that additional expense may be well worth it—depending on the likes, talents, and obligations of the owner. But there is one step further removed from day-to-day involvement: the syndicate.

Syndicate is the term applied to a limited partnership formed for the purpose of owning and operating a real estate investment. There are two main objectives to this form of ownership: it allows owners to have the income tax benefits of operating gains or losses as their own and thus avoids the double taxation of business profits that takes place, for example, in corporations; and it permits the owners to avoid any personal involvement in the day-to-day operation. The syndicate device is widely used outside the field of real estate, too.

The syndicate will consist of a general partner, who often is a real estate management firm or building contractor, and the individual investors, who are limited partners; that is, the individual's liability is restricted to the amount of his investment or contribution to the partnership. Established properly, the limited partnership itself pays no income tax. The operating gains or losses pass through to be reported by each investor; this device consequently has been widely used for tax sheltering.

A limited partner in a real estate syndicate enjoys all of the advantages of current income or tax sheltering, *plus* long-term capital gain prospective benefits without having to find the investment or tenants or manage or, eventually, sell the property to realize the gain. Obviously the people who perform these functions must be paid, and that cost is borne by the limited partners. In theory, however, through management expertise, volume buying, and other economies of scale, the cost should be minimized. A major objective is to run the syndicate in such a way that the individual partner-investor makes even more profit than he would if he were to do everything himself. Some syndicates have achieved that objective; many have been serious failures.

Another form of non-participative investing is provided by the Real Estate Investment Trust—REIT. One of the disadvantages of the syndicate is that a limited partner may have trouble liquidating his investment because there normally is not a market for partnership interests. This problem is overcome, in theory if not in practice, by the REIT, an organization formed to invest in various forms of real estate and to hold in trust the assets of those who put up the money. The investors buy "shares of beneficial interest" in the trust; a group of experienced and reputable persons serve as trustees. Once the trust is off the ground, the shares may be marketable in a manner similar to shares of stock. Many REITs obtain listings on the major stock exchanges for that purpose. Under federal income tax laws, if the income of the trust comes from specified forms of investment—primarily ownership of real property or mortgage loans—and each year at least 90 percent of the income is distributed to shareholders, there is *no* tax assessed on the trust. In turn, the shareholders declare income from the trust, and such income is taxed to the individual on a current or long-term capital gain basis, according to the way in which the money is earned by the trust. Thus double taxation is avoided as long as the trust continues to qualify.

Both investment objectives we have been considering—current income and long-term capital gain—may be achieved through investment in a REIT. Some REITs are operated primarily for current income and concentrate the use of the investors' funds in long-term real estate mortgages. Others buy and operate income-producing properties and expect capital appreciation. However, the REIT may not be as suitable for tax sheltering as a syndicate because of the restriction on passing tax losses as freely through to the investor.

The trustees of a REIT contract for services to be provided by specialists in property management and mortgage servicing. As a general rule, it is not the function of the trust to do other than provide the funds for purchase or lending, make the decisions with respect to the investments, and supervise the independent contractors who take care of the day-to-day activity of running the trust properties or investments. The closest the shareholder of the trust gets to the action is when he votes on the election of the trustees, who are his representatives much the way directors of a corporation represent the stockholders. The REIT appeals to the investor who wants to have his money work in real estate but who does not want to be involved personally with the actual process.

Is a REIT a good investment? The REIT is as good as the people operating it, a truism applicable to all situations. That does not say much, however. Note that the investor has little or no opportunity to influence the nature of the investments made by the trustees or the decisions concerning contracts for services or the disposition of assets. Further, it is essential that the investor understand the objectives of the REIT and match them with his own. If he wants only long-term gain and no current income, only a few REITs currently in operation are suitable. Many have been established to obtain relatively high yields for current income in competition with other types of lenders such as life insurance companies and banks. One risk REITs run is that of becoming locked into fixed-return investments that fall in value relative to alternative forms of investment. There is little opportunity for capital appreciation for REITs operating as lenders; that happens only if the REITs buy mortgages at a discount and they are paid off without loss—and this is not customary REIT practice.

Most REITs established for capital appreciation invest funds in operating properties from which current income, or at least no operating loss, is expected. The expectation is that the trust will ultimately sell the asset for more than its cost, thus obtaining the long-term gain. The proceeds would then be distributed to the shareholders.

Complex real estate projects require large sums of money. The purchase and conversion of a large acreage into a regional shopping center or the construction of a fifty-story office building involve cash requirements that far exceed the capacity of most financial institutions operating by themselves. Often several banks or life insurance companies may go together to put up the needed resources. A REIT that has amassed fairly large sums by widespread sale of its shares may have the ability to finance projects too large for institutions on their own or even in concert. But not all REITs are that large, and even if a particular REIT is, it is unlikely to concentrate too heavily in single projects.

All the same, the REIT device has made it possible to finance larger developments than have generally been possible without it. Extra earnings often are possible because of size, and some REITs will make them; this quality, therefore, gives the individual investor an opportunity to participate in huge projects. Conversely, the larger a project, the further it has to fall if things go wrong. The extra profit potential carries with it extra risk.

A final note on non-participative investing: either a syndicate or a REIT may allow you to meet your investment objective without "getting your hands dirty." But perhaps you would prefer a middle-ground position that allows you to make more decisions with respect to the operation. In that case, you should employ a manager or property management service to do "the dirty work" while you maintain the major decision-making authority.

The costs of professional management are easily ascertainable. Often the charge is based on a percentage of the rents collected, but the percentage will vary with the services to be rendered, which vary according to the contract you enter into. We will go into more detail on this subject later when we discuss what an owner does for himself. For the present we can list the following areas:

1. *Find tenants.* Your goal will be to reduce to zero the time elapsing between the departure of one tenant and the arrival of

the next. There is no way to recover rent for vacancies. This requires that you know in advance when a tenant plans to leave, a matter usually taken care of by the terms of the lease or rental agreement requiring notice of termination. Then you need to know where to find prospective tenants. If the property management service is also in the real estate business, it may have a ready source of prospects. If you do this work yourself, you will have to advertise and do whatever is necessary to bring the property to the attention of those who might rent or lease it.

Not every property is automatically rented to the first prospect. Showing property to a succession of "suspects" can be a time-consuming and even frustrating job. On the other hand, many people enjoy that type of contact and challenge. You need to decide how you stand on this. Property management services may be employed to find a tenant, in which case they would show the property and arrange for the paper work as well. The fee for this in some areas is paid by the tenant; in others, by the owner. It may also be lumped into an overall property management charge. Check for local conditions.

2. *Collect rents.* The majority of tenants pay their rent on time *and* with checks that do not bounce. Even a few bad tenants present a problem, however, and it is well to assume the worst. Some tenants respond better to the pressure applied by a third-party property manager as opposed to the owner. When contracting for property management services, specify whether the rent collection responsibility includes getting the rent regardless of difficulty or just collecting the rents the tenants offer.

3. *Repairs.* In some states, if the property is large enough, a resident manager is required by law. In addition to being a rent "cashier," the manager will ordinarily be expected to fix leaky faucets, have broken windows replaced, and so on. Otherwise, the owner must respond to requests from tenants for items of this nature. There is also the matter of decorating. You can redecorate on a regular basis—all units once every three years, for example—thus maintaining the property to a fairly high level; at the end of each lease (especially before re-renting the accommodations); or only when tenants complain. You can also advise the tenant that you will buy the materials if he will do the work.

Under your property-management service contract you should specify all the above, as well as anything else you want settled. Then problems not covered will be referred to you.

After reviewing the foregoing, you should be able to reach a decision as to how far you would like to "get involved" in operating your investment in real estate. The discussion has been general enough to apply to most forms of property to be considered for investment; it likely is most applicable to residential property.

Lending on Real Estate

Perhaps the foregoing has led you to conclude you want no part of directly managing property. You are attracted to the non-participative aspects of the syndicate or REIT but still feel either device does not give you enough control. You want control but no involvement with those using the property. There are other ways.

The traditional real estate loan is called a "mortgage." When a lender puts up funds and the borrower offers an interest in real property as security, we say that the *note*, which is the evidence of the debt, is *secured* by a *mortgage,* which is the term applied to the document in which the borrower agrees that the lender has a security interest in the property. Title to the property is vested or recorded in the name of the borrower. The lender does not acquire title and cannot sell or transfer title in the absence of a default by the borrower. As long as the indebtedness is paid off according to the loan agreement, the lender has a passive role. He just collects the payments, watching to make sure that they are made on time if the loan is to be repaid in installments, or that the principal is repaid on the date agreed upon. Borrower and lender are free to agree on repayment terms; there may be a statutory limit on interest rates, late charges, and repayment penalties. For our purpose we will consider only the typical mortgage to be repaid in monthly installments that cover repayment of principal and interest on the unpaid balance.

How can this be of interest to you as investor? Perhaps you have spent a good part of your life up to now *paying off* a mortgage and you would just as soon forget mortgages. But consider how much interest you have been paying. That was income to the lender. Why not be a lender yourself?

From the lender's point of view, the risk is that of potential default—nonpayment by the borrower. Necessarily, therefore, the loan must be secured so you will be able to obtain the amount of the unpaid balance of the loan. The mortgage provides you with a legal right to force the sale of the real property, with as much of the proceeds of the sale going to you as the debt is outstanding. If the proceeds are less than the amount needed to settle the debt, the chances are you will be out of pocket for the balance. This involves what is known as a "deficiency judgment"—getting the court to allow you to go after the borrower to recover the balance of the indebtedness over and above what was obtained from the sale. In most states the law holds that the creditor has *only* the value of the property as security, and you should realize that many things can happen to cause the value of an asset to sink below the unpaid balance of a mortgage.

Your goal, therefore, is to lend money and to have the security of a piece of property that can always be sold for enough to pay off the debt, but never to have to "foreclose" on the mortgage. The interest you charge is simply the "rent" for the use of your money.

The best kind of mortgage is a "first" mortgage, because the *first* charge on the proceeds of a foreclosure sale, after delinquent state and local, if any, property taxes have been paid, is to the unpaid balance of the *first* mortgage. If the sale does not produce enough to cover that and the expenses, there is nothing left for a second mortgagee or any other creditor. It is therefore best to be first in line, though relative to other mortgages, the first mortgage carries the lowest rate of interest because the risk is smaller than for "junior"—meaning "coming after the first"—mortgages. To lend your money for mortgages, although you can handle the advertising and, far more important, checking on the prospective borrower yourself, you may be better off going to a mortgage loan broker. This businessman who specializes in matching those having funds to lend with those who want to borrow funds charges a fee, often to the borrower, for his services. Alternatively, you can make arrangements instead with real estate brokers to call on you when loans are required in real estate deals.

Because conventional lenders such as banks, savings associations, and life insurance companies are the regular market for many types of real estate loans, the private investor is competing with some pretty heavy guns. He may have to accept more risk, but to compensate he usually can charge a higher rate of interest. Private investors also can qualify as lenders under the Federal Housing Administration (FHA) and Veteran's Administration mortgage insurance programs. For these loans interest rates generally are lower than for non-insured loans, but of course the risk is reduced.

A private lender may be able to arrange with a savings association or bank to act as a collection agent for the mortgage payments. The borrower is then instructed to make his payments accordingly. As a general rule, these arrangements do not include following up if payments become delinquent and the lender will need to establish his own procedure for learning when he should take action either to collect delinquent payments or institute foreclosure proceedings. The cost, if any, for the collection activity will simply be a charge against the investor's income, and after expenses the rate of current income on a first mortgage loan will likely exceed less risky investments. Hence mortgage loans are attractive, particularly to those wishing to maximize current income.

How can you do better? Increase the risk and you can increase the rate of return. There is considerable activity in second and even third mortgages. Remember: foreclosure could wipe out the junior mortgages. Yet those who invest in second mortgages may realize not only higher interest rates but also a gain from another feature of mortgages—purchase of the mortgage at a discount.

An additional risk factor—and, as we will see, profit potential—in all mortgages is prepayment. The basic goal of a lender is to have a safe, secure investment with repayment on a timely basis. There is expense incurred in obtaining the loan, and as long as the payments are being made the lender usually does not want the loan to be paid off in advance. If it is, he must set about to find another investment, and he may not be able to earn as much in a new situation. (The reverse of that may also be true, of course.) The risk is there. To compensate it is customary to include in the mortgage terms a penalty to be paid by the borrower if the loan is paid off in advance. This is the prepayment penalty. It may appear in any mortgage—first, second, and so on—and it usually is a percentage of the original loan or of the balance at the time of payoff, ranging from, say, 1 percent to 3. In other cases, the lender may have a sliding scale with the penalty reducing as the regular termination approaches. Others may allow for limited repayment of principal each year without penalty and charge one only if the entire loan is paid off at one time. As a borrower you will want to avoid a prepayment penalty; as a lender you'll have a different attitude. As a lender you may obtain, in addition to interest income, a lump sum amount of income or profit if the loan is paid off and a prepayment penalty exacted.

Assume you become concerned that the borrower will repay the money early. At that point you may decide you would like to get rid of this prospective bad debt by selling the note and mortgage to another investor. You would be willing to sell it for less than the outstanding balance because you are eliminating the risk. The purchaser would buy if he felt that the amount of the discount was enough to make the risk of nonpayment attractive. He would then hold the mortgage, expecting the borrower ultimately to settle the debt. The excess of payments to principal over the cost of the purchase of the mortgage would be his extra gain. There are some investors who specialize in buying mortgages at discount. Because the rewards are higher than for other types of investment, it goes without saying that the risks are greater and you really need to know what you are doing.

In all cases, all mortgages should be filed with the county recorder or registrar so their existence is a matter of public record. The lender is then protected to the extent that the title holder cannot pass clear title and thus defeat the mortgagee. He may be able to pass title—that is, sell the property—but the title will be subject to the outstanding loans; so the lender will still be in the picture. The lender may insert in the mortgage agreement a provision calling for accelerating the payment of the balance if the original borrower conveys title to someone else; the unpaid balance then becomes due and payable in full at the time the sale occurs. This device gives the lender the opportunity to evaluate the new purchaser and to decide whether he wants to have him take over the loan. We will see later the role played by title insurance in this matter.

Up to this point we have spoken in terms of you putting up funds as a loan on real estate. You may do something of the same thing, but by means other than a mortgage. Assume that you own some property, perhaps your home, and you plan to sell it; but you don't want all cash from it, preferring to use it as your real estate investment as a lender. As described, you could take back a mortgage from a purchaser. But, also, you could sell on a sales contract. The purchaser would agree to a stipulated purchase price, cash down payment, and balance in monthly payments for a designated term and rate of interest. This agreement would be in the form of a sales contract and you, the seller, would retain title to the property. In this case the buyer would record the sales contract so you could not pass clear title subsequently. At such time as the contract is fully paid you would then execute a deed to pass clear title to the contract-purchaser. Beforehand, you control title, and it might look as though you would not even have to foreclose in the event of default. All you would have to do is get the defaulter out of the property and sell it to someone else. Originally, in fact, that was the whole idea of a sales contract and the way it worked. However, generally today the contract purchaser has the same rights of redemption as a mortgagor and it would take just as long to get rid of a defaulting contract purchaser as a mortgagor. The sales contract does, however, at least give some psychological benefit for the contract seller and, other things being equal, that might be reason enough to be an investor-lender on that basis.

The question of foreclosure is replete with myth and bad odor. In days gone by when foreclosing on a mortgage was a cruel and melodramatic event, an effort was made to overcome the cumbersome and adverse nature of the mortgage financing device. The solution was third-party participation. The parties nowadays agree, at the time the loan is made, that if there is a default, the lender will be able to recover the property with a minimum of fuss. This agreement is incorporated into a deed, which is held by a disinterested trustee, such as a title insurance company or corporation set up for the purpose. If the debtor pays his obligation, the trustee then reconveys title back to him. If there is a default—and the trustee has to make sure it is a legal default—he then allows the deed to be used to convey title to the lender, who can then proceed to do whatever he wishes with the property to recover his unpaid balance. As a practical matter, the trustee may be employed to make the sale and give the proceeds to the lender.

Apart from the legal technicalities that separate the two—mortgage and deed of trust—they are really the same thing. In fact, in some states, at least for first liens or encumbrances on real property, only the deed of trust is used, not a mortgage. Although the trust deed was invented to overcome difficulties lenders felt they had with mortgages, in those states where trust deeds rather than mortgages are used, lenders still must allow for redemption by defaulting borrowers; thus as far as protecting borrowers is concerned, state laws have equalized the two devices. For our purpose, mortgage and trust deed are interchangeable terms.

We have now discussed many of the aspects of investing in real estate by way of lending money with the use of property as security. Before that we covered many of the types of real estate you can buy to realize an investment return in the form of income and/or long-term appreciation. For each of the alternatives we treated briefly the pros and cons. Now it is time to look at some of the risks inherent in real estate investment on a general basis.

Risks Involved in Real Estate Investment

Basically, an investment in real estate—whether you function as owner or as lender—is a long-term proposition. It is not reasonable to expect a profit from turning over the investment in a few days, weeks, or months. That is a characteristic of other forms of investment, but certainly not of real estate. The prospective investor who must have liquidity should stay away from real estate. Once the investment is made, freeing up the funds in the short term will ordinarily involve a loss.

Although an owner, as opposed to a lender, carries the major portion of the risk (because, at least in theory, the borrower is obligated to pay off the debt even if the project is a disaster), from a practical point of view a lender should consider all of the risks inherent in the investment even though he may have some protection against loss by way of the mortgage.

First, *before investing*, find out about zoning, planning commission regulations and plans, environmental controls, potential annexations, presence of easements and availability of utilities. A major expense is property taxes. The property may be overdue for reassessment. The tax rate for the next year may be substantially higher than before. The extra rental unit in the basement, garage, or attic may not be legal. You may not be able to get a permit to remodel the large, single-family building into a pair of flats. The vacant land may not in fact be served by water and power, and the cost to extend such facilities in order to develop the land may exceed the value of the improved property. The seller may not be able to pass clear title. The local government may plan to condemn the property and obtain it under its rights of eminent domain. Will the appraised value under these circumstances be in line with your investment? The attorney fees to protect your rights may turn the investment into a financial nightmare. The building may need a new roof, new plumbing and new wiring, all just waiting to be installed at your unplanned expense. In many areas the building code requires bringing older properties up to code even if only modest repairs are to be made. The owner and his lender face any number of surprises. *In-depth checking before buying or lending is essential to successful investing.*

Second, assuming that all possible precautions have been taken, other matters must be taken into consideration:

For *rental property* the key is avoiding vacancies. Property that "has never had a vacancy all the time I've owned it" may suddenly develop halitosis, under-arm odor, or leprosy. It is impossible to recover lost time. Being able to fill vacant units promptly is vital. But how about the tenant who is happy to keep your property occupied but somehow just can't pay the rent? He is not much of a bargain. You must be prepared to eliminate the credit risk.

This will require checking references, getting rent deposits, and being tough on the day when the rent is due. It takes time to evict a tenant who does not want to leave. Repairs can be expensive, particularly those you cannot do yourself. To have a satisfactory return on the investment, operating expenses must be carefully controlled. Rents must be set to allow for maintenance (and of course be realistic as far as the marketplace is concerned).

Having a tenant bound to a lease has some advantages. On the other hand, in the absence of an escalation clause—rare in most leases—the owner is caught in a bind if expenses increase, and he has no way to raise rents. Property taxes can increase, and the owner has little or no control over that expense. He may not be able to have his assessed value reduced if he feels it is too high. He may even wake up some morning to find that rent controls have been imposed either by Uncle Sam or by a local municipality. Mortgage payments and other costs must be met regardless of what has happened to his income. If he abandons the property to the lender, he sacrifices his equity.

Third, in the case of investments for tax sheltering, the spread between income and expenses must be watched. The spread becomes undesirable when the actual expenses, as opposed to the "paper" (depreciation) expenses, get out of line. When there is an operating loss requiring more cash to be paid out than comes in, without regard to the taxable income, the investor will have to provide the cash and thus increase his investment. That may not be what he had in mind. Particularly in tax-shelter investments, the balancing of cash income and outgo is a delicate operation.

Fourth, the aim of real estate investment is the long-term gain to be realized on disposition of the investment. You are counting on the asset's appreciating in value. This plan may be interfered with by a number of factors.

Timing of the resale is important. If you are forced to liquidate the investment, it may come at an inappropriate time insofar as the market is concerned. It may happen that when you want to sell, somehow there are a large number of similar properties, all apparently more attractive than yours, available on the market at ridiculously low prices. You may find that by the time you allow for the cost to fix the place up to put it on the market and the cost to sell it (payment of real estate commission), the sales price is not going to be high enough to give you any gain over your original cost. Economic conditions beyond your control may serve to eliminate the appreciation you were counting on and you are left only with depreciation. That seems to go on regardless. Even the neighborhood may be against you. If other owners have allowed their property to go to rack and ruin, you can be sure that factor will have a depressing effect on the value of yours. You may find that you overlooked a strenuous prepayment penalty in your financing.

Finally, experts are not always right. Real estate syndicates and REITs all face *precisely* the same problems. The people who operate them are expected to be expert enough to avoid unsatisfactory results. Some of them are and do, but the investor must, before giving them his money, assure himself that they are in fact expert. What has been their track record in other projects? If they had failures, why? If they are new at the job, what has been the business experience of the organizers? Are the prospective benefits reasonable? Don't let your desire for an above-average return interfere with your judgment. Outrageous returns simply are not available, except by luck, which you cannot count on. And there is always a problem in interpreting rates of return. As we will see more clearly in subsequent chapters, there are several ways to measure returns, but *any* syndicate, REIT, or individual real estate investment offering to provide, say, 15 percent to 20 percent annual returns on a basis to compare with, say, 6 percent on a savings account is hardly to be believed. Extravagant claims need to be recognized, though it is also true that you can make satisfactory investments in real estate through a syndicate or REIT.

Let's assume you do at least want to try your hand and go all the way. You investigate investment opportunities, make arrangements for the financing, prepare a financial plan for the operation, estimate your current and long-term results, and undertake to manage the property yourself. You might even have a good set of tools and are all ready to answer a tenant's call for help with a leaky faucet or sticky window. It is further assumed you intend to continue to be employed and this property investment project will require only spare time. Your goal is to take a sum of money and through this venture generate an attractive current return and be in the position to reap a capital gain some years hence.

You will need to decide on just what type of residential income property you should buy. There are several to choose from: single-family, duplexes, and larger multiple units. What are the considerations?

The larger the property, the greater will be the amount of money needed to buy it. The more tenants, the more property management effort will be required. As long as you are going to be a part-time manager while holding down a job (with a safe, secure paycheck), there is a limit on how big the project should be. Rate of return is also an important matter. Which type yields the most?

For the beginning amateur income property investor, the smaller the project the less frightening the problems appear and presumably the smaller the financial risk. That might lead you to conclude you should start with a single-family house. Let's look at that possibility.

This type of income property investment, except under the most unusual circumstances, will provide the least satisfactory return. The income, relative to land and other costs, is at the minimum. To demonstrate this point, consider a single-family dwelling for which the fair rental value is, say, $200 per month. If you could, zoning allowing, convert the building to two rental units, would you expect the rental income to remain the same? Not if you know what you should know. It is likely you could rent each unit for $125 so now you have 2 times $125 to equal $250 gross income per month. You will find that the additional costs to operate, apart from the conversion expense, would not increase in the same proportion as the increase in income. Property taxes might go up slightly if it was reassessed as income property. If the rents included utilities, two families would incur greater expense than one but only perhaps. The single-family property would likely be rented to a family, whereas two apartments under these conditions would be more suitable for only adults. As we will see shortly, the value of income property is determined basically by the amount of net income available from it, so if that income is increased, its value will increase.

If, on the other hand, you have lived in a single-family home for many years and have either paid off the mortgage, or the mortgage payments are quite modest, you might obtain an attractive return by renting it. Realize, of course, that this is possible only because you have a significant equity; otherwise the mortgage payments for a large loan, plus the other expenses, would preclude you from having a surplus from the maximum rent you could get. And if you have a big equity why not release those dollars and use them in conjunction with borrowed funds and thus use leverage to maximize your return?

Faced with investing today in residential income property, you can invariably do better with multiple units than single-family dwellings.

The Case for the Fourplex

Frequently a fourplex is built on a lot perhaps originally intended for a single-family home. At any rate, a fourplex typically uses relatively little land and as a consequence, on a per-rental-unit basis, there is a minimum cost for land, thus a maximum return from the land value. The proportionate share of property taxes per unit is also at a minimum. Yet the rental charge is not subject to reduction, because each unit is complete—living, dining, sleeping—and justifies an appropriate charge. By spreading land cost and other expenses over four units, the maximum return is possible.

By applying what has just been said, you might conclude the maximum return would be available from the largest possible residential building. Not quite so. As the size of the project increases, there are additional expenses for management, for example, that serve to offset some of the advantages. As you move from the fourplex to, say, six units, the lot size must increase and then you find that you are not making the most use of it. Larger properties will have swimming pools and other amenities that add to their desirability but also increase cost and reduce, relatively speaking, the return. On the other hand, while you as an individual could expect to have a minimum of trouble in managing a fourplex yourself, it is not economical for a commercial property management firm to operate several small scattered properties when compared with the large-scale project.

If it is excitement you are looking for, along with investment returns, a fourplex ought to provide all you want, at least at the outset.

Now that it has been decided you are going to consider investing in a fourplex, you will have some questions. They are posed and answered next. Meanwhile, you probably have seen a fourplex in your travels. Keep such a building in mind as we discuss your prospective venture into the world of real estate investment.

So on to the questions: how much money will I need, and where on earth will I get it—not to mention whatever I will need to borrow? Read on!

2

Financing a Real Estate Investment

How much cash—meaning your own funds—will be needed, and how can you raise cash in addition to the mortgage? What are the factors that enter into obtaining real estate loans? What is meant by the term "amortization"? That's what this chapter is all about.

Cash Required

The purchase price of the property generally will govern the amount of cash needed to swing the deal, because lenders determine the amount they will lend on the basis of the appraised value of the property. These percentages vary with the supply and demand for money as well as with the nature of the borrower and type of property.

Most real estate investors start at what is probably the wrong end—they find a piece of property, learn how much can be borrowed and then start to scramble for cash to make up the difference. This way works, but there is a more scientific way to approach the problem. Determine first the maximum amount of money you can scrape together for the investment; then go looking for property.

First, however, a general rule: unless you have at least $5,000 in cash, beyond the liquid assets needed to cover any personal emergencies, you probably should not consider making a *purchase* investment in real estate. You may be able to put smaller amounts to work in real estate syndicates, REITs, and second mortgages— but not as a purchaser of income property. You may be able to buy a small plot of undeveloped land for less than $5,000, but to realize a return it probably will require a further investment to develop it.

This does not mean that you could invest with a *down payment* of $5,000. There are costs associated with the purchase that must be met at the time it is made. Your cash must be enough to cover not only the down payment but these costs as well. The down payment is the difference between the sales price and the total amount to be borrowed for which the property is used as security. For example, take a piece of property going for $60,000:

Sales price	$60,000
Mortgage	$50,000
Down payment	$10,000

Up to this point $10,000 cash will be needed. Then there are the closing costs: loan fees, title insurance, prorated expenses. The total will vary from one transaction to another. Whatever they amount to, they must be paid at the time the deal is closed. If in this example the closing costs amount to $1,500, the total cash needed is $11,500. As far as raising cash is concerned, we will not distinguish between money needed for down payment and for closing costs. It is the total number of dollars needed that we are after.

Sources of Cash—Your Own

You probably have some money in a *savings account*, having accumulated it with the idea that some day you would put it to good use. That day may be close at hand.

Timing of the withdrawal may be important. If you have a

regular passbook account, you probably are earning interest to the day of withdrawal. If you have a bonus or certificate account, there may be a penalty or deduction of earned interest if you withdraw before a due date. This is not necessarily a large amount, nor should it be a factor causing you to give up a project; you simply should check into the situation and find out how you stand. Delaying a withdrawal by a few days might make a difference.

An alternative to withdrawal is to borrow on the account, using the passbook or certificate as security. Many savings institutions make this type of loan and charge 1 percent over the savings rate. Assume you are earning 6 percent on your account. Borrow most of the amount at 7 percent. Your interest cost is 1 percent of the amount borrowed. If the money goes into a good investment, it certainly will earn more than the 1 percent. If you repay the savings account loan out of the earnings from the real estate investment, you will recapture the funds and have both the asset and the savings account balance.

For the sake of an ongoing example, assume you have $15,000 in a savings account. Where else can you raise money?

On your home, to begin with. What is the market value of your property? What is the present balance of your mortgage? *Everyone* has a mortgage on his home. Chances are very good that you have an equity in your present property that can be tapped to provide money for your next real estate investment venture. Then you face two basic choices: re-finance the present loan or borrow by way of a second mortgage.

The most desirable choice probably involves not increasing your monthly cash outlay for housing. If that is the case, forget the second mortgage route. To re-finance the present mortgage you need to find a lender—maybe the lender who made the present loan—to reappraise the property and make a loan in an amount greater than the current unpaid balance, thus giving you the difference in cash.

A word of caution: if you now have a very favorable interest rate, perhaps because the loan was obtained many years ago, in all probability the new loan will be at a much higher rate. To borrow anew you probably will have an additional cost that will have to be recovered out of the investment to be made with the cash. There may also be a prepayment penalty, though this sometimes is waived if the new loan is made by the original lender. There also will be the costs of a new title search as well as an appraisal. Therefore, *before* re-financing, get all your costs lined up so you can see just what expenses will have to be recovered from the investment.

Let's assume at this point you obtain $6,000 in cash from the re-financing.

If for some reason, getting a new first mortgage is not feasible, you can explore the second mortgage alternative. For this loan there will be expenses for appraisal, title search, and title insurance. The interest rate will be higher and the term shorter. The monthly payment will have to be met either by way of increased living expenses or from the real estate investment; do not forget this aspect if you raise part of the cash for the project from this source. Finally, as with all loans of this nature, they have to be repaid even if the investment into which the money goes is not profitable.

For well-situated property, owned by persons with satisfactory credit records, second mortgage money is generally available. It costs more than many other alternatives; we won't use it here in our continuing example.

How about getting out your life insurance policies? Unless you bought the no-cash value of term-type life insurance, your life insurance policy has a cash surrender value, on which you can obtain a policy loan. If you bought the policy many years ago, the policy loan rate, which is stated in the contract, will likely startle you—it will be quite low in comparison with current interest rates.

In view of this you may wish to consider raising some cash by borrowing on, *not canceling,* your life insurance. Again, you will incur an interest cost, to be recovered from your investment. But you will not have appraisal and title costs. Usually the loan can be paid off in amounts and at times you choose; in particular, monthly repayment of principal is not usually required. Interest is often paid annually. If you are confident about paying the interest out of other income (should the investment turn sour), and if you are confident that having the amount of life insurance payable reduced by the amount of the loan does not present a problem, then you should seriously consider raising cash in the manner outlined.

If you want the full amount of life insurance protection restored, the loan will have to be paid off. Otherwise, in the event of the death of the life assured, the beneficiary will receive the amount of insurance *less* the unpaid balance of the loan and accrued interest. If the policy is allowed to lapse, the loan balance and accrued interest will be charged against the cash surrender value. The balance will then be available to be withdrawn in cash; it might automatically be used as a loan of premium to keep the policy in force until that amount is used up.

For our example, assume you do not use your life insurance as a source for cash to invest.

You may have other investments for which the outlook is not as favorable as for a real estate venture; for example, shares, especially shares of a stock or of a mutual fund that, if sold, would give you a loss for income tax purposes.

An investment in real estate, as is the case with *every* investment, should be made *only* after you have taken a good look at your investment objectives, what you have in current investments, and what the outlook is for your future. It is a mistake to make any investment, forget it, *and* expect to make a handsome profit when you pull it out—at retirement, say. Investments must not be neglected; they need to be reevaluated periodically.

In our example, so far you have raised $15,000 from liquidating a savings account and a further $6,000 by re-financing your home, for a total of $21,000—well beyond the minimum. But what if you could raise only $2,000 or $3,000 this way? Where else can you raise money?

First, you can get together with a few other people who are in the same boat. Obviously, troubles can arise when two or more human beings try to make decisions about handling money, but it may be practical for a small group to pool their resources. The easiest way to handle the contractual arrangements would be for one person or couple to represent the group. The other "investors" could have a contract with the representative, spelling out the obligations. The alternative method is to form a partnership and have all parties named in deeds, mortgages, and so on executed in connection with the investment. This latter route is perhaps more secure, but certainly it is cumbersome.

Second, if you find your present housing has outlived its usefulness—kids have gone and Mom and Dad rattle around in a big house—how about selling it? The cash raised could then be invested. In turn, you could rent an apartment. Whether you rent from someone else or use a part of your own income property, selling your present home will give you cash to invest. As stated earlier, if you live in part of a building and rent the balance to others, you will lose a small part of the income tax advantage but that is not a serious consideration.

There are, then, many ways of raising cash, and we will assume you can raise at least $5,000 and thus have enough to make a purchase on your own. Now, how do you finance the balance needed for the project?

Borrowing on Real Estate

If your investment objective is to maximize long-term gain and minimize current income subject to income tax, you should utilize *leverage*. As a general rule, the maximum investment return is obtained when you secure the largest possible—in terms of dollar value—property for the cash dollars you invest. This involves *borrowing the balance needed to make the purchase, using the property itself as security for the loan:* this is called using leverage. When you borrow money at a fixed interest rate and invest it in a project where the prospective return is not limited or guaranteed, you hope for a good spread between what it costs in interest expense and what your realized profit is. If you borrow at 8 percent and earn 12 percent, you earn 4 percent on the funds invested. This is one example of leverage. (Note, however, that if the venture does not fare well, the borrower will still have to pay the fixed interest cost even though there is little or no return from the investment to cover it.)

An example of the foregoing involves borrowing $20,000 at 8 percent and investing it; the investment turns out very well and we earn 15 percent.

Earnings	$3,000
Interest cost	1,600
Gain	$1,400

Nothing has been said about your own share of the investment. You usually are not able to borrow 100 percent. Let's assume you make a $50,000 investment that actually produces a profit of 12 percent, $6,000. If you borrow half, $25,000, at 8 percent, your interest cost is $2,000, leaving $4,000 profit on your half, or a 16 percent return on your investment.

Now, if you can borrow 80 percent or, conversely, invest as little as 20 percent in your own funds, interest cost at 8 percent on $40,000 would be $3,200. If investment earnings are $6,000, the net profit is $2,800. But the $2,800 is profit on an investment of only $10,000, or a whopping 28 percent.

The idea of leverage involves borrowing as much as you can at the lowest interest cost and investing it to produce the greatest return. *The greater the proportion of borrowed funds, the greater will be the percentage return on your invested cash,* assuming the rate of return exceeds the fixed interest cost. The motivation to invest in the largest possible project in terms of dollars cost comes from the fact that rates of return tend to increase as the size of the project increases. For example, the rate of return from a $25,000 duplex generally will be smaller than from a $500,000 apartment complex.

Factors in Borrowing

A mortgage lender recognizes how leverage works. He does not begrudge your 12 percent and 15 percent return potential. He is glad to lend at, say, 8 percent if he is assured that no matter what happens you will pay off the loan. He is not your partner, sharing in gains and losses. He only wants his interest. With much of the risk removed, the interest rate represents simply the charge made for the use of money.

A real estate mortgage is typically a long-term proposition. Terms of up to thirty years are not uncommon. With repayment spreading over that length of time the lender may want some hedge against inflation. When the prospects for continued inflation are good, long-term interest rates will be higher than for the short term; they include some allowance for the future reduction in value of dollars. The interest rate will also be influenced by the cost of the money to the lender. A savings institution may be paying 5 percent on passbook accounts. If it can lend those funds on mortgages at 8 percent, it has a 3 percent spread. Lenders understand leverage. If the passbook rate goes up, or the demand for commercial loans increases, mortgage rates will go up, too.

Lenders, however, must make loans to stay in business, so there may be substantial competition to lend on real estate from time to time. The situation is dynamic, and a borrower should shop around for the best terms.

Let's look closely at each of the factors: interest rates, borrower's credit, nature of the security, proportion to be lent, and appraisal policies.

Generally, mortgage interest rates are set simply on the basis of supply and demand, but there is more to it than the casual observer sees. We have already noted that the length of the loan term may affect the rate. When the supply of lendable funds is less than the demand, lenders may change the maximum term from, say, twenty-five years to twenty years on certain types of property. That does not change the rate of interest, but it does increase the monthly payment. When funds are borrowed to finance a real estate investment, the income from which is used to repay the loan, the size of the monthly payment can make a difference. A shorter repayment period may, in the eyes of the lender, reduce the risk, so if the interest rate is held steady, but the term cut, the lender in effect is earning a better return.

Lenders prefer not to have fluctuations in the interest rate. They would rather alter the other terms of the borrowing contract to reflect conditions of supply and demand. One such adjustable condition is the point charge or loan fee. A point, or loan fee, is one percentage point of the amount of the loan. If the borrowing is at, say 7 ½ percent and 3 points, and the loan amount is $30,000, the borrower will be charged at the time the loan is made with $900 in points. This fee really is interest in advance, and it is charged because the lender feels that the basic rate of 7 ½ percent is too low. Instead of increasing the rate—lenders do not like to change rates—points are charged, thus increasing the yield or return. In this example, the borrower would receive $29,100 in loan proceeds but would be obligated to repay $30,000; and interest would be calculated at the outset on $30,000. In this situation, the "Annual Percentage Rate" will be more than the mortgage interest rate of 7 ½ percent. The difference is due to the point charge. The only advantage the borrower gets is being permitted by the Internal Revenue Service to charge points or loan fees as deductible interest expense against income.

Conventional financial institutions such as banks and savings or building and loan associations ordinarily grant *only* first mortgages. Individuals and organizations that deal in second mortgages charge higher interest rates and offer shorter repayment terms to offset the risk factor in such financing.

And there is a risk factor. If the borrower finds he cannot make the monthly payments on the mortgage, he may attempt to sell the property and have someone else take over the loan or walk away and abandon it to the lender. Lenders do not like to acquire real estate in the latter way, and they try at the time they make the loan to avoid such adverse consequences by checking credit ratings carefully.

The vast majority of borrowers are conscientious and reliable. Even though things turn out badly, most people will struggle through and find a way to make their payments and fulfill their responsibilities. The best way for a person to demonstrate he has this sense of responsibility is to borrow money and repay it, over the agreed-upon period of time and basis. He becomes a "good credit risk." (Indeed, the person who prides himself on always paying cash is going to have a tough time getting his first loan; there is no way for the lender to know how good a credit risk he is.)

Only a person with a good credit record, employment stability, and other indications of reliability will receive favorable consideration, especially if, in addition, the overall financial position of the borrower and the financial plan for the project are healthy —particularly in terms of estimated income, expense and contingency margin.

Borrowing Proportions

Don't be misled by advertising of 100 percent loans. The qualified purchaser of a single-family home, with Veteran's Administration benefits, may be able to buy without a down payment, but the investor-borrower in residential income property will *not* be able to. The starting point is always the appraised value of the property, and the loan available will be some percentage of that figure.

Conservative lenders have conservative appraisers and will start by suggesting a 60 percent to 65 percent loan. At the other end of the spectrum, a hungry lender may almost automatically agree to the proposed purchase price as the value and grant a loan of 80 percent of that figure. There may or may not be restrictions by the first mortgagee (lender) on the use of secondary financing such as a second mortgage.

The problem is this: the lender *wants* the borrower to have something to lose so that if the going gets tough there will be no incentive just to walk away, leaving the lender holding the property. Further, because of the possibility that the market value of the property may go down, the lender does not want to find, in case of default, that the loan balance is greater than the figure the property can be sold for. As a consequence, the lender wants to start out with a loan balance that is well below the market price, established on a conservative basis, and for the borrower to have a significant stake in the project. Judgment, therefore, enters into the picture, and the amount of the loan and its terms may vary from one lender to another. As we said, you should shop around for the best arrangement.

Now for some interim conclusions. Lenders are fussy about whom they lend money to, the kind of property used as security, and the terms on which the mortgage is made. Having made a good loan, the lender prefers that the borrower simply make payments until the loan is paid off. That rarely happens. In fact, although real estate loans are made typically for anywhere from fifteen to thirty years, the average length of a real estate loan is under five years. In recognition of this kind of turnover, lenders usually include a prepayment penalty in the loan agreement. As described earlier, these penalties may vary from a straight percentage—1 percent, 2 percent—of the original loan amount to less strenuous penalties. If the original loan is paid off, such as would be the case if the property was sold and a new loan obtained or full cash paid by the purchaser, the penalty would be assessed against the seller. There are two alternatives: to persuade the buyer to do his re-financing with the original lender, in which case the prepayment penalty may not be assessed, or for the purchaser to assume the loan. The latter course is possible if the purchaser can pay off the seller's equity without involving the mortgage. Equity here is defined as the difference between the purchase price and the total of the outstanding loan balances. If the new purchaser is to assume the loan, the lender has to agree to take him on; there is no obligation on the part of the lender to consent to an assumption. The lender will probably go through the loan qualification procedure for the new borrower before agreeing to the assumption. If the loan is assumed, the original borrower may still have some contingent responsibility in the event of default. The seller may prefer to have the buyer "substitute" on the loan. In this case, the lender, in effect, makes a new loan to the purchaser; and instead of assumption documents, the purchaser signs a new mortgage or note and deed of trust. This would serve to get the original borrower off the hook.

Sources of Real Estate Finance

If you are a first-time borrower, except perhaps for your own home, you will probably need to rely on the advice of others and to check around to see where money can be borrowed for an investment in income property. A good place to start is the bank where you now have your checking account and the savings institution where you keep your nest egg. You will want to discuss mortgage financing with every real estate broker you meet. Your goal is to gain a feel for the current money market and obtain a recommendation from any and all who might have one to make. Keeping a notebook is a very good idea.

The money market is constantly changing. A lender who turned down every applicant last month may suddenly become the most aggressive seeker of borrowers overnight. The more you learn about how lenders operate, the less you should be discouraged about the chances of lining up financing when you need it. By knowing what you are doing you can put together a loan application package that no lender will be able to resist even when he is refusing others. Until a financial institution closes its doors it must make loans to stay in business. Lending policies clearly change with the ebb and flow in the supply of money, and you will want to time your requirements accordingly, but that does not mean that you will not be able to obtain financing for a well-thought-out, sound project. You may just have to look a little further.

Seller Financing

It may develop that the seller wishes to provide the financing, particularly if the property is free and clear of indebtedness and the owner wants to get out from under the management and operational risk and assume the role of mortgagee. The terms offered must be carefully looked at and compared with alternatives. For example, a seller-lender may be more flexible when it comes to the term of the mortgage and the required down payment than an institutional lender. If banks are limiting mortgages to twenty years, the seller may be agreeable to twenty-five years. (The age of the property has quite a bit to do with the term of the loan. For older properties, say those at least thirty years old, the majority of lenders would likely limit their loans to fifteen years or twenty at the most. On brand new properties the regular lenders will not likely go over thirty years and will more likely limit loans to twenty-five years. The seller-lender may be persuaded to agree to a term longer than is available from other lenders, depending on how badly he wanted to sell.) All in all, it is quite practical for buyer and seller to arrange the financing themselves; there is no requirement that you restrict your borrowing to a financial institution.

An alternative to the procedure whereby a seller takes back a mortgage is the sales contract, referred to earlier. In this case, the seller retains title but signs an agreement with the buyer under which, after all the payments have been made, title will be passed. Buying "on contract" means that the seller is financing the sale, though there may be an underlying mortgage, in which case the seller will be obligated to continue making those payments and the purchaser will want to assure himself that such is the case. From the buyer's point of view the best arrangement is to make his payments to a third party who first makes the payment on the mortgage out of the buyer's remittance and then sends the balance to the seller. With or without an underlying mortgage, the buyer's payments are applied to his total purchase obligation. It is customary for the sales contract to include a rate of interest and other terms, just like a mortgage. The periodic payment serves to pay the interest and a partial payment on the principal. In fact, as we have seen, except for some technical matters, the only practical difference between a mortgage and a sales contract is the way in which the title to the real estate is handled.

In this context, a related device has recently been introduced, particularly in the financing of larger properties. It is called the *"wrap-around" mortgage*. Assume the following situation:

You have found an apartment complex for sale at a price that is satisfactory. The seller's equity is greater than the cash you have available, so some special arrangement must be made if the deal is to go through. The mortgage already on the property can be assumed. The seller could take your cash and a second mortgage and have you assume the first mortgage. On the other hand, he might prefer to sell on a sales contract, retaining title and control. You would prefer the first plan because it gives you title and freedom from any control of the seller. Under the second plan you might be exposed to a problem if the seller did not keep the mortgage current even though you made your payments. The seller's preference and your preference are not the same. Enter the wrap-around mortgage. Under this plan, you agree to buy the property for the total price with a specified cash down payment. The seller takes back a mortgage for the entire balance, including the amount of the existing first mortgage. This new mortgage, between the buyer and seller, is actually a second mortgage because the first still applies. The payments on the wrap-around mortgage are applied to the total indebtedness, and the seller must keep the first mortgage payments current, as under a sales contract. The main advantage to the wrap-around is the flexibility provided to the seller. He then will more readily be able to sell the mortgage if he wants to cash out than he would with a sales contract.

Caution: there may be a provision in the first mortgage that serves to accelerate it if there is a further encumbrance such as a second or wrap-around mortgage. If accelerated, the unpaid balance becomes due immediately the second mortgaging occurs. That would defeat the whole idea of the financing plan, which calls for the continuation of the existing loan.

In addition to the three methods of seller-organized financing discussed above, there is one more method, involving the straight assumption of the existing loan.

In an era of rising interest rates, buyers look for chances to assume loans with lower than current interest rates. When the rate is low enough, in fact, a larger than customary cash down payment may well be justified. A careful check should be made to determine whether in fact the loan can be properly assumed by the buyer and what fee, if any, is to be charged by the lender. The cost involved in assuming existing financing ordinarily will be substantially less than the cost of obtaining a new first loan. It will be no bargain, however, if the interest rate is too high, the term is too short (high monthly payments), or there is an unfavorable prepayment penalty.

A word of caution against doing what many do when they find that assumption is not permitted. To get around this, a seller may suggest that, even though a deed is executed and recorded, thus passing title, the buyer make the payments on the loan in a fashion such that the lender is not aware of the sale. This calls for a subterfuge in the handling of the payments. This plan will not likely stand up for long. Once the deed is recorded—if it is not, the buyer has no protection against the seller's selling the property again to someone else—the property tax records will be changed and the chances are good the lender will learn of the transaction. That will likely result in the loan balance being accelerated, and the buyer will be in the soup.

Assume now that the first loan can be properly taken over but that the seller's equity is larger than the cash you wish to invest. To make the sale the seller may be agreeable to taking back a second mortgage (assume that the first lender is not opposed to this—as is likely if the lender is agreeable to the assumption in the first place).

The seller gets enough cash to meet his requirements, gets out from under the first loan even though under an assumption that he may have a contingent liability, *and* has interest income from the second mortgage. By recording the second mortgage the seller preserves his legal interest in the property so that any future transfer of title is subject to those rights. Thus the financing of the purchase has been provided essentially through the seller and without a need to go elsewhere to borrow funds. (In addition, as we will see, the seller-provided second mortgage can also be used in conjunction with obtaining a new loan.)

Astute real estate buyer-investors look first for opportunities to finance their acquisitions along the lines discussed in the preceding sections. Failing that, they go outside for finance.

Commercial Banks

Commercial banks lend money on residential income property, though banks often are more interested in making business loans than property loans because the interest rate often is higher, the terms often are shorter, and the money turns over, therefore, more quickly. Find out what the conditions are where you live. On the other hand, a bank that does mortgage financing often offers lower interest rates, though to justify a lower rate, the bank probably will require the purchaser to have a larger equity than some other lenders.

As we have seen, in the case of *dwelling* mortgages—the type of financing you are most likely to be familiar with already—the lender may be willing to lend as much as 80 percent of the appraised value, sometimes 90 percent if there is mortgage insurance available. Under some FHA and VA programs the amount may be even higher. However, when it comes to residential *income* property, the practice differs. Generally, for individuals investing in relatively small apartment projects, no FHA insured financing is available (for developers and large-scale projects, there is).

That brings us back to what is called in the trade "conventional" mortgage loans. Institutions making conventional loans have no reason to share the ownership risk and require, therefore, that the investor-buyer's equity be sufficient to justify the risk to the lender. This is reflected in the practice followed by the majority of banks, savings institutions, and life insurance companies; these rarely lend more than 75 percent of appraised value and, more typically, about 70 percent.

Investors seeking to minimize taxable current income and maximize long-term capital appreciation usually wish to maximize leverage and therefore want to borrow the maximum possible. In arranging for financing, then, the investor should negotiate for a relaxing of the usual rules and try to obtain a higher percent of the value to be borrowed. Different lenders will have different ideas, and it will pay you to shop for your loan.

If in fact you need the maximum possible amount of funds, it is not likely you will get it through a bank. A bank, even if it will match a competing lender as far as amount is concerned, may not be willing to make the loan for as long a time period. This will mean that payments on a bank loan will be higher but that, in the long run, the total interest cost will be smaller. As will be seen later, the cash flow from a project is very important, and there may be a problem for you if your cash expenses are larger than they would be under alternative financing. Further, if you are seeking a tax shelter, the lower interest expense will increase the taxable income and lower the shelter benefit. (Of course, no matter what tax bracket you are in, the tax man "pays" only a part of any dollar spent for expenses. It still costs you *something* when you pay interest or for repairs and so on.)

We must not, needless to say, lump all commercial banks together. Some banks prefer certain types of loans to others. At a point in time, some banks have more funds to lend than others. Not only should you explore borrowing from a commercial bank as well as other types of financial institutions; you should talk to several banks.

Savings Banks

The comments concerning commercial banks generally do not apply to savings banks. The latter are more like, for our purpose, savings and loan and building and loan associations. These all are financial institutions established for the purpose of giving those with money to save a place to deposit it and earn interest and to channel funds into real estate loans, particularly single-family residences. In relating your needs for mortgage money to these sources, we will refer to them simply as *savings institutions*.

Although savings institutions lend money primarily for single-family residences, they also are an important source for mortgages to finance apartment houses. Their emphasis is on long-term lending, and they are particularly interested in new construction. As before, these lenders do not wish to become "partners" with an investor and look for adequate borrower-equity, particularly in residential income projects not occupied by the borrower. Except for some unusual situation, you should not expect to be able to borrow more than 80 percent of the appraised value and more likely only 70-75 percent. Again remember: conditions change, sometimes very rapidly, and you will need to keep yourself informed.

If you are seeking maximum proportion and maximum term, a savings institution may be your best bet. Their interest rates, however, may be somewhat higher than those charged by banks. You will need to balance each of the factors in your financial plan; compromise will be in order.

Insurance Companies

Life insurance companies make a large number of mortgage loans. Most operate through loan correspondents, and you will not likely deal directly with the mortgage loan department of a life insurer. Many correspondents represent several different life companies and also other sources of loan money such as pension plans. Be sure to check out this source, project by project and company by company. Generalizations work only to the extent of saying that long-term real estate mortgages are important to life insurance companies and such companies always are interested in making good loans.

Mortgage Loan Brokers and Private Investors

As suggested earlier, many people with funds to invest prefer to be involved in real estate by way of lending rather than owning. As a prospective buyer-investor, you need to know where some of these people are. You may just prefer to deal with an individual (learning how to do it yourself in the process). More importantly, you may want to locate a private investor because he may be a better lender for your project than any of the others. Realize that the private lender will want all the advantages any other lender wants: maximum rates, minimum terms, lowest proportion of loan to value, highest prepayment penalty, highest quality credit risk and brand new property as security. So why bother with him? He may be more flexible.

Individuals wishing to make mortgage loans often advertise in the newspaper. They also spread the word to real estate brokers. The prospective borrower may also use the same media. A real estate broker usually will know a great deal about the local money market, and if you are making the purchase through him, you may be able to reach a private lender in that way. (We'll have more to say about the role of real estate brokers in the next chapter.)

Some private investors prefer to rely on the expertise of others in making a loan decision, so they contract with a mortgage loan broker to obtain prospective borrowers, appraise properties, and handle the paper work. You should be acquainted with mortgage loan brokers in your area. The fee for their services is normally paid by the borrower; it may range from 2 percent to 5 percent or more of the amount borrowed.

Private investors and mortgage loan brokers are not just sources for first mortgage money; additionally, second or junior mortgages (even third and fourth!) can be obtained from these sources.

We have already discussed the risk involved in second mortgages. If there is a default on the first and the property value has dropped, the interest of the second mortgagee may well be wiped out. The person making second mortgages is, or should be, very much aware of this risk, but as a prospective borrower you should also recognize what is involved. When the second mortgage is used to supplement maximum first mortgage financing, obviously the risk for the second mortgagee is potentially serious. In a declining market, the total of the first and second mortgages can easily exceed the possible sale price. You can therefore expect to pay the highest allowable interest rate on a second mortgage in this category. It will also have a fairly short term. That is, even though the payments on the second mortgage are calculated on the basis of an extended period of time, the balance of the loan may be payable on a due date in the fairly near future. This feature is often described in the following way: "Second mortgage for $10,000 at 10 percent interest on unpaid balance, with monthly amortization over fifteen years, due date in five years, no prepayment penalty."

If the loan is to be repaid in monthly payments for the full fifteen years, no principal would remain outstanding at the end of that time. With a five-year due date, however, the balance of the principal is due and payable at that time.

When you borrow with this type of due-date situation, you must plan on re-financing the project by the time the due date arrives. This is a quite feasible and widely used financing technique.

Amortization

If you borrow a sum of money, agree to pay interest, and repay the loan in a lump sum at some date in the future, you are *not* involved in amortization. The interest charge is computed by multiplying the rate times the term times the amount, and the repayment amount will be the same as the amount borrowed, the principal.

Example: Borrow $5,000 at 6 percent and repay in lump sum two years hence.

Interest $5,000 × .06 × 2	$ 600
Principal	5,000
Principal & interest combined	$5,600

The interest of $300 each year may be paid separately. That is an example of a non-amortization situation. The principal amount remains constant during the time the loan is outstanding.

But what about paying off the principal in monthly install-ments? As said before, this is the way most real estate mortgages are handled. The key difference to note here is that out of each monthly payment a portion is assigned to repayment of principal and the interest portion is based on the balance of the unpaid principal.

Example: Borrow $10,000 at 7½ percent to be repaid monthly over twenty years.

First we need to find the amount of the monthly payment. Look at Table I (beginning on page 212) and locate a term of 20 years and an interest rate of 7½ percent. Note also that the table is entitled "Payment Amortizes Loan." You are looking for a way to calculate the amount that, paid monthly, is exactly enough to pay all the interest that is due and all of the principal so that at the end of 20 years, after you have made the last (240th) payment, the principal is completely repaid. Table I indicates a monthly payment, per $1,000, of $8.05639. The monthly payment amount for our problem here is

$$\$8.05639 \times 10 = \$80.56$$

If it takes $8.05639 to repay $1,000, then it takes ten times that for a loan of ten times $1,000.

In each succeeding month the interest portion is less and the principal reduction is more. The monthly payment amount remains constant. (As a service to the borrower, most lenders provide a statement at the end of the year showing the total amount of interest paid; this figure will be needed when preparing an income tax return.)

Insurance

As long as the market value of the property is equal to or greater than the loan balance, in the event of default it can be sold and the lender's interest restored. What about the possible destruction of the property? Loss or damage by physical perils such as fire, windstorm, explosion and others can be insured against by obtaining a fire or multiple-peril insurance policy. The lender obtains protection by requiring that the policy include a loss-payable clause naming the lender. The policy should always be written in the name of the titleholder. Usually the lender holds the original policy and the borrower-insured has a copy. Under these circumstances the lender is protected against the insured's canceling the policy and leaving the property uninsured. The amount of the insurance should be not less than the amount of the unpaid loan balance.

Now what if the premium is not paid when it is due? The insurance company will cancel the coverage. Under FHA and VA rules for mortgages, lenders are required to maintain impound or loan trust fund accounts and collect each month from borrowers the amounts needed to pay insurance premiums and property taxes when they are due. This money belongs to the borrower but is administered by the lender to guard against nonpayment of taxes and insurance, thus protecting the lender. Some mortgage lenders extend this practice to non-FHA and VA loans as a matter of convenience for both lender and borrower.

As a borrower you will have to have property insurance. If your lender is agreeable, you will be able to keep this reserve yourself. You may wish to set up a savings account for the purpose and thus earn some interest.

One final word about loan trust fund or impound accounts. Earlier we stated that in amortizing a mortgage, the periodic payment remains constant. If the lender requires a loan trust fund, the amounts needed for it to build up reserves for payment of insurance and property taxes will be added to the payment amount for principal and interest. If the cost of taxes or insurance changes, so will the amount to be accumulated in the loan trust fund. When this happens, the lender will send a notice of a change in the monthly payments. This does *not* change the payment on the mortgage, even though you now must send a different amount each month.

We now know that if our investment objective is to maximize current income, we need to minimize expenses and therefore will *not* borrow funds if it can be avoided. On the other hand, if we need to borrow money, which will be the case if we are seeking long-term capital appreciation and minimized current income, there are many different ways in which to do so.

Because the amount of money we can borrow is very much related to the amount of our own funds we invest in the project, the first step is to establish just how much cash we can put into the investment. Assuming we can borrow at least 75 percent of the smaller of the purchase or appraised price, once we know how much cash we have we can estimate closely how big a piece of property we can handle. In our ongoing example in this chapter, we finally accumulated $21,000. That would mean we could seriously consider buying property selling in the neighborhood of $80,000.

Note carefully we have not yet looked for property. We want to do this thing properly. Until you know what amount you can invest, you should not get involved in trying to find a piece of property—unless, of course, you are doing so just for the exercise. At any rate, we now are ready to take the next important step: the search for an investment vehicle.

3

The Search for an Investment Vehicle

Iɴ this chapter we will look at how to narrow the field so you can efficiently seek out properties that meet your requirements. Then you will see how to analyze systematically each alternative to arrive at the maximum price to pay and to compute the cash flows, taxable income, and the long-term gain on the resale. Forms and charts created specially for these purposes make it easy, particularly for the person looking at real estate investment for the first time. We will follow carefully a complete example of how to determine if a property offers a satisfactory return.

The First Step

Previously we have decided seriously to consider putting our venture capital to work in owning and operating a fourplex, though that does not exclude other forms of property. It goes without saying that the principles employed and procedures suggested relative to a fourplex all apply no matter what the size of the property.

Before you begin to search for properties, you must first make basic decisions regarding location and price range.

Location is critical, if only because you are going to manage the investment yourself. This means it has to be practical to journey to the property to show it to prospective tenants, perhaps to collect rents, and generally to keep an eye on it. Decide just what is a reasonable distance from where you live and maybe even draw a circle on a map (and remember: gas shortages may continue). In fact, you should pin down the general area in which it is going to be practical to own income property *before* you start looking. Otherwise you will waste a lot of time and effort looking at property in locations that are impractical for you to reach after you make the investment.

Once you have decided upon the general locations, you should decide on your price range. You will recall that we cautioned against looking first and counting your money second. Your available cash—in our example it was $21,000—must cover the down payment *and* the closing costs, and it is wise to have a little cushion so that if you find a really great opportunity and need a few more dollars to take advantage of it, you will be able to do so.

With $21,000 you can expect to be able to borrow at least three times $21,000, or $60,000 from institutional lenders. To extend further your use of leverage, you might be able to arrange either for a private investor to lend more, for the seller to finance more than 75 percent of the price, or to take back a second mortgage. There are other sources for second mortgage financing too, as described before. At this point, however, you know that, given a satisfactory property, you should have little or no difficulty in financing the purchase of $80,000 worth of real estate.

Now that we know we want to examine in detail properties in a specified area of the community, that the type of greatest interest is a fourplex, and that the offering price should be around $80,000, let's take a closer look at the various sources of information we'll use.

Real Estate Brokers

When you buy property through a real estate office you are paying for the services rendered by way of a commission. The rates vary and are subject to negotiation and local custom, though the point at which the bargaining begins is around 6 percent of the purchase price. This sum normally is paid by the seller out of the proceeds of the sale, but inasmuch as the purchaser is providing those proceeds he is really paying the commission. The question then is: are the services of the real estate licensee worth the cost?

The seller offering property other than through a real estate office expects to save the commission, so the offering price, in theory, is going to be the same as if the property is listed with a broker. However, the prudent buyer will make an offer based at least in part on a price *less* the commission, knowing that the seller would receive that amount if he had used a broker. Any compromise will result in a lower price to the buyer and a higher net proceeds to the seller.

Yet many sellers still use brokers. Do they earn their commissions? The answer is: probably so. Many owners do not want to be bothered with qualifying prospects, then showing the property and negotiating a deal directly with a prospective buyer. To them the commission is a reasonable fee. If the broker does in fact ferret out a buyer who would not otherwise be available to the seller, that in itself could be worth the commission. The broker usually advertises the property and incurs expense promoting it. It is his time and effort that goes into finding prospects and negotiating the sale. Unless that is the ultimate result, nothing is paid to the broker. Then, many *buyers* would rather make offers and negotiate with an agent instead of the seller personally—they feel more comfortable with the representative than with the owner.

A qualified real estate person will be familiar with the market and can provide useful advice to both buyer and seller as to the market value of a particular piece of real estate.

Financing is often the most important aspect of the deal. A real estate dealer can be expected to know where the money is and to line up financing on the most favorable terms to the buyer. If you do not have access to the money market, the real estate commission is a small price to pay for overcoming that problem.

Finally, the broker and his staff should be able to handle the paperwork. This may mean obtaining the services of an experienced attorney or escrow agent or title abstractor.

Thus both seller and buyer can get good service out of a broker. But how do you know which office to use? Not all real estate firms are expert in handling residential income property. What you want is one that specializes in the field. Their ad in the phone book may provide a clue. Discussing this question with bankers and savings association people may give you some leads. In a word, if you are going to use a real estate office, find one that knows how to handle *income property*. Otherwise, the chance that you will get your commission's worth is not very great.

Once you have become sophisticated in making investments in income property, you may decide that you will want to use a real estate broker for every investment. The right person can save you time and energy, provide you with information, and generally arrange deals you could never hope to do on your own. Some investors feel just the opposite and much prefer to handle everything they can themselves. There is one nagging reality, however, always to be taken into account: some investment opportunities are available *only* to clients of real estate offices.

Owners as Sellers

If the seller is knowledgeable and wants to provide the financing, you will be ahead in dealing with him. In contrast, an owner who has no idea of what market values are and expects the buyer to figure out how to give him all cash needs to be educated; you will have to decide whether you want to be the teacher. Find out as soon as possible how much the seller knows about the business and take appropriate action. The seller's inexperience can cost *you* money. If the seller obviously is smarter than you, you should run, not walk, to the nearest skilled real estate man.

Basic Analysis

What you need for the decision-making process is information. You need data from each of several different pieces of property, and you need to have knowledge to use in evaluating and comparing. What is market value? What is reasonable financing? What is a good yield? Set up your criteria, then develop real-life data and do an analysis. Investors who do this on a systematic basis find their results are substantially better than if they operate on a hit-and-miss basis, buying and selling on emotion, whim, and fancy.

As illustrated on the following pages, you should use a *Fact Sheet* and a set of *Analysis Worksheets*. The Fact Sheet data are for use in performing the computations required by the Worksheets. Then you pull the results together on a *Summary Sheet*. With the Summary Sheet in front of you, backed up by all the data used to get the entries on it, you can proceed to make a decision as to the property you *should* buy.

Let us take an example.

Using the initial criteria—location, type of property, and price range—we have located a property at 1234 Wistful Vista in the community of Utopia, California. We located this prospective "gem" through talking with Mr. I. M. Realtor, who represents the owner and who showed us through one of the units and provided most of the information we needed. We now are going to verify his data. Wherever possible we are going to get answers to questions from at least two reliable and pertinent sources. The Fact Sheet tells us what questions to ask and gives us a place to record the answers.

Fact Sheet

Referring now to the Fact Sheet reproduced on pages 58 and 70, let's examine each of the major entries that require some comment. (Have a supply of blank forms with you at all times—you never know when opportunity may knock.) The form is designed to be filled in by hand and allows for putting down not only facts such as rents and expenses but also other items you think may be useful in the ultimate decision-making process. You will see more than one piece of property, and you will find it difficult to separate, in your memory, one property from another after you've been looking for a while, so record on the Fact Sheet everything of importance *at the time you think of it and while on the premises.*

Gross Monthly Rents

You want to know the total number of dollars from rent

FACT SHEET FOR PROPOSED INVESTMENT IN INCOME PROPERTY

LOCATION: _1234 Wistful Vista_ OWNER OR BROKER _I. M. Realtor_ PHONE _765-432_
Utopia, California
NUMBER OF UNITS: _4_ DESCRIPTION: _2-1BR, 2-2BR_ GROSS MONTHLY RENTS: $ _900_

LOT SIZE: _60 x 125_ BUILDING SIZE IN SQUARE FEET: _4000_
SQUARE-FOOT COST TODAY: $ _1900_

OTHER FEATURES: _Owner's unit — 1500 sq. ft._
Landscaping worth $500

DESCRIBE EQUIPMENT: _Stove/Ref. in each unit_ ITS CASH VALUE $ _2000_

	ASSESSED VALUE	TAXES FOR 197-	BUILDING AGE _10_ YEARS
LAND	$ _3,750_	$ _511_	ESTIMATED USEFUL LIFE REMAINING:
IMPROVEMENTS	$ _15,000_	$ _2,045_	BUILDING _30_
PERSONAL PROPERTY	$ _500_	$ _69_	EQUIPMENT _5_
TOTALS	$ _19,250_	$ _2,625_	OWNER'S PROPERTY TAX EXEMPTION TAKEN? _No_

ANNUAL OPERATING EXPENSES (ACTUAL _XX_ OR ESTIMATED _____)

PAID BY OWNER:

GAS ____ POWER ____ WATER _X — garden only_

GARBAGE _XX_ OTHER _____

CONDITION OF PROPERTY: _Good._
One unit needs paint.
_____

PAST DEPRECIATION RATE _1_ % PER YEAR

PROPERTY TAXES	$ _2,625_
UTILITIES	$ _240_
INSURANCE	$ _100_
MAINTENANCE	$ _250_
GARDENING	$ _185_
MANAGEMENT	$
	$
TOTAL ANNUAL OPERATING EXPENSE	$ _3,400_

INVESTOR'S DATA:
DESIRED YIELD BEFORE INCOME TAX: _9_ % FEDERAL & STATE TAX RATE: _40_ %

EXPECTED NUMBER OF YEARS BEFORE RESALE: _5_ . ANNUAL APPRECIATION RATE: _2_ %

EXPECTED RESALE EXPENSE $ _1000_ FOR FIX UP; SALES COMMISSION: _6_ %

EXPECTED VACANCY ALLOWANCE WHILE OWNED: _2_ % OF ANNUAL INCOME. MAXIMUM
GROSS MULTIPLIER _8_

REMARKS: _Good rental record. Adjoining property about_
same value - shopping 2 blocks away.

© 1972 D.M. TEMPLE

received from all units, assuming they are all occupied (even if they are not at the time), on a monthly basis. The exact rent per unit is not important at this time, just the total. This is going to be the figure you will use later to arrive at the gross annual income (by multiplying by twelve).

Information about rents usually will be given by the real estate broker; he obtains it from the owner. Whenever possible you should verify, *by talking with the tenants,* the rental figure given. If this is not possible before offering to buy, then put a provision in your offer that your offer is subject to verification that the actual rental income is as stated in the preliminary negotiations. This is only one of several possible qualifications to your offer, all of which will be discussed in the next chapter. There cannot be too much stress placed on the importance of working *only* with accurate data, and accuracy requires checking and double-checking. You may feel some reluctance in speaking to a tenant. Overcome that reluctance by remembering it is *your money* that is going on the line.

Lot Size, Building Size

Later you will use this information in estimating the value of the property. Again, owners and their real estate agents should have this information readily available. You may have to pace off the building and make an estimate of the number of square feet of living area. If the garages are separate, make a note of the size. If they are part of the building, do not include the garage area in the total area figure.

Square-Foot Cost Today

Arriving at this figure may provide a bit of a challenge. Best of all, locate the contractor who built the building and ask him what it would cost *today*, on a square-foot basis, to build the same structure. Note that the lot is not involved here, only the building. If the builder is not available, ask other contractors and obtain building cost data from the local contractors' association, real estate brokers, and mortgage lenders.

Other Features

Record the items you have noticed that relate to the property's desirability from the point of view of a prospective tenant. Also, put down items that should be allowed for in estimating costs or values. Be careful not to inject your own personal likes and dislikes into this project. You are not appraising the property in terms of your own occupancy. What appeals to you may not be of interest to a tenant and what is unattractive to you may not concern tenants. Be as objective as possible in viewing the property and recording data about it.

Equipment Description

Here you are concerned with the equipment either in the individual rental units or in the building for the use of all or some of the tenants—ordinarily, stoves, refrigerators, laundry appliances, and so on. You need an estimated cash value of those items that are not included in the value of the structure. Generally, whatever rule you apply for separating depreciation between building and equipment should be applied here. Units not built-in are clearly equipment. Built-in stoves, for example, may be considered a part of the building although you can, under some circumstances, treat such a unit, for depreciation and tax purposes, as separate. At this time, make a note of what is there in such detail as will be enough for later computation. Estimating the value will not be easy at first, but with practice you will get better at it. *Be conservative.* Be certain to check to see if replacements are needed.

Assessed Value and Taxes

Ask for a copy of the most recent tax bill and copy the information from it. If not available, call the local tax assessor's office and ask for the assessed values and tax amounts. This information is a matter of public record, and you are entitled to it. Be sure to find out if the present owner has obtained any special tax exemptions that have resulted in lowering his taxes but that will not be available to you. Buyers can easily be misled by using tax costs for the seller that will not apply to the new owner—you, the buyer.

A tax assessor is obligated to review periodically the value of each parcel of property and arrive at an updated assessed value. A reevaluation of assessed value frequently takes place just after a property has changed hands. In some states the buyer is obligated to tell the assessor the purchase price and financing details of the transaction. The prudent investor will adjust his property tax expense figure for possible change in the assessed value.

The property tax amount is obtained by multiplying the assessed value by the tax rate; tax rates usually change every year. If the tax rate has not been established when you are evaluating an investment opportunity, you will have to guess at it.

In some states—California, for example—by law the county tax assessor is expected to determine the market value of the property and use 25 percent of that amount as the assessed value. As long as that is done, you can take a current assessed value and multiply it by four to get an idea of what the assessor thought the property was worth. Be aware, however, that this will be *only* a guide. The assessed value may not be up to date; the assessor may not in fact be following the rule; and there may be other good reasons for the market price to be other than simply a multiple of the assessed valuation.

Assessed values are separate for land and improvements (building); personal property is valued by itself. The ratio of the value of the land to the total of land and improvements may be useful later in estimating values. Ultimately we will need a value for the building by itself for depreciation purposes. If, for example, in the assessment, the ratio indicated is four-to-one for the land, you may want to say later that the portion of the total purchase price attributable to the lot is 20 percent. This would leave 80 percent of the price as the beginning "book value" of the building. (More later on the magic of depreciation.) Note: we have ignored, for this simple example, the relatively small amount of personal property when estimating the book value. To be precise you should calculate the percentages of the total assessed value represented by each component: land, building, personal property. Those percentages could then be applied to a purchase price.

Building Age

If you are looking at a brand-new structure, there is no problem. Otherwise, there are several sources of information. The best is the building department at City Hall. Ask for the date on which a building permit was issued for the property. You can assume the building was completed within a year of that date in the absence of information to the contrary. Try looking at the underside of the lid on a toilet tank—it frequently has a date of manufacture and this would give you a clue. If the seller is the original owner, he may recall the date. But if the property is relatively old, don't rely entirely on the owner's memory or the assertion of the real estate agent. You need to get some idea of how old the property is so that you can intelligently estimate the remaining useful life, a figure needed for depreciation computations.

For income tax purposes a new apartment building of the type we are considering will have an estimated total useful life of forty years. Many buildings that are much more than forty years old continue to function quite well. This arbitrary estimated life is only for the purpose of spreading the cost of the building over the future. If you own a building that is ten years old, by applying the forty-year rule, you come up with thirty years remaining.

Equipment such as stoves and refrigerators does not last as long as the building, so there is a shorter period over which to spread its cost. The actual lifetime is dependent in large part on the kind of treatment and use it is given. The shorter the period, the larger each year will be the amount of depreciation to be charged against income, thus reducing your taxable income. In a situation where there is a special difficulty in arriving at estimates, contact the Internal Revenue Service for guidance. Apartment house equipment such as appliances is often depreciated over five to eight years. (The methods used to arrive at dollars of depreciation are covered later in the chapter.)

Annual Operating Expenses

We have already discussed the property tax item. The other expense data will come largely from the owner directly or through the real estate broker who obtained it from the owner. Some investors ask to see the accounting records to verify the information given. As you gain experience, you will be able to evaluate expense data and recognize unreasonable figures. The total of the operating expenses is going to play an important role in our evaluation. The numbers need to be accurate, and you should make some allowance for the unexpected.

Be certain to find out precisely which *utilities* the owner is responsible for and try to avoid those where there is little or no control over the amount of expense incurred. It is best to have tenants pay for their own power, for example.

The *maintenance* figure will be an estimate because you cannot tell in advance what costs you will have. By looking closely at the property at this research stage you should be able to see where there is likely to be some maintenance cost in the near future. Try to guess, based on what you have learned from the seller about his maintenance costs and what you think you will have to do, what a fair expense will be for the first year of ownership. If you underestimate, you will not realize the profit your analysis would suggest. If you overestimate, you may decide against investing in a property that is in fact satisfactory.

For tax purposes you must separate maintenance and repair costs from *capital improvements*. If you install new plumbing fixtures such as a stall shower, or replace the roof, or replace the water heater, such costs are considered capital improvements. The cost would be added to the cost of your investment. Having a plumber clean out the pipes or a glazier repair a broken window would ordinarily be viewed as maintenance and treated as operating expense to be charged against current income. Again, if in doubt about a particular item, ask the Internal Revenue Service.

For the cost of *insurance*, ask your insurance agent. You will need not only fire and other physical peril coverage to satisfy the lender, but also public liability insurance. This is readily available in one insurance policy, and your agent can quickly tell you its annual cost. Even though you might take over the policy on the property and thereby pay out less than a full term's premium, you want to know the *annual* cost for insurance. Note the heading on the form: "*Annual* Operating Expenses."

As to the cost of *management*, we have already decided you are going to run the show yourself. You cannot pay yourself for this work. If you generate a profit and long-term gain, you get paid then, but you cannot charge for things you do. If you pay someone for services in connection with managing the property, it will be a proper expense and you record the expected annual amount. (If the payment is to be in the form of reduced rent, it is good accounting practice to show the gross rent as income and the allowance as an expense.)

Past Depreciation Rate

Shortly, you are going to calculate a value of the property by taking into consideration the extent to which it has depreciated in the past; the present figure, however, is not affected in any way by what depreciation the seller has taken. It is simply your *estimate*, as you look at the property, as to how it has weathered (literally, even) the passage of time. Now for some guidelines. Even though we have said that for tax purposes an apartment house may have an estimated useful life of forty years (a depreciation rate of 2.5 percent a year), we know the actual depreciation may not be that great. Further, a building depreciates at different rates during its lifetime. If a structure has been reasonably well cared for, a rate of 1 percent per year gone by is probably workable. That would mean, for example, that a ten-year-old property would have depreciated a total of 10 percent. For older properties the rate might be higher. Note: if a building has been renovated and remodeled you may require professional help with determining an appraised value.

Investor's Data

You must decide what you think would be a fair yield from an investment in residential income property, and that is not an easy decision to make. What is reasonable? What is par for the course? And even more important, what do we mean by *yield*?

Shortly, we will calculate several different yields; for the time being, however, let's take the desired yield to be a before-income-tax annual rate of return on an investment that has some risk. The rate, therefore, will be greater than we could get by putting our funds in an insured savings account, which, as this is written, is at least 6 percent and can be 7.5 percent. We will also, for the time being, ignore the long-term capital appreciation return and deal only with current income return. We will use the rate we decide on to capitalize the income to arrive at a fair purchase price. If we require a yield that is unrealistically high, we will miss out on some good investments. If it is too low, we might be deluded into paying too much for the property. In our example, we use 9 percent. By experience you will learn whether this is a good rate for you to use.

Federal and State Tax Rate

This is for income taxes. By looking at your last tax return, you can tell what federal and state rates (and city, in some places) applied to the last increment of taxable income. Because most income taxes are assessed on a graduated scale, to know the rate to apply to a particular source of income you must know to what total the incremental income would come. For this purpose make a careful estimate of what your situation would be and use the percentages indicated. Add together the federal, state and city taxes, if any, to get a single rate. In our example, we are using 40 percent.

Expected Number of Years Before Resale

This is the holding period or investment horizon. It is likely to be the same for each investment you are analyzing, but it does not have to be the same. We will see what differences there are in using different holding periods when we consider the comparison process. The time at which you would resell the property is governed by many factors not ascertainable at this time. If you use accelerated depreciation, that will influence your choice of resale date. A future emergency might govern what you would do. Investing in real estate is a long-term proposition. To obtain the benefits of favorable income tax rates on gain you must hold the property long enough to qualify. For federal taxes that is at least six months; in some states it is a longer period. For our example, and to approximate the typical situation, we use five years.

Annual Appreciation Rate

If you assume that the market value of this property will increase in the future, reflect that in your analysis. If it is likely to go down, you want also to reflect that. How do we know what to do here? If you look around you, it will be apparent that property values have been increasing steadily in most areas for the past thirty years or more. Will this continue? Will inflation continue? If the past is an indicator of the future, the answer is yes. By how much? Compare selling prices of similar properties over the past several years. Discuss this subject with real estate brokers, bankers, and builders. The actual rate will vary from one area to another, even within a community. Be conservative when you pick a percentage.

Here we use 2 percent. Remember, this is saying that each year the value goes up 2 percent of the preceding year's value. In five years that will be more than 10 percent. If you think values will go down, then choose a rate but apply it as a negative.

Expected Resale Expense

The work to be done to make the property presentable when you want to sell it is often referred to as "deferred maintenance." You will have to decide on your maintenance policy. Either keep the property painted and fixed up all the time or let things go until they have to be done. Even then you may decide to offer the property in an "as-is" condition rather than pay the cost of a thin coat of paint to make it look good to prospective buyers. You cannot really know what shape the place will be in five years hence. Even though you plan now to keep it painted, if you run into cash flow problems, you may not be able to implement such a policy. Be conservative and put something into your figures for fix-up. If you do not have to spend it when the time comes, you will simply be ahead further than you expected.

Here we are using $1,000.

Sales Commission

You are planning at this point to use a real estate agent to find a buyer. If you manage to do that yourself, you will have saved the commission—usually, though not always, 6 percent.

Expected Vacancy

You can have rent loss either from vacant units or from occupied units for which the tenant does not pay. Some investors use as much as 10 percent of gross rental income as an allowance to cover their losses. If demand for housing is strong and is expected to remain strong and you plan to avoid bad debt losses, you may want to use a nominal rate.

Here we have 2 percent.

Maximum Gross Multiplier

The computation and use of the gross multiplier are covered later in the chapter. Through experience and analysis of the market place, you will reach a conclusion as to how high you should go. In most areas a multiplier between six and eight will be reasonable. For use in the analysis to be made from the Fact Sheet data you will enter here the maximum multiplier you feel is right for your purposes.

Remarks

A place to record other pieces of information you may need when evaluating the property and choosing one out of several.

Now that you have some idea of what goes into the first page of the Fact Sheet, look at a checklist of some of the things you need to look for—plan on adding to this list as you learn from experience.

Things to Look For When Gathering Facts

1. A termite inspection report should be obtained and studied before deciding on purchase. Local custom will determine whether buyer or seller

pays for this type of report. It may also be important to get a soils engineer's report or one from a structural engineer. In some areas building inspection services will provide a complete report on the soundness and condition of the property. The cost will vary by area and size. Expect to pay at least $100 for a properly done report.

2. Are there local problems with sewage, drainage, streets, earth movement? Septic tank or public service? Adequate? Cost to service septic tank?

3. Is property due to be annexed to adjoining city? Other change in taxing jurisdiction?

4. Improvement bonds or other assessments outstanding?

5. Are all apartment units "legal"? This is a prospective problem particularly for remodeled property. Even though occupied and tenants pay rent, the apartment may not be legal and owner may not be permitted to continue to rent it. Apartment may be deficient with respect to building and health and safety code requirements.

6. Condition of appliances? Will you need to make replacements soon? Check water heaters, furnaces, cooling equipment.

7. How about the roof? It never lasts as long as the building.

8. Why is the owner selling? What's the *real* reason?

9. How does the value of this property compare with others in the neighborhood? If it is out of line, there may be a problem. A luxury apartment in a depressed area will not command adequate rents.

10. What features are likely to appeal to tenants?

11. What has been the rental or vacancy record?

12. Are present tenants on lease? Provisions for changing rents?
13. Have any tenants given notice of leaving?
14. Any unresolved disputes between present tenants and landlord?
15. Any special "understandings" between present tenants and landlord?
16. Will landscaping require attention? Has enough allowance been made for gardening in expense estimates?
17. Have tenants paid a rent deposit to be applied to last month's rent? (Buyer to receive this on purchase.)
18. How about damage deposits? Which tenants have paid and how much?
19. If needed, is TV cable available? How about non-cable reception?
20. Did you get *all* the information needed to complete the Fact Sheet?

(Fact Sheet, Continued)

Financing

Either the seller or the real estate broker will indicate the nature of the financing he has lined up. You may want to arrange your own, but at least for now you should record what others have available. To show some of the options, the example covers a first and second mortgage for a total borrowing of nearly 80 percent. In your efforts to maximize leverage you may be able to raise this to 90 percent.

As discussed previously, a lender will obtain an appraisal and use that figure in determining the amount to lend. Here we assume the first mortgagee will lend just under 70 percent of the offering price. The interest rate is 8 percent and the term of the loan is 20 years. The monthly payments, the first of which is payable about a month after the date the loan is made, cover both prin-

FINANCING: (FACT SHEET, CONTINUED)

LOAN	AMOUNT	RATE	TERM	PAYMENT	FEES OR POINTS	DUE DATE
FIRST	$ 54000	8%	20	$ 452	1%	
SECOND	$ 7000	9%		$ 70		6/80

COMMENTS ON PREPAYMENT PENALTY

First mtge – 1% on unpaid bal.

ASKING PRICE $ 79,000

TOTAL BORROWING $ 61,000

CASH DOWN PAYMENT $ 18,000

ESTIMATED CLOSING COSTS:

PRORATIONS $ 50

MORTGAGE POINTS/FEES $ 540

TITLE INSURANCE/ESCROW FEE $ 500

OTHER ONE-TIME FEES $ 60

TOTAL CLOSING COSTS $ 1,150

TOTAL CASH REQUIRED: $ 19,150

CALCULATION OF MORTGAGE PAYMENT:

$ 54 (LOAN IN 1000s) x 8.364758 (FACTOR) = $ 452

COMPUTATION OF FUTURE DEPRECIATION:

BUILDING: VALUE TO BE DEPRECIATED IS $ 60,000 OVER 30 YEARS

STRAIGHT LINE RATE= 100% ÷ 30 (NUMBER OF YEARS) = 3⅓ % PER YEAR.

METHOD *straight line*

ANNUAL DEPRECIATION CHARGE IS $ 60,000 (VALUE) x 3⅓% (RATE) = $ 2,000

EQUIPMENT: VALUE TO BE DEPRECIATED IS $ 1,800 OVER 5 YEARS.

METHOD AND COMPUTATION: *straight line – $200 salvage*
1800 ÷ 5 = $360 each year

DATE PREPARED 4-20-7-

cipal and interest, with interest computed on the unpaid principal balance. This is an amortization-type loan. Because the lender feels that 8 percent is not high enough, he is asking for a loan fee of 1 percent. This is in effect interest in advance.

When discussing a loan, the lending officer simply looks up a table to give you the amount of the monthly payment. Use the tables in the back of this book either to confirm information given you or to compute alternatives. For example, in order to reduce the monthly payment, you may want to try to persuade the lender to make the loan for 25 years instead of 20. Look up the "amortization" table for the interest rate and term to find the factor to apply to the amount borrowed, in thousands, to calculate the monthly payment.

For the second mortgage in our example we are assuming the payment is "stipulated" to be 1 percent of the amount borrowed, a typical condition for second mortgages. That will mean that the monthly payment will not fully pay the loan by the due date and that, therefore, on that due date the borrower will be faced with paying off the unpaid balance in full. In making your plans for this prospective investment, you might expect to sell the property before the due date and thus pay off both mortgages. Otherwise, you must make necessary provision for taking care of this second mortgage. Of course, the lender might be willing to rewrite the note, particularly if you have been making the payments on time.

Also under the heading of advance planning, you will want to make a note of the prepayment penalty, if any. Here it is 1 percent of the balance due at the time the first mortgage is paid off. That is a very liberal type of penalty. As discussed in the preceding chapter, you should aim for financing without a prepayment penalty, but that may be hard to obtain. When you compute the gain on the resale five years from now, you will want to include the impact of the prepayment penalty.

In this section you calculate the total amount of cash the project requires *for the asking price.* You, of course, are not going to offer to pay the asking price (wait until you come to the next chapter to see how you do that) and hope to get the property for less if you decide you want to buy it at all. A lower purchase price will not automatically reduce the amount of cash required. Recall that the amount of the first mortgage is related to the lender's appraisal. It is also related to the purchase price the buyer and seller have agreed to. If it goes down, so may the lender's first mortgage.

Here, we see that we should have around $18,000 in cash to swing this part of the deal. Is there more needed?

Closing Cost

More dollars over the cash down payment will be needed to pay the mortgage loan fees or points.

Here, $540.

In addition, there will be title insurance or fees to abstractors and attorneys for handling the title search and documents and perhaps appraisal, inspection, and recording fees. Finally, we may have to reimburse the seller for property taxes or insurance he has paid in advance.

In our example we have assumed a purchase as of December 31 with property taxes paid to that date, but we are going to take over an existing fire insurance policy that has been paid in advance to the extent of $50.

All told here the total for closing costs is $1,150. This could have been a great deal more, and you should make liberal allowance in any analysis for closing costs. You will need *cash* for these expenses. Shortly, you will see that you will be able to recover some of these costs almost right away, but they will have to be covered at the time the purchase is made.

On the form is an example of how to compute a mortgage payment. For use in the subsequent financial analysis we also calculate the depreciation charges at this point. The basis for the computation is to be found in the information recorded on the first page of the Fact Sheet.

Future Depreciation

Digressing somewhat from the example, you cover here the essential elements of depreciation for income tax purposes. These elements must be considered when you make decisions as to how you will treat depreciation either in analyzing a prospective investment or in reporting income from property you own. The ultimate authority for information on this subject is the Internal Revenue Service and your tax accountant or attorney.

The basic premise is this: when you invest in an income-producing asset, such as an apartment house, the taxable income is basically the difference between the income you receive from it and the expenses incurred in generating the income. It is easy to state the income. It is the sum of the dollars paid to you by your tenants during the accounting period. That usually is a calendar year—January 1 to December 31. You may have some other incidental income—such as from coin-operated appliances. From the grand total you deduct the operating expenses. These include maintenance, insurance, interest expense, property taxes, utilities, gardening, management, travel, postage, telephone, advertising, and so on. Any expense incurred in connection with generating the income can be deducted. But what about the cost of the property in the first place? (If you were in the business of selling merchandise, you certainly would include in your deductions from income the cost of the goods.)

How do you properly apportion the cost of this type of capital asset over time? The goal is to match the cost of the building and equipment against the income. The cost of the land does not enter into any of this because it is not "used up" the way the building and equipment are. If you knew with certainty exactly how long the building could be used, and that it would then become worthless overnight and that the value of its use was uniform throughout its very distinct lifetime, the problem would be easy to handle. In fact, even though the use and value of a structure do not turn out that way, in effect we pretend that they do and allow for making an adjustment at some time in the future to take care of what the end result really turns out to be.

The portion of an asset used up with use and passage of time is called *depreciation*. By careful calculation after making certain assumptions you arrive at a dollar amount of depreciation for a given time period, usually a year, to serve as the "cost" of the building. This amount then becomes an *expense* to be charged against income.

Two aspects should be apparent at this point. The larger the amount of depreciation, the greater will be the total expenses and the smaller the income or profit. In turn, there will be a smaller amount of income tax to be paid on the income. Second, this expense does not involve the payout of cash in the same manner as for other expenses. In a sense, it was paid out beforehand when the property was purchased. From these two aspects flow the procedures we are concerned with, particularly in the case of real estate investments.

The fact that you can charge as expense the amount of depreciation, yet not disburse funds, means that you may have a surplus of cash from income over expenses that differs from the calculated net income or profit. This will later be described as "cash flow," and we will look at it more closely. For now, concentrate on the methods we can use to compute the amount of annual depreciation, keeping in mind we are looking for a way to apportion the total cost over the life of the property and thus avoid distorting the picture of the results of ownership provided by accounting records and reports.

Until you sell the property and compare the price realized with the original cost, you have no way of knowing what *actual* depreciation (or appreciation) in value has taken place during the period of ownership. As a consequence, depreciation amounts are estimates. (Note there can in fact be an appreciation in the value of the property. As a general rule, you assign the appreciation to the land and consider that the building is wearing out with the passing of time.)

From a practical point of view, the primary reason to concern yourself with trying for an accurate estimate is to take advantage of the income tax rules administered by the Internal Revenue Service and state offices. In addition, the prudent investor or businessperson wants to get a realistic picture of income and therefore needs a way to apportion costs accurately. The question is: how to do it?

Straight Line. There is a certain amount of logic associated with simply charging the depreciation in equal amounts, spreading the total cost over the lifetime. For example, if you expect to use an asset for 20 years, then you would charge 5 percent a year of its original cost, provided there is no value left. For assets other than buildings it is customary to estimate the ending salvage or scrap value, deducting that value from the cost and depreciating the difference. For real estate investments, by custom you ignore the salvage. As we will see later, for tax purposes we depreciate the building during the time we own it, but on the resale, we calculate the long-term gain on the basis of the selling price of the whole property—land *and* structure.

If you use straight line, the term applied to the equal apportionment of the cost over the lifetime, all you need is an estimated remaining useful life. That can be expressed as a percentage for each year.

Let's assume you are looking at a newly constructed apartment house. To maximize the amount of depreciation and to minimize the amount of income tax, you want as short a life as possible because that will give you the most depreciation to charge each year. The IRS has decreed that you may use forty years as a maximum useful life for a new building of this type; you would have trouble, on the audit, if you tried using less. For forty years the annual straight line depreciation rate would be 2.5 percent (40 × 2½ = 100 percent).

For used property you use another figure. If the building is, say, ten years old, you might consider using thirty years remaining useful life. But this will depend upon the condition of the property. It might not have thirty years left because of abuse or other factors. Whatever number you use, you must be prepared to justify it to the Internal Revenue Service.

Accelerated. Assets do not necessarily depreciate at an even rate, and you may use methods other than straight line. For new construction, in part to recognize a variation from straight line and, probably more importantly, to provide incentives to build new housing, the income tax rules include optional depreciation methods called "accelerated." The "declining balance" and "sum of the years' digits" formulas are available to increase the amount of depreciation in the early years of the lifetime of a capital asset. Their use will reduce the amount of tax payable in the beginning. There is a day of reckoning, however.

Overall, the rules are too complex for treatment here, and it is sufficient just to realize that if you use an accelerated method, you may have to adjust your declaration of taxable income at some future time to offset partially some of the advantage gained earlier.

You and your tax adviser may well decide to make a particular investment because the property is eligible for accelerated depreciation, especially if it is newly built. In such cases, you may be able to charge twice the straight line rate of depreciation. Used property is subject to lower accelerated rates and only under certain conditions. Full and current information is readily available from the Internal Revenue Service.

For our purposes we will stick to the straight line method. You can't go wrong. It will give conservative results. As you progress in your investment activities, you will want to see how you can use accelerated depreciation rates and increase your immediate returns.

If you are considering a property that contains any significant value of equipment, use an accelerated formula, probably the sum of the years' digits method.

Assume you have equipment worth $5,000, and it has an estimated remaining useful life of five years. To calculate the first year's depreciation charge, you need a factor or ratio to apply to the total amount to be depreciated. Assume you can sell the used equipment at the end of five years for $500. You have $4,500 to depreciate.

The formula requires that we add the years' digits: $1 + 2 + 3 + 4 + 5 = 15$. (For eight years, it would be 36.) The factor for the first year is 5/15; second year, 4/15. Note that the numerator is the number of the years of useful life for the first year, and one less for each succeeding year. The denominator remains the same and is the sum of the years of useful life.

For the first year's depreciation then:

$$5/15 \times \$4,500 = \$1,500.$$

For the second year:

$$4/15 \times \$4,500 = \$1,200.$$

During the last years of the asset's life the accelerated depreciation charge would be *less* than what it would be under straight line. For example, take the fifth year. Under straight line we would have taken the $4,500 and divided that sum·into five equal parts: $900 would be the annual depreciation charge. Using the sum of the years' digits method:

$$1/15 \times \$4,500 = \$300$$

In total, under *both* methods, $4,500 would be depreciated, but by differing amounts each year and, therefore, with different effect on your tax status. The sum of the years' digits method can be used for any capital asset including buildings provided it meets the eligibility requirements and a new asset is a likely candidate. Most of the time, however, in practice this method is used on new equipment rather than buildings.

The declining balance method is widely used by aggressive investors to maximize early returns from newly constructed apartment projects. Assume that the asset meets the eligibility requirements and we can use the formula producing the maximum amount of depreciation—the "double declining balance" method. Another way of saying the same thing is to state that the depreciation rate is 200 percent of the straight line rate. But, unlike the straight line procedure, the declining balance formula requires that the rate be applied to an amount reduced by the depreciation charge of the preceding year, hence the expression "declining balance." This will produce a much larger depreciation charge in the early life of the asset than does straight line, and that is the whole idea. Let's look at an example.

Assume we have a new building used for residential purposes and from which at least 80 percent of the income is from such residential use. The first user could elect to use the double declining balance method. The cost is $100,000 for the building (ignore land and equipment). The estimated remaining useful life is forty years, so the annual straight line rate would be 2.5 percent. We double this to get 5 percent (200 percent of 2.5 percent = 5 percent). This rate will be applied to successive ending book values.

First year depreciation charge:
  5 percent of $100,000=$5,000   Ending Book Value $95,000
Second year depreciation charge:
  5 percent of $95,000=$4,750   Ending Book Value $90,250
If we had used straight line:
  2.5 percent of $100,000=$2,500 each and every year.

In our example, we have opted for straight line for both building and equipment. To depreciate the building over thirty years (even though we have no intention of owning it for thirty years), we use an annual straight line rate of 3.3 percent. That rate times the value of the structure gives us $2,000 as the charge to be made each year we own the property. If we were to remodel or extensively repair the building, we would change the $60,000 base, which would in turn change the depreciation charge. For the equipment, we started with a $2,000 value and estimated $200 salvage. Over the five-year period we want to allocate the difference, $1,800. This gives us $360 to be charged each year. As we replace the equipment with new units, we recalculate, using new costs and perhaps different lifetimes. We could use, say, the sum of the years' digits method on the equipment even though we use straight line on the building. We could even use a different method on different pieces of equipment.

We have now completed our examination of the two-page Fact Sheet. All the data needed for the analysis of the investment opportunity now is available.

Analysis Worksheets

The analysis of the property is divided into four parts: Indicated Economic Value, Cash Flows, Yields, and Resale Results.

By using the information gathered and the tables provided you can forecast the financial picture according to the assumptions made. In this manner you can obtain an idea in advance of what the situation would be if you bought the property. You are truly looking before you leap!

Refer to the example reproduced on pages 80-90.

Purchase and Financing Data

For convenience, show clearly the total of the down payment and costs to arrive at the total cash required. You had better know where that sum is coming from, or the analysis will be just an exercise, no matter how good an investment it appears.

Indicated Economic Value

Since you intend never to pay more for something than it is worth, you must find out what a particular piece of property is worth. There are three different computations to make and when you have made them, the figures can be averaged. The goal here is to arrive at values using the customary approaches for valuation and then to be able to compare the offering price.

The offering price is simply a beginning point. Investors generally determine independently what they think a property is worth and prepare an offer accordingly (making sure they do not offer more than what the seller is asking, of course!). You must not feel any compulsion to accept the seller's idea of value. Find out for yourself.

Cost Approach. The objective is to find out what it would cost today to replace. Start by computing the current cost to build the structure today, using the square-foot area and building cost. Then estimate what percentage of that value has disappeared through usage. Recall you examined the building to see if you could judge a rate of past depreciation. Now use that rate and apply it to the current cost. To the depreciated cost of the building add values not a part of the structure but a part of the total property. When these are added together, you have a total reproduction cost.

Recall the earlier instructions on how to estimate the value of

ANALYSIS OF PROPOSED INVESTMENT*

LOCATION: _1234 Wistful Vista, Utopia, California_

PURCHASE AND FINANCING DATA

ASKING PRICE		$ _79,000_
FIRST MORTGAGE	$ _54,000_	
SECOND MORTGAGE	$ _7,000_	
TOTAL BORROWINGS		$ _61,000_
	DOWN PAYMENT	$ _18,000_
PRORATIONS	$ _50_	
MORTGAGE POINTS/LOAN FEES	$ _540_	
TITLE INSURANCE/ESCROW FEE	$ _500_	
OTHER ONE-TIME FEES	$ _60_	
TOTAL EXPENSES		$ _1,150_
	TOTAL CASH REQUIRED	$ _19,150_

INDICATED ECONOMIC VALUE

A. COST APPROACH: _4,000_ SQUARE FEET   @$ _19.00_ EACH = $ _76,000_

LESS DEPRECIATION @ _1_ % YEARLY FOR _10_ YEARS = $ _7,600_

DEPRECIATED COST OF BUILDING $ _68,400_

ADD: EQUIPMENT/LANDSCAPING $ _2,500_
         LAND VALUE $ _15,000_
         TOTAL ADDITIONS $ _17,500_

TOTAL REPRODUCTION COST $ _85,900_

B. GROSS MULTIPLIER

$$\underset{\text{ASKING PRICE}}{\$\ \underline{79,000}} \div \underset{\text{GROSS ANNUAL INCOME}}{\$\ \underline{10,800}} = \underline{7.3} \text{ TIMES}$$

$$\underset{\text{YOUR MULTIPLIER}}{\underline{8}} \times \underset{\text{GROSS ANNUAL INCOME}}{\$\ \underline{10,800}} = \underset{\text{MAXIMUM PRICE}}{\boxed{\$\ 86,400}}$$

C. CAPITALIZATION OF INCOME

GROSS ANNUAL INCOME LESS VACANCY $ _10,600_

LESS ANNUAL OPERATING EXPENSES $ _3,400_

NET OPERATING INCOME $ _7,200_

$$\underset{\text{NET OPERATING INCOME}}{\$\ \underline{7,200}} \div \underset{\text{DESIRED YIELD}}{\underline{.09}} = \underset{\text{MAXIMUM PRICE}}{\boxed{\$\ 80,000}}$$

$$\underset{\text{NET OPERATING INCOME}}{\$\ \underline{7,200}} \div \underset{\text{ASKING PRICE}}{\$\ \underline{79,000}} = \times\ 100\% = \underset{\text{YIELD}}{\underline{9.1}} \%$$

*ASSUMPTION: PURCHASE MADE AT FIRST OF YEAR; ALL ANNUAL FIGURES the lot by using data on the property tax bill. If there is a similar vacant lot on the market, use the sales price as the value of "your" lot. Because a number of factors have a bearing on the market price, the cost approach value often is not the same as the offering price.

Gross Multiplier.   This method allows you to compare this property with other similar properties. If you could go around and locate other properties identical to the one being studied and determine what they sold for recently, you would have a good way to compare the offering price. That is not practical, however. Instead, you look for a *common denominator* and find it in the relationship of gross rental income and sales price. Because property rented to others is being used to generate a return on the investment, it is reasonable to think that the level of rents is related to the value of the property, though the net return will vary according to expenses.

By reading newspaper classified advertising you will be able to find offering prices and gross rental income data. Divide the gross income into the asking price to obtain what is called the "gross multiplier." Some ads will even state: "Selling at 6.5 times gross." Enough checking will reveal what the going gross multiplier is in your area. It will vary slightly for different types of property, so, if your interest is in fourplexes, try to use only data for fourplexes.

The smaller the number, the better the deal, all other things equal. But be careful. Property offered at, say, five times gross may have some serious deficiency. Very high gross multiples may indicate either a very tight rental market or an owner who does not know what his property is worth. Any property having a multiplier of 8 or less will be of interest. Properties with much higher multiples may not be worth investigating. Use the gross multiplier as a means of sorting out properties you hear about, going after the lower multipliers first.

In our example, the subject property has a 7.3 multiplier, the right side of our criterion of 8. Going one step further, we compute the maximum price to pay for the multiplier we have chosen, and, not unexpectedly, it is greater than the offering price.

So far so good. The property offered at $79,000 is favorable when measured against both cost and market as calculated by use of the gross multiplier. How about net income?

Capitalization of Income.   Many analysts feel that the most useful and important measure is that on net income. They argue that when putting money to work to produce a return, it is the return that counts, relative to dollars invested. So they capitalize that net income.

Assume you have not borrowed any money and have used all cash to buy the property. Out of rents you pay all expenses. Without regard for income taxes—no depreciation charge—what does the property provide in the way of a net income? If you put $10,000 in a savings account and receive $600 at the end of a year, the rate of return is 6 percent. How about the apartment house? Note we are working only with current income and have not allowed for long-term potential capital appreciation. We are assuming either that we will not sell the property or that, if we do, we get back only what we paid.

In the example, we see that the net operating income is $7,200. This is our return on an investment of the purchase price. What should we pay for this asset? That depends on how much we want as a yield. Previously we had decided on a 9 percent yield, and we use that figure here. By dividing the yield into the income, we get a value of $80,000. If you put $80,000 to work at 9 percent per annum, the income would be $7,200. This gives us another benchmark. We compare the $80,000 against the $79,000 asking price. We could go as high as $80,000. The other way of looking at it is to see that the operating income related to the asking price will give a yield of 9.1 percent.

Our goal was to reach indicated economic values. We now have three. If they are averaged the result is $84,100. When this is measured against the asking price of $79,000 plus the closing costs, other than prorations, we can conclude that we would have a satisfactory investment if we bought at the asking price—better if for less. But there is more to check first.

Cash Flows

If you owned the property, collected the rents, and paid the expenses, would you have enough cash? Ordinarily you want an investment to be self-sustaining, though it is not automatically bad if the investment is not. If the expenses exceed the income, you will have to put up the difference and that would be viewed as simply increasing your cash investment. In some situations this would make sense. Ordinarily not so.

In our example, we already have decided on the vacancy allowance so we can calculate the expected rental income after vacancies. The cash-paid operating expenses have been totaled on the Fact Sheet. Because we have borrowed funds for the project, we will make the mortgage payments out of the rental income. The annual mortgage disbursement is twelve times the actual monthly payments of $452 and $70. If all goes well and our operating expenses turn out to be what we estimated, we should have a surplus of $936 at the end of the year. We conclude the property will be self-sustaining on a cash basis.

But, as everyone knows, the only useful dollar is the one remaining *after* taxes have been settled.

Annual Taxable Income

You need to compute, for tax purposes, the return. From the actual income deduct all those expenses deductible under the Internal Revenue Service rules. The first computation is that of mortgage *interest*.

In our example, what part of the $5,424 paid in first mortgage payments was applied to interest? What part of the $840 for interest on the second mortgage?

You could laboriously calculate each separate payment. Much easier just to look up a table. Turn to Table I for an interest rate of 8 percent and term of 20 years. Table I gives you a factor to be applied against the number of thousands you have borrowed. Under the column heading "INTEREST," and for the end of year 1, you see the multiplier factor, 79.23451. When we multiply this factor by $54 we get $4,278.66. Why, then, has $4,282 been entered on the form? We rounded the monthly payment to an even $452, so we made a slight adjustment. This would not really be necessary when preparing estimates.

ANNUAL CASH FLOW - BEFORE INCOME TAX

GROSS ANNUAL RENTAL INCOME	$ 10,800	
LESS VACANCY ALLOWANCE OF 2 %	$ 200	
NET ANNUAL SCHEDULED INCOME		$ 10,600
LESS: ANNUAL OPERATING EXPENSES	$ 3,400	
1ST MORTGAGE (12 X MONTHLY PAYMENTS*)	$ 5,424	
2ND MORTGAGE (12 X MONTHLY PAYMENTS)	$ 840	
TOTAL ANNUAL CASH EXPENSES		$ 9,66-
NET ANNUAL BEFORE-TAX CASH FLOW		$ 93●

*PRINCIPAL AND INTEREST ONLY - DO NOT INCLUDE PROPERTY
TAXES AND INSURANCE.

ANNUAL TAXABLE INCOME

NET ANNUAL SCHEDULED INCOME		$ 10,60
LESS: ANNUAL OPERATING EXPENSES	$ 3,400	
FIRST MORTGAGE INTEREST	$ 4,282	
SECOND MORTGAGE INTEREST	$ 621	
DEPRECIATION:		
BUILDING - $ 60,000 OVER 30 YEARS	$ 2,000	
EQUIPMENT - $ 1,800 OVER 5 YEARS	$ 360	
TOTAL ANNUAL DEDUCTIBLE EXPENSE		$ 10,66●
ANNUAL TAXABLE INCOME		$ <63●
TAX LIABILITY** - FEDERAL AND STATE COMBINED RATE OF 40 %		$ <25●

ADJUSTMENTS FOR FIRST YEAR

MORTGAGE POINTS/FEES	$ 540	
TITLE INSURANCE AND ESCROW FEES	$ 500	
OTHER ONE-TIME FEES	$ 60	
TOTAL ADDITIONAL DEDUCTIBLE EXPENSES		$ 1,100
INCOME TAX CREDIT -- COMBINED RATE TIMES PRECEDING TOTAL		$ 440

INCOME TAX PAYABLE ON OTHER INCOME FOR YEAR IN WHICH
THESE ADDITIONAL EXPENSES ARE INCURRED WILL BE REDUCED
BY THE AMOUNT OF THE INCOME TAX CREDIT SHOWN.

**IF ANNUAL TAXABLE INCOME IS NEGATIVE, THE AMOUNT OF THE TAX LIABILITY
IS YOUR TAX SHELTER BENEFIT.

The second mortgage in the example came with a *stipulated* payment so we have to use the appropriate table. In this case, turn to page 275. For a rate of 9 percent, the interest expense factor is 88.72974 to be applied to $7 for total interest expense of $621, as entered on the form.

The depreciation charges were calculated on the Fact Sheet, so now we can make the necessary entries of $2,000 for the building and $360 for the equipment. After deducting all expenses, both those paid in cash and the depreciation not paid in cash, the *net annual taxable income* amounts to a loss of $63.

We have assumed all along you have other income and that this investment was to help you accomplish a goal of minimizing current income and maximizing long-term gain. You can charge a loss against your other income and thus reduce the number of dollars paid out for income taxes. Here the loss of $63 is actually worth $25 to you because your total income taxes will be less by that much because of owning this property for the year.

In addition, under the *current* income taxes rules, you can charge against income certain other expenses in the year in which they have been incurred. At the time of purchase you spent money for mortgage loan fees, which was interest in advance, and title insurance and other costs. The $50 for prorations has already been recovered out of income during the year because it was for prepaid expenses. The total of $1,100 is deductible expense, increasing the first year's operating loss. The value of this is the tax rate (state and federal) times the loss.

Here we reduce income taxes by a further $440. This loss, of course, is only to be taken in the first year.

Now we have some results to evaluate. Leaving for later the long-term aspects, let's state these returns in a form easier to use in comparison—percentages.

Yields

In this section we deal only with current income yields. The long-term results will be handled later.

On the previous sheet we determined the income would be

YIELDS

A. **ANNUAL**

NET ANNUAL BEFORE-TAX CASH FLOW $ *936*

INCOME TAX LIABILITY (DEDUCT IF TAXABLE
INCOME IS POSITIVE, OTHERWISE ADD.) *add* $ *25*

NET SPENDABLE CASH AFTER TAX $ *961*

B. **FIRST YEAR**

ADD INCOME TAX CREDIT FROM ADJUSTMENTS $ *440*

TOTAL SPENDABLE CASH FIRST YEAR* $ *1,401*

*PRESUMES PROPERTY OWNED FOR FULL 12 MONTHS.

C. **TYPICAL ANNUAL RETURNS ON CASH INVESTED**

1. BEFORE INCOME TAX:

$$\frac{\$\ 936}{\text{NET ANNUAL BEFORE -}\atop\text{TAX CASH FLOW}} \div \frac{\$18,000}{\text{CASH DOWN}\atop\text{PAYMENT}} \times 100\% = \boxed{5.2\ \%}$$

2. AFTER INCOME TAX:

$$\frac{\$\ 961}{\text{NET SPENDABLE}\atop\text{CASH AFTER-TAX}} \div \frac{\$18,000}{\text{CASH DOWN}\atop\text{PAYMENT}} \times 100\% = \boxed{5.34\%}$$

3. INCLUDING MORTGAGE REDUCTION:

NET SPENDABLE CASH AFTER-TAX $ *961*

MORTGAGE REDUCTIONS FIRST YEAR $ *1,361*

TOTAL RETURN $ *2,322*

$$\frac{\$\ 2,322}{\text{TOTAL RETURN}} \div \frac{\$\ 8,000}{\text{CASH DOWN}\atop\text{PAYMENT}} \times 100\% = \boxed{12.9\%}$$

NOTE: YIELDS FOR SUBSEQUENT YEARS WILL NOT BE THE SAME IF THERE
IS A MORTGAGE NOR IF THE INCOME AND EXPENSES DO NOT
RETAIN THE SAME INITIAL RELATIONSHIP.

enough to produce a surplus of $936 after all bills were paid but before income tax. Because we have a loss, there is also a tax shelter benefit of $25. The "net spendable" is an important figure because of its widespread use in real estate investment analysis.

For the first year we have an additional tax saving of $440 (for our tax bracket and one-time expenses). The total first-year spendable cash figure, $1,401, is important if we used some short-term borrowing to scare up the cash needed to swing the deal; this sum is a source for repayment.

Now let's move to a *typical* annual result. After all, you are considering the investment for the long term and want to compare against alternative properties and alternative investments. What will you receive typically each year?

Compute the before-tax yield of cash as to down payment, not to total cash invested. You could do the latter, but the smaller figure generally is used because of the partial recovery of the closing costs in the first year. True, there is some remaining money at risk, but most investors ignore that minor matter and prefer to make comparisons relative to different down payments at risk.

The most important yield is that on an after-tax basis. Here we have a yield of 5.34 percent *after taxes*. That certainly compares favorably with savings accounts at 6 percent or even 7 percent *before taxes*. But there is more. As pointed out before, the mortgages are being reduced each time a payment is made. As the rental income is the source of the funds to make the mortgage payments, the reduction is a form of yield from the investment.

When we computed the interest expense, we also computed the figures needed for entry here. The sum of $1,142 and $219 is $1,361. We should consider this a return, however, *only* if we are confident that the property will ultimately sell for *not less* than we paid for it. Otherwise, the loss will cut into the equity provided by this mortgage reduction. Given that assumption, we now have a yield of 12.9 percent from current operations. If there is capital appreciation, the return will be greater.

We now have simulated the results from owning this apartment house. If we have no alternatives that will provide better than a 5.34 percent after-tax return of cash or 12.9 percent return including equity build-up, we will want to consider seriously making the purchase. But before we make up our minds, let's look at the long term.

Estimated Results from Resale

The investor in real estate expects, as a general rule, that the market value of the property will increase over time. If that gain is realized, it supplements the annual gain. In evaluating the opportunity, you should make some assumption concerning appreciation and reflect it in the statement of overall results.

Here we assumed 2 percent annual appreciation rate and recorded it in the Fact Sheet. We assume that the market value each year will be 2 percent greater than in the preceding year, so the increase is compounding. Referring now to our example, you can see that we have used a factor applied to the original purchase price to obtain the figure of $87,000 as an expected selling price.

The table of appreciation factors, Table III, starts on page 278. Having selected a 2 percent annual rate, we go to the number of years held—five—and find the factor of 1.104076. You certainly would not be wrong in using a straight 10 percent—2 percent a year for ten years. The expected selling price at best is a rough estimate, however; many factors determine the ultimate value.

When you sell, there will be expenses to pay. The real estate commission amount is governed by the sales price; we originally felt that the usual 6 percent is the rate that likely will apply. If you can negotiate this downward, or make the sale yourself, the difference is a saving. The expected fix-up expense of $1,000 may turn out to be a different amount when the time comes; experience will guide you here. Then there is the prepayment penalty.

When gathering the data for this evaluation, we found that we would be subject to a penalty of 1 percent of the loan balance at payoff time. In this resale forecast we are assuming the purchaser will obtain new financing, thus resulting in a payoff of our loans. So we need to know what the loan balance would be at the end of five years. Again we can use the tables.

Table 1 for 8 percent and 20 years will provide a Balance Due

ESTIMATED RESULTS FROM RESALE

EXPECTED SELLING PRICE:

<u>1,104076</u> x <u>79,000</u> = $<u>87,000</u>
APPRECIATION FACTOR   PURCHASE PRICE

LESS: SALES EXPENSE @ <u>6</u> % COMMISSION = $ <u>5,220</u>

FIX-UP EXPENSE $ <u>1,000</u>

PREPAYMENT PENALTY $ <u>473</u>

TOTAL EXPENSES $ <u>6,693</u>

GROSS CASH PROCEEDS $80,307

LESS: FIRST MORTGAGE BALANCE $ <u>47,262</u>

SECOND MORTGAGE BALANCE $ <u>5,680</u>

TOTAL AMOUNT PAID OFF $ <u>52,942</u>

NET CASH PROCEEDS FROM SALE $27,365

COMPUTATION OF LONG TERM TAXABLE GAIN:

BEGINNING BOOK VALUE (ORIGINAL COST) $ <u>79,000</u>

LESS ACCRUED DEPRECIATION - BUILDING $ <u>10,000</u>
                           - EQUIPMENT $ <u>1,800</u>

TOTAL DEPRECIATION $ <u>11,800</u>

ENDING BOOK VALUE $ <u>67,200</u>

TAXABLE GAIN: GROSS CASH PROCEEDS $ <u>80,307</u>

LESS ENDING BOOK VALUE $ <u>67,200</u>

GAIN/LOSS ON SALE $ 13,107

INCOME TAX ON GAIN/LOSS:

$ <u>13,107</u> ÷ 2 = $ <u>6,554</u> TAXABLE AMOUNT.
GAIN/LOSS ON SALE

INCOME TAX LIABILITY = $ <u>6,554</u> x <u>40</u> % = $2,622
                         TAXABLE   RATE

NET CASH PROCEEDS FROM SALE $ _27,365_

LESS: INCOME TAX LIABILITY $ _2,622_

        CASH DOWN PAYMENT $ _18,000_

        MORTGAGE FEES AND TITLE INSURANCE
        LESS TAX CREDIT TAKEN PREVIOUSLY $ _660_

        TOTAL DEDUCTIONS $ _21,282_

NET GAIN AFTER TAX AND RETURN OF FUNDS INVESTED $ _6,083_

ADD ADJUSTED ANNUAL NET SPENDABLE CASH GAIN:

        $ _900_   X _____5_____   = $ _4,500_
           ADJUSTED   YEARS HELD
           CASH GAIN

TOTAL AFTER-TAX GAIN FROM THIS INVESTMENT $ _10,583_

TOTAL YIELD

AVERAGE ANNUAL YIELD:

        $ _10,583_   ÷   _____5_____   = $ _2,117_
        TOTAL AFTER-TAX GAIN   YEARS   ANNUAL GAIN

        $ _2,117_   ÷ $ _19,100_ X 100% =   _11.1_%
          ANNUAL GAIN   CASH INVESTED   YIELD AFTER
                                                              TAXES

COMPARISON WITH SAVINGS ACCOUNT:

        TOTAL AFTER-TAX GAIN FROM INVESTMENT $ _10,583_

        IF YOU DEPOSITED ORIGINAL CASH INVESTED
        TO EARN _6_ %, COMPOUNDED DAILY FOR
        _5_ YEARS IT WOULD HAVE GROWN TO

        $ _19,100_   X _1.349618_   = $ _25,778_
          CASH INVESTED   FACTOR

                        LESS DEPOSIT $ _19,100_
                     TOTAL EARNINGS $ _6,678_
        LESS INCOME TAX @ _40_%   = $ _2,671_

                NET AFTER-TAX EARNINGS $ _4,007_

                DIFFERENCE BETWEEN GAINS $ _6,576_

factor of 875.2207 for each $1,000 of the original loan at the end of five years. By multiplying this factor by $54 we get $47,262 for the unpaid balance, for a prepayment penalty of $473—thus making the total expenses to be deducted from the sales price $6,693. Gross cash proceeds are $80,307.

The mortgages also are to be paid off out of the proceeds. The first mortgage balance is already known—$47,262. We use Table II for the second mortgage. Recall the payment was stipulated and the amount does not amortize the debt in a specified term. Using the same procedure, we find a factor of 811.4309. Multiplying it by $7, we obtain a payoff amount of $5,680. If we do not sell the property and pay off the second mortgage prior to the due date, we will have to settle this debt anyway. Computing the amount due on the due date is done in the manner just described.

We now find, after paying off the mortgages, we have net cash of $27,365.

Because this is a capital asset held long enough to qualify, the profit or gain will be taxed on a long-term basis. We can apply our regular income tax rate to half the gain *or* half the rate to all the gain. That is a generalization that would apply to the vast majority of taxpayers. Those in a tax bracket greater than 50 percent and with other capital gains and tax preference income may have to calculate their tax on a different basis, coming up with proportionately more tax to pay. In our example we have assumed none of that would apply. The first step, in any event, is to calculate the taxable gain. This amount will depend on the way in which we have handled depreciation.

In the example, depreciation was figured on a straight-line basis. For the building it was $2,000 each year, for a five-year total of $10,000. For the equipment, depreciation will be complete in five years and will total $1,800. Because these amounts of depreciation have already been charged against income, we must reduce the book value or "basis" accordingly. The ending book value represents, in a sense, the *cost* of the property for use in computing how much we have gained by selling it. The difference between what we sell it for and this adjusted cost will be the gain or loss on the sale. Note that the expenses incurred in connection with the sale are deductible, and that we get the benefit of those costs when computing taxable amounts. Here we arrive at a $13,107 gain to be shared with income tax collectors.

If we had used accelerated depreciation, the foregoing computations might have been different. The rules are complex, however, and it is not worthwhile to try to discuss them here. Recall, simply, that accelerated depreciation gives you larger amounts to be charged in the early years. On the other hand, if you sell the property before you have owned it—under *current* rules—at least 100 months, some of the accelerated depreciation may have to be charged back as current income, thus reducing the benefit. In given cases it will be worthwhile to use accelerated depreciation, but careful study is required to know just when. We have kept our example simple by using straight line depreciation. In most cases this will produce the most satisfactory investment return.

How much of the gain must we share? In the example we have divided the gain by two. To this we apply the full ordinary income tax rate to reach a tax amount of $2,622. This would take care of both state and federal taxes if our 40 percent rate is the correct total of the two rates. There is another consideration. If in the year we make the sale we have a substantial change in our other income, the estimated rate we chose when gathering data may not be usable. Tax rates apply to "marginal" income. For example, assume your taxable income from all sources other than this investment is $28,000. Using rates applicable to income in 1973, federal income tax would be charged at the rate of 36 percent on the last $4,000 of income in that $28,000 total. If you add another, say, $2,000 of taxable income, it would be taxed at the next bracket of 39 percent. You can see, then, the actual tax to be paid on the long-term gain from the sale of a capital asset such as this apartment house will depend on rates applicable at the time the sale is made, your other income, and the way in which you computed depreciation. Notwithstanding these complexities, you can prepare forecasts along the lines illustrated. As long as you use the same assumptions as to income tax rates for *each* property analyzed, you will have a proper basis for comparison.

The next item to compute is the net gain *after* paying income taxes and recovering the investment.

Referring to the example, note the $660 for mortgage fees and other costs. Certain one-time expenses were deducted for tax purposes the first year. By way of the tax credit we recovered part of that money—$440, to be exact. The original amount was $1,100; we have recovered the "missing" $660. The original total closing or settlement costs were $1,150. What about the $50? We had to pay it at the time of purchase to reimburse the seller for fire insurance paid in advance; we recovered it out of income during the first year.

So now, after getting our money back and paying income taxes on the gain, we have $6,083 in hand. This is only part of the gain, however. How about the amounts each year during the holding period? That is a return also. Because, however, the interest expense will be less each year as the mortgage principal is reduced, even though income and expense remain in proportion, the dollars of gain in subsequent years, after income taxes, will be fewer. The tax shelter benefit might even be eliminated. When we add the annual income to the gain on resale, we must make an adjustment—we cannot just multiply the annual return by five. An arbitrary procedure is simply to take 90 percent of the annual amount and then multiply that figure by the number of years the property is owned. Here we have adjusted the $961 down to an even $900, not 90 percent but used for the sake of simplicity. When this total of the expected annual return is added, we have a grand total after-tax gain of $10,583.

Total Yield

We started out to determine just what kind of overall return we could achieve by investing in this property. The best measure is the number of dollars you have more than you started with, after all obligations are settled. Here we have $10,583 in hand as well as all of the money we invested: the dollar return. All taxes are paid. To compare this gain with investments that employ different amounts of money, we need a percentage, obtained by dividing the cash invested into the net gain, expressed in annual terms, even though, actually, most of the gain was realized at the sale of the property.

We received, on the average, $2,117 each year ($10,583

divided by 5), on a total initial investment of $19,100. The return represents a yield of 11.1 percent per annum *after* taxes. We can use that figure to compare against other properties and even other types of investment for which an annual return has been computed allowing for the same considerations.

For example, if we had put $19,100 in a savings account that pays 6 percent compounded daily for the five-year holding period, it would have grown to $25,778. (See Table IV for factors to use.) Of course, the interest earnings are subject to income tax as current income, hence at the full rate. When we deduct income tax and the deposit, the net gain is $4,007. The real estate investment, given the assumptions used in our computations, would provide $6,576 more.

So we are dollars ahead. What did we give up or contribute to earn this difference? We took a risk. The results *could* be quite different. There could be vacancies and unexpected expenses that would eliminate or reduce seriously the annual gain. At resale time we might have found that the market value had dropped substantially or that we simply could not find a buyer at any price and so were locked into a losing proposition. Finally, when we add up the number of hours devoted to the project and divide it into the dollars of gain, we may find that we worked for a ridiculously low hourly rate.

The Third Step

The third step is to analyze carefully the results obtained for each property evaluated and reach a conclusion as to which one you want to buy. Repeat the Fact Sheet and Analysis Worksheet procedures for each of several similar properties. From this work you can take appropriate data to complete an *Investment Analysis Summary*. This summary will enable you more clearly to see which property offers the best returns. After reaching your conclusion, you can go ahead to obtain the property. A word of caution: numbers can fail to disclose pertinent factors. You would not want to decide on a particular property solely on the basis of the yields or dollar calculations. Be certain your assumptions are reasonable and that you are comparing comparable oppor-

Date __4-25-7-__

PROPERTY ADDRESS	PRICE	CASH REQUIRED	AVERAGE INDICATED ECONOMIC VALUE	YIELD REQUIRED	NET ANNUAL SPENDABLE CASH	TAX SHELTER VALUE	ANNUAL YIELDS AFTER TAX	ANNUAL YIELDS AFTER INCLUDING MORTGAGE	HOLDING PERIOD	TOTAL AFTER TAX GAIN	AVERAGE ANNUAL YIELD
1234 Wistful Vista	79,000	19,150	84,100	9%	961	25	5.34	12.9	5	19,583	11.1%
1111 Gold St.	49,000	5,080	43,850	8%	392	176	9.8	23.4	5	5,916	24.74%
536 Mission St.	84,000	16,400	85,000	9%	765	200	5.1	8.2	5	7,455	9.09%

tunities—apartment houses with apartment houses and so on. You can use different size projects and even different holding periods; you can vary the financing.

Finally: do not expect to gain the moon! This type of investment is a long-term proposition offering very good but *not* fantastic returns.

4

Making the Offer

AFTER considerable searching and extensive analysis we have decided to buy the property at 1234 Wistful Vista. We must prepare a formal offer, in writing, and be prepared to "sell" the seller on our proposal. There are several points to be kept in mind in this important phase, and they will be reviewed along with an illustration of a typical purchase contract. If the seller accepts we then prepare to "go into escrow."

Formulating the Offer

The price we will offer is very important but not the only item that matters. However, it is a good starting point. Going back to our analysis of each of the properties we have been considering (as set forth on the Investment Summary discussed in the preceding chapter), we find that we prefer 1234 Wistful Vista because it offers the greatest return on the funds we have available to invest. From the calculation of indicated economic values we know the offering price of $79,000 is below what we can pay. The cash flow analysis and computation of long-term gain were made on the basis of a purchase price of $79,000. Is that the amount we should offer?

There's an old, highly revered law of bargaining: Never pay the asking price! Does that apply here?

Obviously the seller wants the highest price possible. When he set the $79,000 figure we do not know whether he planned to stand firm or was simply hoping he could get it but would settle for less. If you offer $79,000 you will never know whether he would have taken less. One way to find out is to offer less. For our part, we want to obtain the best deal possible and certainly do not wish to pay more than we have to. If the prospective returns are good at $79,000 they will be even better at a lower purchase price. All of this points to an offer of something less than the asking price.

Possibly even more important than getting a reduced price is obtaining maximum financing. Perhaps we would prefer to borrow even more than the amounts we used in the analysis. If so, we want to redo the analysis on the new basis of financing to see what the results would be.

In formulating the offer we want to ask for the best terms possible while leaving ourselves open if we don't succeed on all points. That is accomplished by making the offer "subject to" specified conditions. To illustrate:

Before setting into motion an action designed to result in purchase, you should have clearly in mind exactly how you want the offer to be framed. If you are using the services of a real estate broker you will be able to ask his advice on various terms. If he also represents the seller, he should be able to judge the acceptability of your ideas. If you use an attorney he will know how to frame the offer in legal terms to protect you, but he is not likely to be familiar with the market situation or the seller's position. Just how feasible is it for a lay investor to formulate an offer, write it up, and present it on his own?

The most conservative approach is to use a real estate broker and employ an attorney to draw up all the papers. Assuming both are competent, the job will be done in the best possible fashion. It will also cost the most as far as fees are concerned. As a general rule, the real estate broker does not charge a fee for drafting the offer, but of course the attorney does. After you run into trouble while trying to do all of this on your own, you might feel that an attorney's fee would be a small price to pay to save yourself grief. If you are dealing with an owner directly and not through a real estate broker, you might save the real estate commission; but, then again, you might not, and you will not have had the benefit of his financing contacts, knowledge of the market, and his advice and expertise.

At most, we can say it is *possible* for you—on your own—to prepare an offer, present it to a seller yourself, have it accepted, and complete the purchase. Whether that is the way it would work for you is unknown. Regardless of who is involved, you must make certain basic decisions with respect to the details of the offer. We will concentrate on those, leaving unresolved the question of using brokers and attorneys. That's your problem.

So now we need to formulate the offer and communicate it to the owner and/or his agent. This should be done in writing. It is probable that an oral contract either would be unenforceable because a written contract is required by law, or would be unsatisfactory because of misunderstandings due to the absence of written terms. The written offer may be called a "purchase contract," "contract of sale," or "deposit receipt." The terms will vary according to local custom and practice. We will use the term "purchase contract."

Purchase Contract

The form reproduced on pages 102-103 has been created by the California Real Estate Association for use by its members. The blanks have been filled in to illustrate possible terms to be offered in purchasing the property we have been considering. In California it is customary to prepare four copies of the contract. When signed by all parties, the copies are distributed to buyer, seller, real estate broker, and, usually, the title insurance company or escrow agent. A reproduction may be used for a lender.*

---

* We have indicated it is feasible for some investors to handle all aspects of a real estate investment by themselves; in this example, however, we have made certain assumptions concerning your use of the services of others. When a real estate broker takes

Read the form through carefully, then come back to the following description.

Deposit Amount

This is sometimes called the "earnest" money. How much? The buyer should make this amount as small as possible, because it will be tied up either until the offer is rejected and the deposit returned, or until the deal is closed and the money is applied to the purchase. The seller wants as large a deposit as possible. If he accepts, he does not want to find that the buyer has subsequently reneged and that he has no way of recovering whatever loss that has caused. The deposit is subject to forfeiture if the buyer does not proceed once the offer is accepted. The real estate broker may receive some part of a forfeited deposit. He has earned his commission when he brings buyer and seller together. He will want the deposit to be large enough so if there is a default it will be relatively easy to collect something for his efforts. You will note this is covered in the form we are using. If you are dealing directly with the owner-seller he will want a deposit large enough to provide you with an incentive, faced with forfeiture, to complete the transaction.

Recall that you will need enough cash to cover the down payment and the closing or settlement costs. Many buyers consider the deposit made at the time the offer is drawn up to be simply an advance payment on the closing costs, and some real estate brokers make it a practice to ask for a deposit equal to the estimated

---

a listing, he may also obtain a preliminary title report from the title insurance or abstract company. He may also obtain a pest control report, or the owner may already have done so. These reports will be of considerable use to all parties. If they are not obtained before the execution of a Purchase Contract, they will be afterwards. In our example, we are assuming, for instance, that the pest control report shows only minor damage and that the inspector will issue a report that the property meets the standards of state law after work costing less than $500 is performed. Further, we know from the preliminary title report that there are no special features of the record title to be handled in advance of the transfer of title when the deal is closed. As a general practice, the real estate broker will prepare the purchase contract after discussion with the parties. The buyer must, of course, know what he wants and communicate it to the person preparing the contract. The seller must be certain he understands the terms of the contract before he accepts the offer by signing the documents.

amount required for such costs. As you can see, the actual amount for a given case is a negotiable one. Here we decided $1,000 was a good, healthy amount, one that would tell the seller we were serious. This is important, especially when we are asking the seller to reduce his price. The sign of a serious buyer is the placing of a sizeable sum of money on the line. We might even have gone to $2,000 to impress him further. The assumption is that we want the property on our terms and will do what we can to persuade the seller to accept.

Who should get the deposit? Ideally an escrow has been opened so that the deposit is placed in those neutral hands. A real estate broker serves quite well as a holder of deposit funds when he is involved in the transaction. You may even find yourself making the deposit check payable to the seller. Unless you have reason not to trust the seller—in which case you shouldn't be trying to buy from him—there is nothing wrong with giving him the deposit. The risk you take, of course, is that it might be difficult to get your money back if he does not do his part in the transaction. You can ask a bank or an attorney to serve as a third party if none of the other alternatives appeals to you.

If you either postdate your check or ask the person who is to take care of the deposit not to cash it, then you probably have not given a valid deposit, and a seller might have grounds later for rescinding. On the other hand, two parties can agree on a course of action, and if the seller accepts a postdated check, knowing and acknowledging the conditions, there may be no problem.

Purchase Price

We are going to try $77,000. There is no special reason for thinking the seller will take $2,000 less, but we know for sure that if he will, we have saved $2,000. At worst, he can reject the offer; at best, he can accept it and we are ahead.

Property Description

It is customary to use both the legal and common description to avoid a controversy later over which piece of property was intended. The legal description, exactly as it appears in the public

CALIFORNIA REAL ESTATE ASSOCIATION STANDARD FORM

Real Estate Purchase Contract and Receipt for Deposit

THIS IS MORE THAN A RECEIPT FOR MONEY. IT MAY BE A LEGALLY BINDING CONTRACT. READ IT CAREFULLY.

Received from ____ John A. and Mary B. Investor _____ Utopia _____ California, ____ May 1 ____ 19_7_.

_____ herein called Buyer,

the sum of ____ --ONE THOUSAND DOLLARS ONLY-- ____ Dollars ($1,000.00 ____)

evidenced by cash ☐, personal check ☒, cashier's check ☐, or ____

as deposit on account of purchase price of ____ --SEVENTY-SEVEN THOUSAND DOLLARS ONLY-- ____ Dollars ($77,000.00 ____)

for the purchase of property, situated in ____ Utopia ____ County of ____ Glory ____ California, described as follows:

____ 1234 Wistful Vista, Utopia, legally described as
____ Lot 4 in Block 20, as designated on the map entitled
____ "Happy Haven, City of Utopia, County of Glory, State of
____ California," filed in the office of the Recorder of the County
____ of Glory, on August 10, 1960, in Volume 3 of Maps, at page 9.

Buyer will deposit in escrow with ____ ABCDE Insurance and Trust Company ____

the balance of purchase price as follows: Subject to: (1) Buyer obtaining a first loan secured by this
____ property of not less than $54,000 at interest not more than 8% plus loan fees
____ of not more than 1% of loan, with a prepayment penalty not greater than 1% of
____ unpaid balance for a term of not less than 20 years; (2) Second deed of trust
____ to seller for not less than $7,000 with interest at 9%, payable $70 per month,
____ principal and interest combined, with unpaid balance due on June 30, 1980.

~~This loan to be without encumbrance, existing, refinance, With unpaid of record, lien, seller other loan these due other than~~

____ covenants, easements and restrictions shown in
____ ABCDE Insurance and Trust Company preliminary report #48756

Seller shall furnish to Buyer at ____ Buyer's ____ expense a standard California Land Title Association policy insuring title in Buyer subject only
to liens, encumbrances, easements, restrictions, rights and conditions of record as set forth above. If Seller fails to deliver title as herein provided, Buyer at his option may terminate this agreement and any deposit shall thereupon be returned to him.

2. Property taxes, premiums on insurance acceptable to Buyer, rents, interest, and ____ XXX ____ (insert in blank any other items of income or expense to be prorated) shall be

prorated as of ~~XXXXXXXXXXXXXXXXXXXX~~ (2) ____ close of escrow ____ (Strike (1) if (2) is used).The amount of any

bond or assessment which is a lien shall be ~~paid~~ (Strike one) by ____ seller. ____ Seller shall pay cost of revenue stamps on deed.

3. Possession shall be delivered to Buyer (Strike inapplicable alternatives) (a) on close of escrow, or ~~XXXXXXXXXXXXXXXXXXXXXXXXXXXXXXX~~

(c): ____ XXX

4. Escrow instructions signed by Buyer and Seller shall be delivered to the escrow holder within ____ 14 ____ days from the Seller's acceptance hereof and shall

provide for closing within ____ 30 ____ days from the opening of escrow, subject to written extensions signed by Buyer and Seller.

5. Unless otherwise designated in the escrow instructions of Buyer, title shall vest as follows:

____ John A. Investor and Mary B. Investor, his wife, as joint tenants

(THE MANNER OF TAKING TITLE MAY HAVE SIGNIFICANT LEGAL AND TAX CONSEQUENCES. THEREFORE, GIVE THIS MATTER SERIOUS CONSIDERATION.)

6. If the improvements on the property are destroyed or materially damaged prior to close of escrow, then, on demand by Buyer, any deposit made by Buyer shall be returned to him and this contract thereupon shall terminate.

7. If Buyer fails to complete said purchase as herein provided by reason of any default of Buyer, Seller shall be released from his obligation to sell the property _____ and may proceed against Buyer upon any claim or remedy which he may have in law or equity; provided, however, that by placing their initials here _____ Buyer and Seller agree that it would be impractical or extremely difficult to fix actual damages in case of Buyer's default, that the amount of such damages is a reasonable estimate of the damages, and that Seller shall retain the deposit as his sole right to damages.

8. Buyer's signature hereon constitutes an offer to Seller to purchase the real estate described above. Unless acceptance hereof is signed by Seller and the signed copy delivered to Buyer, either in person or by mail to the address shown below, within ___three___ days hereof, this offer shall be deemed revoked and the deposit shall be returned to Buyer.

9. Other terms and conditions: (Set forth any terms and conditions of a factual nature applicable to this sale, such as financing, prior sale of other property, the matter of structural pest control inspection, repairs and personal property to be included in sale.)

This offer is subject to Seller paying the costs of repairs indicated by a structural pest control inspection report but not to exceed $500. Seller to provide a bill of sale for all items of personal property of his ownership currently at the premises, the consideration for which is included in the purchase price.

10. Time is of the essence of this contract.

Real Estate Broker ___I.M. Realtor, Inc.___ By ___I.M. Realtor___

Address ___321 Main St., Utopia, CA___ Telephone ___765-4321___

The undersigned Buyer offers and agrees to buy the above described property on the terms and conditions above stated acknowledges receipt of a copy hereof.

Dated ___May 1, 197-___

Address ___220 Angus Crescent, Utopia, CA___

Telephone ___123-4567___

John H. Investor
Mary B. Investor
Buyer _____

ACCEPTANCE

The undersigned Seller accepts the foregoing offer and agrees to sell the property described thereon on the terms and conditions therein set forth.
The undersigned Seller has employed the Broker above named and for Broker's services agrees to pay Broker, as a commission, the sum of ___Forty-Five Hundred ---___ Dollars ($ ___4,500.00___) payable as follows: (a) On recordation of the deed or other evidence of title, or (b) if completion of sale is prevented by default of Seller, upon Seller's default, or (c) if completion of sale is prevented by default of Buyer, only if and when Seller collects the damages from Buyer, by suit or otherwise, and then in an amount not to exceed one half that portion of the damages collected after first deducting title and escrow expenses and the expenses of collection, if any.

The undersigned acknowledges receipt of a copy hereof and authorizes Broker to deliver a signed copy of it to Buyer.

Dated _____

Address _____ Seller _____

Telephone _____

Broker consents to the foregoing.

Dated _____ Broker _____

A REAL ESTATE BROKER IS THE PERSON QUALIFIED TO ADVISE ON REAL ESTATE. IF YOU DESIRE LEGAL ADVICE CONSULT YOUR ATTORNEY.

record, will be stated in the title company report. It may be copied
from the deed produced by the seller. If you use the latter source
you should take some action to confirm that the deed actually
relates to the physical premises you have been looking at. If the
seller happens to own more than one property and has several
deeds lying around, you will have to make sure you have the right
one. Deeds do not include street addresses.

Escrow

You are cautioned against not using an escrow. Both buyer
and seller need the protection afforded by a competent escrow
agent. In the next chapter you will see what else the escrow agent
does.

Balance of Purchase Price

The essence of our offer is this: we expect to be able to
borrow at least $54,000 on a first mortgage or trust deed basis from
a financial institution. This might be financing the seller has arranged in advance, a source the real estate man has, or arrangements we have made ourselves, preliminarily.

Before formulating the offer you should have some idea of
how the financing can be done. Even though the deal is subject to
obtaining the loans stated, you do not want to include "wild"
terms that have little hope of being realized. We want the seller to
take back a second mortgage of $7,000. It is likely we were told the
seller would entertain such an idea. If the seller is not a candidate
for a second mortgage, we should have another source lined up. By
borrowing a total of $61,000 we will then have to put up in cash a
down payment of $16,000 plus the closing costs. It is presumed
that we know where this cash is coming from—at least in time to
meet the closing date. If the proposed purchaser fails to keep his
part of the bargain, most likely he will lose his deposit. Don't
make offers lightly unless you don't mind forfeiting money.

Although we believe at the time of making the offer we can
obtain the financing as stated, we want the seller to share the risk
that we might not. We do that by using the expression "subject
to." When the seller signs the purchase contract, he is agreeing, for

example, that he cannot hold us to the offer if it turns out that the only first loan we can get is at 8.5 percent (or any other adverse variation from the terms stated in the offer). You might wonder if this provides a loophole for the buyer to use to back out if he simply changes his mind. It probably does. Some sellers might ask that the offer include a provision such as: "buyer to use all diligence in arranging financing." Then, if the buyer backs down and it can be shown he really could have obtained financing on the terms stated, presumably the seller would be sustained in keeping the deposit.

Title

No title is entirely clear. At a minimum, the property is subject to current taxes, which until paid are a lien against the property. Frequently there are easements for utility companies. There may have been covenants and restrictions with respect to the use of the land recorded when the ground was originally subdivided. This is another reason for obtaining a preliminary title report whenever possible. The buyer, however, is protected by providing in the purchase contract that he is agreeable only to certain "clouds on the title." To the extent there are other liens, such as mortgages or trust deeds, the seller will have to satisfy them as a part of completing his side of the transaction. Otherwise he cannot pass "clear" title. In our example, we don't know what loans are on the property before the sale and we don't care. The seller is going to pay them off, probably out of the proceeds of the sale. This will be shown in more detail in the next chapter.

Title Insurance

The cost of this is negotiable between the buyer and seller. By custom—in California, for example—for property located in the southern half of the state, the seller pays; in the northern half, the buyer; and in the middle of the state (wherever that is), they share this expense. Then again we find—in new residential subdivisions, for example—the developer-seller pays the cost.

Taxes and Rents

The owner of property must pay certain items in advance,

such as property taxes, insurance premiums, and perhaps interest. Adjustments will be needed between the buyer and seller as of the date the deal is closed. We refer to that as the "close of escrow," which will ordinarily be the date on which the deed, transferring title, is recorded. Rents are invariably payable in advance so the seller should have some funds to be applied in the future, and these should be passed to the new owner. The customary basis for these adjustments is proration. For example, the property taxes are proportioned at so much a month, or day, and the time period between closing and the date to which the taxes have been paid is used to determine how much is owing to the other party. Note that in some cases money is due the seller because he paid items in advance. In others, where payment has been deferred and the new owner will have to pay the bill, a charge is made against the seller for his proportionate share. The details of these computations are set forth in the statement of the transaction prepared by the escrow agent.

The total amount of credit or charge will be governed largely by the time of the year the sale is made. If we assume a December 31 date and payment of property taxes by the seller for only the first half year, no adjustment would be needed. If all tenants had paid one month's rent in advance the total would be credited to the buyer. As a consequence, the cash required by the buyer may be less than otherwise expected.

Bonds or Assessments

In order to finance the cost of improvements a municipality may float a bond issue and charge the repayment to the property owners whose property has been improved. This may be for street lighting, water or sewer systems, or street paving. You may insist that a seller pay off this obligation and base your offering price accordingly. On the other hand, you may reduce the price and agree to assume the indebtedness. Your decision is reflected here.

Revenue Stamps

A levy is made now by some states on transactions involving transfer of title. Until 1968, the federal government required that documentary stamps be applied to all deeds on the basis of $0.55 per $500 of value of equity transferred. Many states have continued on the same basis from the time the federal government relinquished this taxation. By custom the cost is borne by the seller in most localitites.

Possession

The normal arrangement is for the buyer to obtain possession of the property as of the date the escrow is closed.

Escrow Instructions

The escrow or closing agent cannot proceed until instructions from the parties have been received, and some time thereafter must be allowed for the work to be performed. If necessary, this time provision (and others) is subject to extension by agreement of the parties or on the authority of the real estate agent. The most important time provision, however, is that for the close of the escrow relative to the acceptance of the offer. This should be stated clearly in the purchase contract. Enough time must be allowed for the financing and so on to be arranged. The seller, of course, will want his money as soon as he can get it. Thirty days is often not too long a time in which to do whatever has to be done.

Vesting of Title

The buyer should give careful thought to this subject and obtain legal counsel if necessary. We will defer a discussion of this technical point until we reach the next chapter. In our example, we have shown "joint tenants" as a typical way in which a buyer takes title where it is possible to do so.

Damage or Destruction

Until title passes the seller retains the insurable interest, and no action should be taken with respect to changing the fire insurance until the escrow is closed. Meanwhile, a buyer may choose to obtain insurance, but it is unlikely that he will be able to show an insurable interest prior to the date when title passes, and therefore he would not be able to collect if a loss occurs. Unless you suffer the loss you do not have an insurable interest. Of course, if the property is substantially damaged or destroyed, the buyer may rescind the contract and get his deposit back, at his option.

Failure to Complete

You will recall that the purpose of the deposit is primarily to protect the seller against loss due to nonperformance of the prospective buyer. When the seller signs a purchase contract, he cannot realistically continue trying to sell the property to someone else. So, during the time it takes the buyer to come up with the funds, the seller just has to wait. If the deal falls through because of inaction on the part of the buyer, the buyer should have to pay damages to the seller. The measure of damages is difficult to make. If in fact the seller could not have obtained another buyer in the meantime, it could be argued that the seller had not suffered any damages at all, but no one will ever know. The parties can agree— and this is customary—that the amount of the deposit is a fair measure of damages and thus will be forfeit if default by the buyer occurs. If the seller defaults, the buyer would have ordinary legal remedies for damages by bringing a law suit.

Time for Acceptance

From a practical point of view, as well as the legal requirement, there must be a time limit on the offer. It is automatically void or revoked if not accepted by the time stated in the contract. There are many legal niceties to refer to if there is an argument over whether the offer was accepted within the time, or in the manner prescribed by contract or law. For our purposes, the seller either signs within the time limit or rejects. As a practical matter, if the seller doesn't care much for your proposal he will let you know, directly or through the intermediary, what he would like instead. In effect, the seller now makes a counter-offer. In these circumstances, either the original offer is modified on its face, with the parties initialing appropriately, or you start all over with a new contract document. Your goal is to have a meeting of the minds with such meeting duly reflected in written form. It is common practice to give the seller a short time only in which to make up his mind. In our example, we use the customary three days.

Other Terms

In areas where termite infestation is common, it is customary to have property inspected by a licensed pest-control inspector who prepares a report showing how the building measures up to the standards set forth in the applicable state law. The parties are free to agree on who will pay for the work to be done if the report specifies corrective action. Lenders often make loans subject to the completion of such work. Buyers and sellers not subject to outside lenders' requirements are free to buy and sell on an "as is" basis. It is still a good idea to obtain a "termite report" and if there is a significant problem, it can be reflected in the price. If the buyer suspects an earth movement or other structural problem, he should ask for an appropriate inspection and make the offer subject to resolving whatever problems are identified. In addition to regular soils engineering inspection services there are structural inspection services available. Particularly for older properties, it would be prudent for the investor to spend a few dollars (perhaps $100) to obtain an expert's opinion. This, of course, either would be done before the offer is prepared, or the offer would allow for the prospective consequences of such an inspection.

As a general rule, it is customary for the buyer to pay for inspections and for the seller to pay for the work to be done.

Personal Property

We are speaking here of the appliances and other equipment not considered a part of the structure. Technically, there should be a bill of sale to establish transfer of title and value or cost. In practice, this step is often ignored. The bill of sale can be set forth as a straight statement on a piece of paper; blank printed forms can be purchased at stationery stores.

Real Estate Broker

At this point in the purchase contract, the name and address of the broker are recorded simply as information. Technically, the broker is not a party to the contract; he has been serving as an agent for one or both of the principals. As will be seen shortly, he may be a party to a contract between the seller and himself.

Buyer's Signature

This is important. The date here starts the time running for the seller's acceptance and should be clearly stated. Sometimes even the time of day is included. To avoid possible legal entanglements, it is best that all buyers sign and the signatures be in the same form as identified at the top of the contract. The same form should also be used for vesting title.

Now we have finished the first part and the waiting begins. Will he or won't he accept? What about a counter-offer? We will find out in 72 hours.

Acceptance

As a general rule, the commission payable to the broker will be spelled out (as in our example), thus disclosing the amount. If the seller and broker wish to keep that information confidential, they can do so by preparing a separate contract. If that is the case, the seller would simply accept the offer and cross out any reference to the payment to the broker.

By signing the contract the seller acknowledges receipt of the deposit and agrees to the terms and conditions stated. When this is handled by the real estate agent, a signed copy will be returned to the seller and a copy given to the buyer. Now the process of completing the transaction begins.

It is probably a rare event when the original offer is accepted exactly as made and without changes. Just for the sake of simplicity, we will assume in our example that the seller does agree, and will conclude the transaction accordingly. You should be prepared, however, for much bargaining and negotiation. If you are not a good face-to-face negotiator, you should use the services of an agent, whether a real estate person or an attorney.

The Counter-Offer

We have prepared our offer to provide for the most advantageous terms from our point of view. It should be no surprise, however, that the seller may have other ideas. When we learn what terms are acceptable to the seller, we may need to reevaluate the deal.

If the change in terms will not affect basically the financial returns, we will not need to do any refiguring. On the other hand, for a different price and/or financing arrangements, we should go back to the analysis and work out the results using the new figures. Then, and only then, can we determine whether we should accept the counter-offer. It may be better to consider one of the other properties we analyzed before but did not consider to be the number-one opportunity. We can maximize our return from the effort expended on the evaluation only by using the analyses and comparing against a new set of figures for the seller's offer. Avoid making any decision solely on the basis of emotion. Be a rational decision-maker.

After analyzing several pieces of property, we have narrowed our interest to the one we think is best. We have obtained as much advance information as possible, perhaps even an inspection report and preliminary title report. We have been working with a Realtor who has done a professional job in getting information, lining up financing, and above all persuading the seller to accept the offer we put together. We now have a signed and accepted purchase contract. We can hardly wait to "go into escrow."

5

Closing the Deal

You and the seller have agreed on the terms and signed the purchase contract; you have put up your earnest money or deposit. You both now need an independent third party to do all the things necessary to complete the transaction on the terms agreed upon and to protect the rights of all parties involved. As the buyer, you will need to come up with the balance of the money; the seller will have to execute a deed that will be satisfactory. Once documents are prepared and recorded, money is available, and keys are turned over, the buyer takes possession, makes contact with the tenants, and is then a landlord.

The Buyer's Side

We have assumed the real estate broker opened an escrow with a title insurance company and obtained the preliminary title report. This is not always done in advance and in fact is more frequently done following the signing of the purchase agreement by buyer and seller. The buyer's deposit is normally placed in escrow.

In sections of the country where title insurance companies do not also provide escrow service, this service is provided by attorneys. It is commonplace for the buyer to retain an attorney who will prepare all the papers, obtain an abstract of title, handle the money, deal with the seller's attorney, and see that the deed is recorded. Although in theory a buyer can do all of these things himself, he is much wiser to use the services of professionals; the cost is minor indeed, especially when compared to the cost when things go wrong.

There will be one or two things for the buyer to do, aided by his real estate broker, but most of the activity will involve the escrow agent's following the buyer's and seller's instructions. We will discuss each of the items in some detail shortly. Meanwhile, there is a step to be considered by the buyer.

Opening the Escrow

As indicated, the practice in most areas is to have the title to the property searched or abstracted to determine not only who has title but what liens, encumbrances, easements, or other "clouds" may be on the title. For the sake of simplicity, we will use the procedure followed by title insurance companies, including escrow services; but in doing so we do not mean to slight abstractors and abstract companies. For all practical purposes the process is the same. When an escrow is opened a preliminary title report is ordered. This report will show the manner in which the title stands, a brief comment on encumbrances, etc., and a sketch of the parcel of land showing survey indicators. But there may be a problem. You have looked at the property and are certainly aware of its address— 1234 Wistful Vista. You recall we said that the legal description does not include the street address. How can you be sure that the legal description used on the purchase contract, and later to be used on the deed, actually represents the property you think you are buying?

Obtaining a Land Survey

As you look at the sketch on a copy of the title company's preliminary report, and then compare it with the property as you stand on the street in front of it, you ordinarily will not be able to confirm that they are one and the same. If you go looking for the surveyor's monuments, don't expect them to be easy to find. You have a nagging feeling that although the documents suggest Lot 4 in Block 20, Happy Haven, and 1234 Wistful Vista are one and the same, perhaps they are not. Are you about to obtain title to some other property? When the documents are recorded, you will have title to the property represented by the legal description on the documents, and no other, regardless of the agreement between the parties. Correcting this kind of mistake will cost money.

Even if the legal description is in order and you are in fact getting the property you think you are getting, there is another question. Just where are the lot lines and property boundaries? There are fences, perhaps, but what does that prove? It may prove that the guy who put up the fence didn't know what he was doing. To find a way to solve these problems, you hire a land surveyor.

The surveyor will take the legal description, obtain official survey data for the area, and go to 1234 Wistful Vista. His job is to mark off on the ground the boundaries of the property in such a way that these boundaries can be compared with the legal description to be used on the deed. If he finds an inconsistency between the two descriptions, he will soon let you know. He will also determine where the lot line is and thus confirm whether the fencing is in order. Depending on how complex the survey is, the cost will range from $100 on up—well worth it if you avoid more costly trouble later. When you buy a car, do you not verify by visual inspection that the serial number on the vehicle matches the title document you receive from the seller? This is the equivalent of confirming the physical location of the property against the legal description, except it will ordinarily take a land surveyor to do the job for you.

Clouds on the Title

A primary reason for obtaining a preliminary report is to determine whether the seller can in fact produce a marketable title. This may be the time the seller learns he has a problem. Perhaps there is some unsatisfied debt still standing against the property. It might be his, or it may have been the previous owner's. If the current owner did not obtain a title search at the time he bought the property, he may have taken over an unsatisfied obligation. That will have to be taken care of by the seller before he can pass clear title and get his hands on your money.

If there *are* title defects, ordinarily the real estate broker or escrow agent will contact the seller and let him know about them. Of course, if it will take a lot of time to clear the title and if the time is important, the purchaser can decide against going ahead with the deal. Let's go into the subject of clear and not-clear titles a little further.

The underlying law and practice is that interests in property are established by "recording"—making a part of the public record—a document such as a mortgage, deed, judgment, or contract. In the case of a mortgage, for example, the original lien or encumbrance will be recorded at the time it is originally executed and the money lent. When the debt is paid off, a satisfaction or release should then be recorded to show to the world that the property is no longer subject to the debt because the debt has been settled. All of these documents are recorded in chronological order in the public records office.

An abstractor or title searcher literally searches the public records for any and all filings pertinent to the legal description you started with. He then prepares a copy or note of what he finds. When this is all put together it is called an "abstract" or "title search." Some title insurance companies obtain copies of all filings each day and sort them out, first rejecting any that have nothing to do with property. The remainder then are noted in records by property description. This makes it much easier to prepare a title report when the time comes.

But even with microfilm and other automated processes, title searchers are human, and humans can make mistakes. Assume you have gone through the process of buying the property and a title search was made and a deed recorded transferring title to you. Everyone assumes all is in order. Later you decide to sell and another title search is made that uncovers an unsatisfied mortgage in addition to the ones you know about. It becomes clear that the first searcher was not very efficient and he missed the item. Who is responsible? If you had the foresight to purchase *title insurance*, the title insurance company would be faced with paying the cost of whatever was necessary to clear the title. That could even involve paying off the amount of the debt.

Title Insurance

One risk you take when buying property is that a defect in the title you obtain may show up later and you will be unable to obtain redress from the seller. In theory, if all title searching was perfect, all clouds on the title would be disclosed and there would be no problem. Not all searches are perfect, however, so there is a risk in transferring title. When you buy title insurance you are transferring the risk or uncertainty of loss to the professional risk-bearer, the insurance company. You pay a premium for title insurance as for any other form of insurance. There is one difference, however: the premium is paid only once and the protection stands for as long as you own the property.

There also may be some legal encumbrances that are not required to be recorded in the public record. Unless the title insurance policy provides otherwise, these would not be covered. This is not a very real problem in the vast majority of transactions. Further, the title insurance may protect only the lender, or may be written to cover both lender and owner. As a broad general rule, financial institutions require title insurance; private lenders may not, but they certainly should have it.*

Completing the Financing

The seller has agreed to take part of his price in the form of a second mortgage. A second mortgage is easily handled. Those documents will be prepared by the real estate broker, the title company or escrow agent, or the attorney handling the paper work. We know how much the first mortgage is to be, so now we go to the lender.

---

*In some areas a title insurance company automatically provides both escrow service and title insurance; in others, the services are separate and are charged for separately. You will not have any trouble finding out the local practice. Ask a real estate broker, banker, or attorney who specializes in real estate, or a title company.

As a part of the negotiations leading up to the signing of the purchase agreement, either we as prospective buyers, or the real estate broker, had discussed the loan with a financial institution. Sometimes a real estate broker will obtain a commitment from a lender that it will make a loan on a specific property if the buyer qualifies. These are all preliminary steps.

If we have not already done so, now is the time to prepare a financial statement and submit it to the lender. We would show as part of our assets the deposit of $1,000 made on the property. The lender would obtain a credit report on us and do what is necessary to confirm the information we provided, including verifying the bank balances and other assets and liabilities shown on the financial statement. We probably also ought to show the lender our analysis of the property and therefore show clearly why the lender can expect to get his money back.

The lender will now obtain an appraisal of the property, if he has not done so already. Lenders employ professional appraisers either on contract or as employees. As a general rule, you will not be told what the appraised value is. If the lender agrees to make the loan for the amount requested, you can assume that the property appraised for enough. Although the ratio of loan to appraised value used by lenders will fluctuate from time to time, the loan officer will probably give you some indication of the ratio he is working with at the time. Assume for the kind of property we are expecting to buy, the lender we are dealing with uses a figure of 75 percent. This will mean that for each $100 of appraised value—appraised by the *lender*, not the buyer or seller—he will lend $75. We need $54,000. We would not have made the offer without obtaining at least some tentative indication from a lender that we can raise the necessary amount. Lenders generally will not obtain an appraisal and firm up the loan amount before an offer has been made and accepted. The loan ratio is also applied to the purchase price so regardless of the price agreed to by the parties, the lender's loan will not exceed 75 percent of the appraised value or the purchase price, whichever is smaller.

If, after getting an appraisal and evaluating our loan application, the loan officer says he will grant the $54,000, we are all set—

except for the terms. Those will be checked shortly. What if he says he will lend only $50,000? This would probably mean that the appraised value was less than $72,000. (75 percent of $72,000 = $54,000.) If this is the case, we probably goofed in offering to pay $77,000. But we have some protection. We offered to buy *subject to* certain conditions including obtaining a first loan for $54,000. It was also subject to interest rate, term, and loan fee conditions. If one or more conditions cannot be met, we do not have to go ahead with the purchase. Of course, we are free to go ahead anyway, but those purchase contract provisos give us a chance to take another look and back away if we want to.

We have assumed the lender was agreeable to our use of secondary financing by way of a second mortgage from the seller. It is customary to provide the banker with a copy of the purchase contract at the time of applying for the loan so that he is aware of the terms of the purchase agreement. He will also need a copy of the title report.

If the loan is not approved, what is next? We can always go to another lender if we fail to get what we need from the first one. Not all lenders take the same position, and it is quite possible to get a loan from another lender if we are turned down initially. However, this takes time, and we agreed to take care of our part of the bargain within a time limit stipulated in the contract. To avoid forfeiting the deposit we will have to show that we tried, in good faith, to obtain the financing stated. It is important to make all possible preliminary arrangements for financing before making an offer to buy contingent upon loans.

We will assume instead that the loan for $54,000 has been approved. The lender will prepare the mortgage loan agreement and promissory note and either have us sign them at the lender's office or forward them to the escrow agent's office, where we will sign them. Prior to this time, we have an important decision to make, however. In what form do we want to take title?

Form of Title

You will want to consult with your attorney before making a final decision on this point. The following comments are offered to assist you in gaining an understanding of what is involved so you can consider the matter more intelligently. The entity to which title is to be passed will also be exactly the same entity borrowing the money. Your lender will have something to say about the form of the entity. What are the possibilities?

In the majority of cases relevant to this book, the purchase is made by a husband and wife. In most states the purchase would be made either as community property or in joint tenancy. The law is quite specific on this point in every state and you may not have this choice. The legal standing of the title is governed in large part by the wording on the deed and other documents. If you choose to take title in joint tenancy, the deed in particular would read:

John A. Investor and Mary B. Investor, as joint tenants
In some areas the expression "with right of survivorship" is added; it is probably unnecessary.

The alternative:

John A. Investor and Mary B. Investor, his wife, as community property.

What is the difference? It all has to do with what happens if one of the two parties dies. As joint tenants, the survivor automatically acquires 100 percent interest in the property. As community property, the interest of the surviving spouse is subject to the community-property laws of the jurisdiction and the last will and testament of the decedent. Some say that under joint tenancy, probating the estate can be avoided, but as community property, probate may be necessary. There may be other reasons, in both situations, for probating to be required.

Remember: consultation with your attorney in advance is a good idea before deciding this important matter. There are also some important income tax considerations as well as estate and inheritance tax angles.

While both parties are living, both must sign a deed if title is to be transferred. Under both forms, each has an undivided half-interest in the property. This presumes that the property was purchased with community-property funds. Property acquired before marriage would have title vested in one party. Subsequent to marriage the property may continue to be held as "separate property," but that status might be affected by community-property laws and the manner in which earnings from the property were handled.

For property held in joint tenancy by other than husband and wife, the extent of the individual interests would also be equal in the absence of an agreement to the contrary. Upon the death of a joint tenant, the survivors automatically acquire the interest of the decedent. On the death of a spouse, the simple filing of a "termination of joint tenancy" supported by a death certificate is frequently all that is required to clear title for transfer. (In our example, we are taking title as joint tenants.)

A final point. It is imperative that all documents relating to the title be uniform in the manner in which the parties are designated. The escrow agency checks for this sort of thing and a lender will be very specific. This uniformity includes insurance, the subject to be treated next.

Insurance

We will have an asset to protect, and even if the lender were not standing at our elbow, we would want to have, as a minimum, fire insurance on the building and some liability coverage against loss arising from accidents connected with the property.

Fire

The lender will require that the amount of fire insurance be at least equal to the unpaid balance of the loan. The second mortgagee will also want protection. Both will want their names to appear on the policy. First, the amount.

Basic property insurance policies cover the "actual cash value" of the property. This value, arrived at when the loss occurs, is the current replacement cost, less depreciation. This is the maximum amount payable. The cost to repair will always be greater than the actual cash value unless the damaged property is brand new. The value of the land is not included; land cannot be damaged by the perils we insure the building for, so we have to have a separate structure value. All of this means, for example, if the roof is damaged, we will have to add our own funds to the insuranc~

settlement to pay for the repairs. Of course, we end up with a new roof, so we are ahead and thus our contribution is justified. Insurance is not designed to afford a profit. If written properly, it is to put us back in the position we were in the moment before the loss —no better, no worse. But if the roof is ten years old we cannot put on a ten-year-old roof. So we have to take the new one, like it or not.

The insurance industry has found a way around this problem by offering "replacement cost" coverage, sometimes called "depreciation" insurance. By agreeing to buy an amount of insurance that is related to the entire replacement cost value of the building, we can have the benefit of replacement cost coverage for our apartment house. That will mean that in the event of a loss, if our coverage amount is in accord with our agreement, depreciation will *not* be deducted and the insurance settlement will be equal to the repair bill.

As the value of the structure changes with time we will want to make sure we adjust the amount of the policy. This is obviously much more important if replacement costs are increasing rather than decreasing. Going on our own figures for the property we want to buy, we would consider buying a policy based on a replacement cost of $72,000. In some areas this coverage is available if the insured buys not less than 80 percent of the replacement cost; in others, 100 percent is required. You will be discussing all of this with your insurance agent or broker and he can tell you what the situation is. In our example, if we bought a policy for $72,000 we would have enough to satisfy both lenders, but even more important, for any losses up to complete destruction, the insurance settlement would take care of the entire cost of repairs. We could even get a new building out of it.

Perils

The minimum coverage is fire and extended coverage endorsement; the latter is a group of perils such as windstorm, explosion, riot, and so on. Most lenders will settle for the minimum—"Fire and ECE," as it is called. You should seriously consider buying a policy containing additional perils such as water damage, vandalism, and others. You also should have coverage on whatever personal property you own, such as equipment. But the most important coverage of all is liability insurance.

Liability

If someone other than your employee is hurt on the premises, you may be sued for damages. Initially, the liability coverage will provide the cost of legal services to defend you. In fact, if the claim alleges that you were negligent and were the person responsible for the injury or damage, the insurance company will hire the attorney and undertake your defense at no cost to you. If there is a settlement, in or out of court, the company will pay the amount, up to the amount of insurance. So that raises the question: how much liability insurance should you buy? You can never have too much, because you cannot know in advance how big the claim will be. No doubt you have seen newspaper accounts of lawsuits in which the amounts claimed, or the judgements awarded, probably scared you. The more the claimant thinks you have in assets—or the more serious his injuries—the greater will be his claim. The amount of coverage is somewhat dependent on the extent of the assets you have to protect. But don't be misled into thinking that if your net worth is modest you do not need much insurance. Without enough insurance you could spend the rest of your life working to pay the person you injured. And bankruptcy is not likely to get you out from under. Liability limits of, say, $300,000 are considered modest and limits of $1 million are not unusual. Talk to your insurance man.

Perhaps you are not enthusiastic about buying all these policies. Would it be more palatable if all you needed came in *one* policy and at a reduced cost? Most property and casualty (to distinguish them from life) insurance companies offer a package policy for apartments. You can get one for your home, too. It covers the building, equipment, rents, and liability exposures. If there is a fire or explosion and some of the tenants cannot continue to occupy the property, during the time the repairs are being made your loss of rents is covered by the rental income coverage of the policy. There is a choice of perils. A package like this is by far the best way to insure your investment.

If you are concerned about earthquake or landslide or flood damage, you may also be able to insure against those kinds of losses. They are not covered by the standard policy, but coverage is available. See your insurance man. If you have a resident manager and want to cover the burglary or robbery exposure, policies are available. If you employ someone, you may need workmen's compensation coverage to take care of injuries incurred on the job. If you need to protect against the dishonesty of your employees, you can buy a fidelity bond.

The lender will require the escrow agent to see that proper insurance is in force before the escrow can be closed and the loan proceeds given to the seller. You will want to arrange for the original policy and a copy for the second mortgagee to be delivered to the escrow company in time. The policy, regardless of the type of coverage, is to be endorsed to show that the first and second mortgages have an interest in the subject insured. They are called "loss payees." How does that work?

When the insurance company prepares a loss draft or check, it will make it payable first to the named insured and also to those entities included in the policy as loss payees. The check or draft will be sent to the insured. He will not be able to negotiate it without the endorsement of the loss payees. This is the way in which lenders can protect themselves. If repairs are to be made the lender can wait until they are completed before endorsing it. If the property is not going to be repaired, the lenders can insist that the proceeds of the loss be applied first to the outstanding loan balances. To avoid problems, the lender will insist, and the escrow agent will check, that the insured's name on the policy be exactly the same as on the mortgage or trust deed documents and that the loss payee's name be exactly as designated by the lender.

The final step for the buyer to take is that of signing the escrow instructions. A copy of this document is reproduced on pages 125-126.

Escrow Instructions

The escrow company is acting as the agent of all the parties. As the agent of you, the buyer, the escrow company will require written instructions; forms are provided for this purpose. They may be prepared either by the real estate broker, by the escrow agent, or by you. The original is filed with the escrow company. You will receive in return a copy signed by the escrow agent. (The seller also is required to specify his instructions to the escrow agent. The form reproduced in this book is multi-purpose and can serve both buyers and sellers, but we have illustrated only the buyer's instructions.)

The objective of the instructions is to give the escrow agent the terms of the agreement between buyer and seller and set forth the conditions under which the escrow agent can release the funds to the seller and other parties. Once the funds are placed in escrow, the person handling the transaction must be sure that all the documents required are in order and all parties have performed all acts required by the escrow instructions before making payments from the escrow account. Probably the most important step is to have the deed and loan documents properly recorded, thus protecting both buyer and lender. When that is done, the funds can be released safely to the seller.

Buyer's Instructions

Refer now to the Buyer's Instructions (page 125). Note that the source of the borrowed funds is stated. When the loan is approved the lender will send the proceeds, together with the note and deed of trust documents (or mortgage papers), to the escrow agent. The lender will stipulate that the money is to be used only after the title to the property is vested in the name of the borrower and the loan security document is recorded as a *first* lien against the property. Further, the title insurance policy ordinarily will apply to the lender as well as to the borrower, and the protection must be effective with the disbursement of the loan monies.

The timing of the acts is very important. Several things must take place simultaneously and all parties must be protected. It is apparent that an independent entity, rather than one of the parties involved, can handle these matters best.

In our example, the seller is providing part of the financing.

ESCROW INSTRUCTIONS

SELLERS ☐   BUYERS ☒   BORROWERS ☐

From: John A. and Mary B. Investor   Order No. 48756

To: ABCDE INSURANCE AND TRUST COMPANY: Date: May 10, 197-

On or before May 31, 197-, we will hand you the sum of $77,000 of which ~~I/We hand you herewith~~ $54,000 will be the proceeds of the first trust deed described below, and of which $7,000 will be the proceeds of the second trust deed described below. The sum of $1,000 has already been deposited with you.

Which you will deliver when you obtain for ~~my/~~our account a grant deed in favor of the vestees herein

and when you can issue your Standard   form of CLTA Owner's   policy of title insurance with liability not exceeding $77,000   on the real property described as Lot 4 in Block 20, as designated on the map entitled "Happy Haven, City of Utopia, County of Glory, State of California," recorded in Volume 3 of showing title vested in   Maps, at page 9 in the office of the County Recorder.

John A. Investor and Mary B. Investor,
 husband and wife as joint tenants

SUBJECT ONLY TO: (1) property   taxes for the fiscal year 197-,
(2) A trust deed to record, executed by above·vestees in favor of the
    Last Savings and Loan Association to secure a note for $54,000, 20
    years, 8%; (3) A trust deed to record, executed by above vestees
    in favor of David M. Seller and Janet R. Seller to secure a note
    for $7,000 payable at $70 per month including principal and interest
    at 9% per annum, due June 30, 1980.

Upon close of escrow, you are authorized to deduct from ~~my/~~our account the following:

1. Adjust property taxes and fire insurance, as of close of escrow.
2. Credit prorations of rents, and security deposits.
3. Fee for termite inspection report.
4. Cost of title insurance and escrow services.
5. Loan fee payable to Last Savings and Loan Association in the amount
   of $540.

Any amendment of, or supplement to, these instructions must be in writing.
The GENERAL PROVISIONS printed on the reverse side of this page of these instructions are by reference thereto incorporated herein and made a part hereof.
All documents, balances and statements are to be mailed to the undersigned at the address shown below.

John A. Investor
John A. Investor
Mary B. Investor
Mary B. Investor

Receipt Acknowledged.

ABCDE INSURANCE AND TRUST COMPANY   Address: c/o I.M. Realtor, Inc.,

By _*J.H. Fee*_   321 Main St., Utopia, CA

Date May 10, 197-   Telephone: 765-4321

GENERAL PROVISIONS

All funds received in this escrow shall be deposited with other escrow funds in a general escrow account or accounts
Title Insurance and Trust Company, with any State or National Bank, and may be transferred to any other such gener
account or accounts. All disbursements shall be made by check of Title Insurance and Trust Company.

Any commitment made in writing to Title Insurance and Trust Company by a bank, trust company, insurance compan
or building and loan or savings and loan association, to deliver its check or funds into this escrow may, in the sole discreti
of Title Insurance and Trust Company, be treated as the equivalent of a deposit herein of the amount thereof.

All adjustments to be made on a basis of 30-day months, based on the latest available tax bills.

Recordation of any instruments delivered through this escrow, if necessary or proper in the issuance of the policy
title insurance called for, is authorized.

No examination or insurance as to the amount or payment of real or personal property taxes is required unless the re
property tax is payable on or before the date of the policy of title insurance.

If any party to these instructions obtains a loan on the land involved, and during the pendency of this escrow, you a
authorized to furnish the lender, or anyone operating on its behalf, any information concerning this escrow, including, b
not limited to, a certified copy of the escrow instructions and any amendments thereto.

Execute on behalf of the parties hereto, form assignments of interest in any insurance policies (other than title insuranc
called for herein and forward them upon close of escrow to the agent with the request, first, that insurer consent to su
transfer or attach loss-payable clause or make such other additions or corrections as may have been specifically requir
herein, and second, that the agent thereafter forward such policies to the parties entitled to them. In all acts in this escr
relating to fire insurance, including adjustments, if any, you shall be fully protected in assuming that each such policy is
force and that the necessary premium therefor has been paid.

Unless you are otherwise specifically requested by written instructions so to do, no examination nor insurance as to t
applicability, amount or payment of any transfer tax, imposed by any local, city or county ordinance or otherwise, is requir
through this escrow, as the same will be taken care of by the parties hereto outside of escrow and you are not to be co
cerned with the payment of any such tax.

The second trust deed documents may be prepared by the escrow agent or by the seller or his attorney. The escrow agent has the obligation of seeing that all the documents requiring execution by the buyers be properly signed and ultimately recorded. No particular action will be needed by the seller beyond seeing that the appropriate documents are delivered to the escrow agent.

Although deposits or earnest money may be held by the seller or the real estate agent, the preferable practice is to place those funds in the escrow. As suggested earlier, the buyer usually will arrange for the amount of the total purchase price to be transferred to the escrow, leaving the deposit to be used for the closing costs. In our example, it is implicit in the instructions that the buyer will deposit an additional $16,000 with the escrow agent before the date given. It is not necessary to specify the precise amount of the balance. As the time approaches to close the escrow, the escrow officer will make up a preliminary accounting and determine whether all funds required are on hand; if they are not, he will advise the buyer. The escrow cannot be closed until all parties have performed. Buyer, seller, and lender will be given a closing statement showing exactly how the funds were handled. The expression "closing the escrow" refers to the process of recording documents, disbursing funds, and issuing the escrow closing statement.

The order number—48756 in our example—is the escrow number, a vital identification when communicating with the escrow agent.

When title to land is transferred, it is said that "title is *vested* in. . . ." The entity to which the transfer is made becomes known as the *vestee*; the transferor of the title is the *vestor*. In our example, the escrow agent knows the deed is to be used to vest title in the names and manner indicated in the instructions.

The form of title insurance policy is governed in part by custom in the area where the property is located and in part by the stipulations of lenders. You may wish to discuss this matter with the title insurance or escrow officer handling the transaction.

The reference to the legal description helps to make sure that all concerned are dealing with the same piece of property. The inclusion of the names of the current vestees provides a further assurance that the proposed sellers are the owners.

The buyers are stating they are agreeable to the release of their funds only if the title they are receiving is clear except for the items listed. Property taxes are always a prospective lien. Here, as is customary, the taxes are to be pro-rated; this was discussed in a previous chapter. Obviously the property is being used as security for the first and second trust deeds, so those obligations will be encumbrances on the title. If there are any other liens or encumbrances, the seller is obligated to clear them because the buyer is specifying that his money is not to be paid out until the title is clear except for the items just discussed.

An escrow agent can act only on the instructions of the parties. The expenses to be paid from the buyer's funds are to be specified, thus authorizing disbursement.

Lenders may simply deduct the loan fee from the loan proceeds. In our example, we are assuming that the entire loan amount is sent to the escrow agent and that the fee will be paid to the lender at the time the escrow is closed. This serves to emphasize that this is an expense to be met by the borrower-buyer and that funds over and above the total purchase price will be required.

So much for the buyer's instructions. The escrow agent, when all the money has been paid in, will be able to close the escrow, assuming the seller has delivered the deed and second trust deed documents. After recording, the documents will be returned to the appropriate parties with notations as to the date and recording reference.

Seller's Instructions

The procedure is basically the same as that described for the buyer, so no example is needed. Out of the funds available, the escrow agent will pay off existing loans, other expenses that are the responsibility of the seller, and in particular, the commission to the real estate broker. The seller may also deliver to the escrow agent such items as keys, bills of sale, and so on, for turnover to the buyer.

The Closing Statement

You, the buyer, will have less interest in this document than the seller. When he receives his, it will usually have a big check attached to it.

Refer to the illustrations on pages 130 and 132. We have shown the other side of the transaction, the seller's statement, as well as your own. From these you can see all of what is involved in both buying and selling.

The Buyer's Statement

We agreed to buy at $77,000. By borrowing a total of $61,000, our cash down payment would amount to $16,000. We knew, of course, there would be certain costs to pay in addition. The initial $1,000 deposit at the time of signing the purchase agreement was available to apply to the costs. In the original analysis we estimated the actual costs to be $1,150. We did not allow, however, for the fact the seller would be holding rents paid in advance as well as damage or security deposits. In the escrow we are credited with these items, and that will reduce the amount of cash actually required to complete the transaction.

Once the escrow officer has a copy of the purchase agreement and escrow instructions, he can estimate just how much money the buyer will have to come up with to meet his obligations. From the illustration of the buyer's closing statement you can see that $15,500 in additional cash was requested, and even so, there was a refund of $232.

The purchase was effective as of May 31. The escrow is closed coincident with the recording of the documents and passing of title. In areas where property taxes are paid in semi-annual installments and the tax year ends June 30, there would be one month's taxes to be charged to the buyer; the seller had previously paid the installment for the second half of the year. In our example the pro-rata tax expense is $218. This is credited to the seller, as can be seen in the next illustration.

By custom, certain expenses are charged to the buyer, others to the seller. Here the buyer is charged with the cost of title insur-

ABCDE Insurance and Trust Company

DATE May 31, 197-   ORDER NO. 48756   ESCROW OFFICER J.H. Fee

ESCROW CLOSING STATEMENT   (For Buyer)

```
.  John A. and Mary B. Investor,
.  220 Angus Crescent,
.  UTOPIA, CA  99999
.
```

ITEMS	DEBITS	CREDITS
SALE/PURCHASE PRICE	$ 77,000	
DEPOSITS		$ 15,500
DEPOSIT RETAINED Earnest money		1,000
EXISTING LOAN		
NEW LOAN First Trust Deed		54,000
Second Trust Deed		7,000
PRO-RATA — TAXES	218	
— INSURANCE	50	
— INTEREST		
— RENTS paid in advance		900
Security deposits from tenants		200
TITLE INSURANCE POLICY FOR $77,000	449	
ESCROW FEE		
RECONVEYANCE FEE		
PREPARING DOCUMENTS	10	
NOTARY FEE	6	
TRANSFER TAX		
RECORDING:	8	
TAX COLLECTOR		
COMMISSION		
INSURANCE		
Termite Inspection Report	50	
Loan Fees--Last Savings and Loan Association	540	
Inspection and Credit Reports	37	
CHECK HEREWITH	232	
BALANCE DUE		
TOTALS	$ 78,600	$ 78,600

SAVE FOR INCOME TAX PURPOSES

ance. He had agreed to pay the termite inspection report fee and, of course, must pay the loan fee.

When it comes time to establish the accounting records the buyer will be able to find some of the figures he will need by examining this closing statement.

The Seller's Statement

The seller owed $38,800 on an existing mortgage and because the buyer was obtaining a new loan the existing loan is paid off in the escrow. By giving the escrow officer the details of this loan, he will notify the lender that there will be a payoff and ask for a demand and reconveyance. Quite simply, this is a request for the amount of the unpaid balance as of a certain point in time, plus a basis for charging interest from that time to the closing, and a document, called a reconveyance, which will be recorded to show that the original loan had been satisfied. The lender is protected by the escrow process.

The seller does not have to contribute the advance rents and security deposits because those amounts will be subtracted from what is otherwise coming to him. He has agreed to pay the cost of the termite repair work and the commission to the real estate broker.

In our example, the transfer tax is shown as $84.70; it is payable by the seller. The rate is $0.55 per $500 of equity transferred. If the buyer had assumed the existing mortgage, the transfer tax would have been levied on the difference between the purchase price and the outstanding loan balance. Here, because of the refinancing, the tax applies to the entire $77,000.

The seller receives a check from the escrow agent in the amount of $25,464.30 *plus* a note and second deed of trust for $7,000. Actually the documents sent for recording will be returned to the seller by the county recorder. The promissory note may not be recorded and therefore will be sent directly to the seller.

The escrow agent has completed his function when the escrow is closed, statements are sent to the parties, and all funds are properly accounted for. If mistakes have been made, there is recourse to the escrow organization. If this service has been rendered as a part of providing title insurance, the escrow agent will

ABCDE Insurance and Trust Company

DATE **May 31, 197-**   ORDER NO. **48756**   ESCROW OFFICER **J.H. Fee**

ESCROW CLOSING STATEMENT   (For Seller)

. David M. and Janet R. Seller,
. 879 Regal Road,
. UTOPIA, CA 99999

I T E M S	DEBITS	CREDITS
SALE/PURCHASE PRICE		$77,000.00
DEPOSITS		
DEPOSIT RETAINED		
EXISTING LOAN	$38,800.00	
NEW LOAN Second Trust Deed to Seller	7,000.00	
PRO-RATA — TAXES		218.00
— INSURANCE		50.00
— INTEREST		
— RENTS paid in advance	900.00	
Security Deposits from Tenants	200.00	
TITLE INSURANCE POLICY FOR $		
ESCROW FEE		
RECONVEYANCE FEE	10.00	
PREPARING DOCUMENTS	6.00	
NOTARY FEE	1.00	
TRANSFER TAX	84.70	
RECORDING: Reconveyance	2.00	
TAX COLLECTOR		
COMMISSION Paid to I.M. Realtor, Inc.	4,500.00	
INSURANCE		
Termite Repair Work--paid to Hungry Termite Co.	300.00	
CHECK HEREWITH	25,464.30	
BALANCE DUE		
TOTALS	**$77,268.00**	**$77,268.00**

SAVE FOR INCOME TAX PURPOSES

also distribute the title policies. Otherwise, the escrow agent will work with the title insurer by providing information and copies of documents, and the title insurance company will issue the policy separately from the escrow handling.

Your Tenants

A notice of change of ownership should be given to the tenants. The seller can do this either orally or in writing. It is best if done in writing and signed by the seller. If there are leases, they should formally be assigned to the buyer and processed through the escrow. In one way or another, tenants should know that after a specified date they are to make rental payments to the new owner. Some buyers prefer to be introduced to the tenants by the departing landlord; others would rather be free to meet them on their own.

It is important to establish contact with your tenants. They will have a chance either to confirm or·allay whatever suspicions they have about the new owner. You can confirm to them you now have their rent and security deposits—if that is the case. You may wish to stress how you feel about people who pay their rent on time and about those who don't. If you have in mind making some adjustments in the rents, you can lay the groundwork for that. Once you have met your tenants you can go back home and prepare to operate your newest money-making machine.

To summarize: closing the deal means exchanging your money (including the borrowed amounts) for a good title and the right to collect rents and earn a return from the investment. Because several things must take place at one time, it is best to employ an escrow agent. It is also wise to obtain title insurance even if a lender has not insisted on it. Both you and the seller employ the escrow organization to protect your interests. Documents are recorded to establish your legal interest in the property, and the seller is assured of receiving his money in exchange for the deed. You have done what you think necessary to be sure that you ended up with the property you thought you were buying, including having a land surveyor mark the boundaries. Now all you have to do is learn how to manage your property.

6

Managing the Money-Machine

Now you are a landlord. This chapter covers what is involved in taking care of your property and the present tenants, how to get new tenants, the difference between leasing and renting, and in general, what to do to maximize your overall return.

Beginning Steps

In one way or another the tenants have been notified there is a new owner. You should make contact and, among other things, confirm with each tenant the amount of rent and when it is payable, and whether there is an advance rent payment in hand. You should also cover the matter of a damage or security deposit if there is one. If a lease has been transferred you should confirm that to the tenant. Probably the very best practice is for the new owner to send a letter to each tenant in which these items are recited and ask the tenant to sign and return a copy, thus acknowledging agreement. This will avoid future problems concerning the amount of rent paid in advance or the amount and conditions for the damage deposit.

If you acquired personal property in the purchase, you should have taken inventory at the time the deal was closed. In turn, if tenants are renting furnished units you should take inventory in their presence and reconcile any differences. The furniture should be listed and its description be made a part of the rental agreement or lease.

You may wish to check whether the keys you received from the departing seller work. You may find a tenant has changed a lock. The owner generally has a right to enter the property in order to safeguard it. To avoid an argument in this connection it is good practice to include that provision in the rent or lease agreement. More on that later.

In some localities a business license is required. Even if the previous owner obtained one, either you will have to have it transferred or you will need to get a new one. A phone call to the city hall will produce the information you need.

You should resolve now to take an even greater interest in civic affairs. You might even want to attend a city council meeting. For all you know, there may be a proposed ordinance that, if passed, will affect your operation. You may want to exercise your rights as a citizen to influence such legislation. Keep in touch by carefully reading the local newspaper. Read the classified advertising for real estate rentals and income property. You are in business now and the more information you can acquire the better off you will be. You may wish to join a property owners' association or the local taxpayers' group.

Particularly if you anticipate expanding your property ownership activities, you should consider becoming affiliated with a national association such as the Institute of Real Estate Management of the National Association of Real Estate Boards. This will require association with a local real estate board. Full details can be obtained by writing to the Institute at 155 E. Superior St., Chicago, Illinois 60611.

For assistance with local matters relating to building ownership, you may want to inquire into membership in the local chapter of the Building Owners' and Managers' Association, known as BOMA. You may find this group listed in your telephone book. You can write to BOMA International, 224 S. Michigan Ave., Chicago, Illinois 60604.

Your objective is to do what is necessary to maximize your ultimate return from this investment. By properly maintaining the property, you should obtain the maximum price on resale. By learning how to handle tenants and maintenance matters, you will minimize operating expenses. By getting the best possible tenants and learning how to keep them, you will maximize rental income. Much of this learning will be accomplished simply by doing.

You should open a new bank checking account. You will find it highly desirable always to pay bills by check and to deposit all rental income in a bank account. We will devote the next chapter to handling the accounting records. Meanwhile, get ready by visiting the bank and opening an account. Your first deposit to the account should be the rent advances and damage deposits credited to you in the escrow. Recall those credits reduced the amount of cash you had to produce in order to complete the transaction. You need the money now and you should resist the temptation not to put this money in your property operating account.

You may think it quite feasible to use your family checking account. With a small apartment building you will have only a limited number of banking transactions each month and you may be able to avoid a bank charge by using only one account for both business and personal activity. As you will see in the next chapter, we recommend you have a savings account into which you transfer the surplus of income over expenses each month from the checking account. Once again, you may not wish to have another savings account if you already have one. But in one way or another, you should have the use of a checking account for processing income and expenditures associated with the investment, and a savings account into which you deposit surplus funds so they will earn interest. Some of the so-called surplus will be surplus only for a time and will be needed to pay property taxes, for example. You can earn interest on the money while it is accumulating. Like it or not, you will require good records of the financial transactions and you should start off your ownership on the right foot by recording everything that takes place in terms of money.

We will assume your apartment is fully occupied and, at least for the time being, you will not be faced with obtaining new tenants.

Minimizing Operating Expenses

As you become thoroughly familiar with your new asset, you may notice things that should be repaired. If you are able to make at least minor repairs yourself, you should take care of as many as you can now, while you are still enthusiastic about being a landlord. You may already be acquainted with a handyman. There are many retired craftsmen who are very good at taking care of repairs and you may find it economical to use one. Because emergencies may arise concerning the plumbing or wiring or even the roof, you should decide, *before* the emergency arises, which plumber or electrician or roofing company you will call when they are needed. Write down the results of your research and put the information in your property operating file folder. You do have one, don't you? If not, stop reading and go make one.

The rule here is: as soon as you become aware of a repair problem, take care of it; acting quickly will probably make you a hero (or heroine) in the eyes of your tenants and it might even cost less if you act quickly. Nothing frustrates a tenant more and faster than a landlord who procrastinates. If the complaint or request for repair, concession, or amenity is not justified, don't stall. Give the tenant your decision as soon as possible. That will give the tenant longer to get used to the idea. Developing your judgment for this kind of problem simply takes practice. It is also helpful to compare notes with other property owners to learn what is the common practice in the area. This clearly leads us to the question of decorating.

Who should paint the apartment and how often should it be done? In relatively tight rental markets you may be able to say to enants that you will provide the paint if they will put it on. First, of course, be aware of the problems. If you don't control colors you may be faced with a serious problem in finding a new tenant. Not everyone prefers black living room walls and a chartreuse bathroom. The quality of the paint is also to be considered—not to mention the quality of the painting. You will have to decide whether the tenant is skillful with a paintbrush; if the conclusion is negative you had better do the job yourself.

Paint stores are known to offer discounts to property owners. Visit some and see how good a deal you can get. Get the color charts and decide on the brand and quality, hence the cost. Tell the paint store they can honor requests for paint and charge them to your account if the tenant presents a written authorization from you. You, in turn, after discussing the matter with the tenant, can write out the appropriate authorization. The tenant then picks up the paint and paints his own apartment. You can offer the tenant a choice of colors, like white. Stick to neutral colors and save yourself some grief after your painting-tenants leave. So much for the inside; what about the exterior?

Work to be done by independent contractors should be subject to bid. Ask two or three presumably qualified firms to give you a bid on the work. You may choose the lowest, but it may not always be the best. Getting references from previous customers is often worth the effort. Watch for ads in the classified section of the newspaper placed by people who solicit work you need to be performed. For fairly small jobs there often are a number of "moonlighters" who, because of limited overhead, are willing to charge less for their work. You may not be able to get them to stand behind their work, of course, as you could with an established business firm. You will have to weigh the risk here. A curious phenomenon: you may find that firemen moonlight as painters, particularly of tall buildings.

It will be important for tenants to let you know about plumbing problems. A leaky pipe can cause serious problems and expense apart from loss of water. Washers should be replaced promptly in dripping taps. Once again, if a tenant complains, and if the complaint is justified, fix whatever needs fixings! You are going to have to do it anyway, so do it now and be a hero.

Be careful not to go overboard. If you are very fussy about your own living accommodations you may drive your tenants up the wall by always prowling around the apartment building, checking taps, picking up litter, and in general being a nuisance. Every once in a while you may want to drive by to see if the building is still there; but be sure you respect your tenants' right to privacy. The best relationship is one in which the landlord responds immediately to a tenant's call—presuming the tenant is being reasonable—but otherwise the landlord is never seen or heard from. *This is not a social relationship.* The tenant is paying for sound and safe living accommodation; he is not buying an opportunity to socialize or be pestered.

So much for repairs and maintenance. You will be faced with spending some money no matter what the age or condition of the property. Relax and enjoy it; don't be a Scrooge. If you handle these matters correctly your tenants will be inclined to stay and the property will sell for the maximum in the future.

How about utilities?

Expense for Utilities

There are two basic types of expense for the landlord: fixed and variable. If you are obligated by law or local custom to pay for some of the utilities, try to pay for those that are fixed. Water, gas, and power are usually variable; the cost varies with the quantity used. The same usually holds for electricity and gas. You should try to avoid renting on the basis of including the cost of variable expense utilities.

In some communities garbage service is provided by the municipality and the property owner has a legal obligation to pay for it. This is such a common practice that the seller of the apartment may have forgotten to tell you about it, and the first you will learn of it is when you get a bill. Keep this in mind when you are doing your evaluation and preparing the cash flow analysis.

If you find you have no choice but to be responsible for the expense of variable utilities you may be able to include a provision in the rent or lease to pass some part on to the tenant. Competition from other apartment owners may limit this opportunity.

Expense Control

What should your costs for utilities, repairs, and maintenance be? When you did your analysis you included certain figures.

These were probably based on information received from the seller. He may have been optimistic about what expenses *you* would have. By keeping complete records you will be able to build up, over time, some information on your actual experience to use for comparison purposes. If you owned one or more large apartment buildings you would soon know what was a reasonable and typical cost for the usual maintenance items, but for a fourplex or other smaller building the range of costs can be great. You could go for a whole year without spending any money on painting, for instance. It will be important to keep track of what you are spending, preferably by each rental unit separately, and by type of repair. The national organizations referred to previously offer cost data to their members and you may be able to compare your experience with that of others. Again, this is not as meaningful for the small apartment owner as it is for the large.

Under income tax laws, expenses incurred in the production of taxable income may be deductible. You have already resolved to pay all bills by check and to obtain receipts. If you have some small items paid for in cash, lump them together and write a check for the total to reimburse yourself. But what about some expenses not so readily identified?

In managing an apartment house you will have postage and telephone expense. You may need stationery and record-keeping supplies. You may use your car and travel in the course of a year a significant distance. Keep a record of these expenses and be able to show them as expenses when it comes time to prepare an income tax return. Don't wait until the end of the year to try to recall what these expenses were. Not only are you unlikely to recall correctly, but you won't have records considered adequate by the Internal Revenue Service to support the deduction. Many investors keep a diary of the activities associated with the property and an envelope in which to place receipts.

Persons new to operating a business, realizing that expenses associated with the business are tax-deductible, often fall into the trap of thinking that they should maximize such expenditures because they are tax-deductible. This is fallacious, of course. No matter how large your tax bracket, the tax collector is paying only *part* of every dollar paid out and the taxpayer is paying the balance. You can never be better off simply by incurring expense. To be sure this is understood, consider the following example:

Assume you are subject to a 40 percent income-tax rate. If you spend $100 on tax-deductible expenses, it is true you reduce your taxable income by $100. You reduce the number of tax dollars, however, by only 40 percent. *You* are paying the other 60 percent, or $60. It is all right to say that Uncle Sam is paying 40 cents out of every dollar of your expenses, but don't forget who is paying the remaining 60 cents. If it makes you feel better you can say that the last plumbing bill really only cost you $30 instead of the $50 you paid. But you had to collect $50 in income to pay that bill.

Another item for expense control is property taxes. By now, as an expert in real estate matters, you know that the amount of your property tax bill is governed by both the assessed value and the tax rate. While you may not individually be able to do much about lowering the tax rate, you can do something about the assessed value if you think it is too high.

Early in the year you should receive a notice from the tax assessor's office advising you of the assessed value for the upcoming year. You have a legal right to the information the assessor used in arriving at your assessment. You can challenge his computation. When it is based on the market value of similar properties you may be able to develop information on other similar properties that would support your contention that yours is too high. Be aware, of course, that a reassessment could result in a higher value. Visit your assessor's office some day and find out the procedure for appealing an assessment. Do that before you need it. That information will be useful to you in knowing what steps you might take sometime to be in a better position to keep your assessment at a minimum. That in turn will result in the lowest tax bill.

Maximizing Rental Income

We are still working on the assumption that your apartments are all filled with rent-paying tenants. If you treat the tenants right they will probably stay longer than otherwise. Turnover is to be avoided unless a tenant is undesirable.

Rents are payable in advance. You may lose income if a tenant decides to leave at the time the rent is payable for the next period and has not given you notice. Most apartments are rented on a monthly basis and a month's notice of intention to leave is expected. One way to protect yourself against loss because a tenant leaves without notice is to require the payment of two months' rent at the time of initial occupancy. This is usually referred to as "the first and last month's rent." This should be stated clearly in the receipt for the funds so the tenant understands how the money is to be applied. Then, if the tenant does not make the usual rental payment and thereby shows his intention to leave at the end of what is now the "last" month, the landlord has the month's notice he should have. Responsible tenants, not motivated by a last month's rental payment, will give adequate notice anyway. You have to protect yourself against the other type of tenant who has other things on his mind besides your welfare. Unless you collect two months' rent in advance you cannot be certain of avoiding a loss. Even at that, you might not be able to get a new tenant; but that is the regular risk you have as a property owner.

From an operating point of view, it is best to have rents from all apartments due and payable on the same date. Under those conditions you can quickly become aware of any delinquency. If tenants are paying rent at odd times during the month, unless you are particularly careful, you can lose track of a non-paying tenant and soon find yourself in the hole. Once time has gone by it becomes very difficult to collect from a tenant who decides he doesn't want to pay you. You should be firm, but fair, in dealing with tenants who do not pay on time. If the delinquency is because pay-day comes after rent-day, you may want to adjust the rental period.

Some landlords prefer to call in person to collect the rents. In some situations this may be absolutely necessary. A better arrangement is for tenants to assume the responsibility of delivering the rents to you or your designate on or before a stipulated time. Tenants who pay by mail and on time, with checks that don't bounce, and who stay forever without making unreasonable demands, are devoutly to be desired.

When you have notice of a prospective vacancy, make appropriate arrangements with the departing tenant for you to be able to show the premises to prospective replacements. Most people will be reasonable about this if the landlord is reasonable. It is helpful if the present tenant was able to see the apartment in advance. It may be necessary to remind a reluctant occupant. Your goal is to line up a new tenant to move in exactly at the time the present tenant leaves, with no gap. If you cannot have access to the apartment until the tenant departs, and his departure date is the date to which rent is paid, you face a loss of rents. Once again, timing is important.

Usually, if you start your tenant-seeking activity two weeks before the occupancy date, you will be all right. This depends, of course, on the current rental market. You may have to compromise and simply be prepared for it. Assume, for example, a prospect says he will take the apartment, but the rent on his present apartment is paid until the 10th. Your unit is available as of the first. What do you do? If the market is strongly in your favor, and the prospective tenant is anxious to have your apartment, you could be adamant and you will not lose any rent—he'll take it as of the first. Otherwise, you may have to suggest that you will split the difference—rent it as of the 5th, say. You may be able to make other concessions such as offering to provide the paint if the prospective tenant would like to choose the color (within your range), and apply it himself. In turn, the tenant would have to take the apartment from the first to have this opportunity. Develop your imagination and bargaining skills. The motivation is the realization that there is no way to recover rent for lost time.

How about the other extreme? The departing tenant has to vacate before the time to which rent has been paid. He wants a refund. You may be inclined to say you will make a refund provided you can find a tenant to take up from the date of vacancy. Under those conditions you will not lose rental income and you may gain some valuable good will. Some landlords have been able to avoid refunds and even keep rents paid for the overlap period. This is known as having a "negative vacancy rate." Don't count on being able to accomplish that.

Eviction

The word conjures up nastiness and a picture of the sheriff carrying the widow and kids into the street. Face it: if you have to evict someone from your property, it is going to be nasty. If the tenants were willing to leave on their own initiative, you would not have to evict them. Timeliness of action is vital if you are to minimize your loss. Not only will you lose rent but you will have the expense of the eviction. The longer you put it off, the greater will be your loss. The law is on the side of the landlord under appropriate conditions. It is also on the side of the tenant—to an extent you will learn about only after you have been involved.

Basically, if a tenant refuses to pay rent or otherwise breaches his rental agreement or lease, you may have a right to evict. The precise procedure varies from one community to another. In general, the following considerations apply, regardless of the way in which it may be carried out in a given jurisdiction. You should consult your local municipal court for exact details.

There are several reasons why eviction action may be taken. If rent is unpaid, that may be sufficient grounds. Tenants who damage the property, invade the privacy of others, or consistently hold noisy, boisterous parties or create disturbances are subject to eviction. The tenant may have some defenses. Rent may be withheld because the landlord has refused to make repairs. The extent to which others are being disturbed will be a matter of opinion. To protect both parties to the dispute, there is a court procedure.

Probably the initial step, once the landlord has checked with the local authorities, is to deliver to the tenants a three-day notice to vacate the premises. If that does not succeed, application should be made to the municipal court. The technical name of the action is "complaint in unlawful detainer." A summons and complaint will be served on the tenant. Local custom governs whether the local authority or the landlord (employing a process server) arranges for this. If the tenant does not respond to this summons and complaint by filing his answer, a default judgment will be awarded to the landlord. The court will issue a "writ of possession" and instructions to the sheriff to remove the tenants and their possessions from the property. The landlord will have to post a bond and pay the expenses.

If the tenant wishes to argue his case, he will be able to present his side to a judge. Meanwhile he will remain in possession of the property and the landlord will undoubtedly not be receiving rent in the interim. It is not unknown for a tenant to stall the eviction proceedings for a great length of time.

How does a landlord recover the financial loss? The assumption is that whatever rent has been paid has been used up by the time we reach this point. A reminder: if you require the tenant to pay the first and last months' rent you have most of the last month in which to find out what the tenant is going to do. It is possible to be badly fooled, of course. The tenant can say he is going to leave and then not do so. If you have not collected the advance payment, your potential loss begins on the first day after the end of the time for which rent has been paid.

To attempt to recover the costs of the eviction and lost rent, the landlord may ask the court to attach the tenants' possessions. In the complaint you would allege damages for lost rent and expenses and ask for the money judgment as well as eviction. The sheriff will seize the personal property and it may subsequently be sold to satisfy the judgment if the court awards it to you. An alternative is to proceed in Small Claims Court.

If a tenant owes for unpaid rent you may wish to sue him in Small Claims Court, where the cost is limited to filing fees; attorneys are not employed in this situation. You tell your story to the judge; and if the tenant responds to the summons, he will tell his. If the judge awards you a judgment your next problem is converting the judgment to cash. You will need to locate some property belonging to the tenant and obtain a legal attachment. Again, it will have to be seized by the sheriff and sold to satisfy the judgment. Note you may be able to use the Small Claims Court when eviction is not involved. Some defaulting tenants don't wait around to be evicted; they just quietly leave.

If your tenant plays hard-to-get you may be glad you obtained some information about him at the time he first came into your life. Shortly we will discuss a rental application form and a procedure to use in screening prospective tenants. The key to avoiding eviction and rent loss is good tenants.

Getting New Tenants

We assumed the apartments were all occupied when you bought the building, but now one of the tenants is moving out and your job is to get a replacement. If you are adequately prepared for this important activity you should have no difficulty. The assumption here is that you are handling all of the property management yourself. Before we explore what you will have to do, let's look at some of the alternatives.

You may decide to employ a property manager; perhaps one of the tenants would like to rent the units, collect the rents, and generally take care of things. You have to decide whether the cost is worth it to you. Even if the payment is in the form of reduced rent, be sure to keep your records as though it were paid-out expense. Real estate offices often provide the service of getting tenants. In some areas the cost for this is paid by the tenants; in others, by the landlord. Before you decide to use someone else, find out what it will cost and be sure you want to reduce your return. The most important property management activity is that of getting new tenants who are satisfactory and renting the units without a lapse of rental income. If you do the work yourself you have complete control. Otherwise you may find the person you have chosen to serve does not or cannot perform as well as you would yourself. At this point you are protesting you don't know what it would cost to have someone else to do this work. Get on the telephone and call real estate offices and ask what their charge is for collecting rents and getting tenants. Call more than one so you can compare. This will be a basis to use also if you are thinking of having a tenant take care of the property.

Rent collection involves two points: safeguarding and promptly remitting the funds, and collecting on time and avoiding rent losses. If you employ someone to handle this part of the work, be certain he understands the need to keep after late-paying tenants and to be aware of the potential need to evict. In some cases all a real estate office might agree to do, for example, is collect the rent if it is sent to them. They may not be prepared to pursue delinquents. This is not hard to understand, because the fees for collection service cannot be great enough to support the expenditure of a lot of effort.

Only you, as the owner, have the incentive to work day and night to get a new tenant. Even if a real estate office can earn a rental commission amounting sometimes to a large proportion of the first month's rent, that may not be enough to prompt superhuman effort. Never forget while you own rental property, rental income for time gone by can never be recouped. Keep this from happening by always renting the property effective with the departure of the previous tenant.

If you decide to do all the work yourself, what is involved? You have to decide on leasing versus renting; you have to have a supply of rental applications and contracts on hand; and you have to have a pricing policy. It will be helpful also if you have some tentative ideas on how to handle prospective tenants when they respond to your advertising. And you have to know how to advertise the property.

Renting versus Leasing

When a tenant agrees to pay for the use of premises and the landlord is in accord, a "rental agreement" is thereby created. This agreement should be in writing, regardless of the length of time involved. If the agreement extends beyond one year, the courts will not enforce it unless the agreement is in writing. This is the effect of what the lawyers call the "Statute of Frauds." For apartment property, the unit of time for a rental agreement generally is one month. This is established by the amount of the payment and the length of time for which the payment is applied. In our discussion we assume a monthly basis.

The landlord may decide that he prefers to rent on a "month-to-month" basis. Good property management calls for collecting, prior to occupancy, a sum of money equal to two months' rent. Local custom may prevent you from doing this, however. But you should, as a minimum, always collect rent in advance. A receipt, if given, should clearly show the time period for which the rent payment applies. By renting on the month-to-month basis, the tenant is obligated to give a month's notice of departure. For example, when the tenant makes a rental payment on the due date he then can say, "This will be my last month" and that would provide a notice in compliance with the usual law governing such matters. Typically the amount of notice is to be equal to the time period for which each rental payment applies. There may be a local ordinance that provides otherwise, so check to see what your specific situation is.

The month-to-month basis also allows for rent increases to be made, but advance notice of a change is also required on the same terms as notice. When you want to raise the rent, you can't just tell the tenant you have raised the rent effective immediately. Always give notice of change in rent in writing and allow more than enough time for the change to become effective. Note also, the same time terms apply to a notice to vacate, other than when the notice is for nonpayment, preceding potential eviction proceedings.

Thus the advantage to the landlord of renting on a month-to-month basis is that rents can be changed, and tenants can be asked to leave, with no more notice than the length of time for which rent is paid. That is usually monthly.

This also means, of course, that the tenant can decide to move on and be obligated for no more than a month's rent. If he wants to leave right away, the landlord could theoretically hold him for rent for the notice period. If you already have the money in hand your position is substantially stronger.

If the basis is month-to-month, there should be a written rental agreement. This is *not* a lease. An example of a typical rental agreement is illustrated on page 149 and can be used by you as a sample in preparing your own contracts.

Either the tenant or the landlord may prefer an agreement that provides for more protection—that is, an agreement that obligates the landlord to maintain the rental terms for more than a month at a time, or for the premises to be retained by the tenant for longer than a month at a time. This means we want a lease.

A lease is the name customarily applied to a rental agreement

RENTAL AGREEMENT

This Agreement, executed on_____between

_____

hereinafter called the landlord, and _____

_____ hereinafter called the tenant,

provides that

1. The landlord rents, to the tenant, the following property:

_____

2. At a monthly rental of _____

3. Beginning on_____

4. Receipt is hereby acknowledged of the sum of $_____
   to be applied: $_____ to the first month of occupancy
   and $_____to the last month of occupancy.

5. Receipt is hereby acknowledged of the sum of $_____
   as a damage and cleaning deposit. This deposit will be returned at the time the tenant surrenders the apartment in a
   condition judged satisfactory by the landlord.

6. The landlord agrees to pay the cost of _____
   _____, said services to
   be included in the rental payment.

7. Tenant agrees to _____

8. Tenant agrees to make rental payments not later than
   _____of each month to the landlord at

_____

_____   _____
        Landlord   Tenant

_____   _____
        Landlord   Tenant

having a rental period of some multiple of payment periods as its term. Assume a one-year contract, with a monthly rental of $200. The lease contract (see pages 152-155) would be written to provide that the tenant agrees to pay a total rent of $2,400. It will acknowledge receipt of the initial payment, which should be $400. This should be stated to apply as follows: $200 to the first month and $200 to the last month of the 12-month term of the lease. Note carefully that the tenant, by signing the lease agreement, becomes obligated for the total of $2,400 less the amounts paid in advance. If he moves out early and breaches the contract, he still owes the balance of the money and can be sued accordingly. The question of whether he continued to use the premises does not become an issue. It is simply a debt to be satisfied.

The landlord, under such a lease, cannot change the rental terms *during the term* other than by agreement with the tenant. Provision is usually made for a renewal of the lease, with the amount of the rent for the ensuing period left open to negotiation. The parties can, of course, agree in advance on a specific amount.

The basic idea of a lease is that the tenant is protected against rent increases but is obligated to stay or at least pay for the term of the agreement. The landlord, in theory, can forget about looking for a new tenant as long as the lease is in force. If his expenses increase he has no way—in the absence of a provision in the lease —to increase the rent to offset such an increase. It is not usual in residential property leases to provide for increases in rents to cover increases in operating expenses. It has been said that a lease protects only the tenant, because if the tenant wants to leave, the landlord probably cannot collect for lost rent, whereas the tenant is guaranteed that his rent will not be increased. You will have to consider the pros and cons and decide. Some landlords offer either a rental or lease basis and let the tenant decide. If the prospective tenant is concerned about increasing rents, he may choose your apartment over a competitor's because you are willing to lease it to him. On the other hand, you may find it more difficult to get an undesirable tenant out of your premises if he has a lease rather than a month-to-month rental agreement.

Rental Application Form

When you offer an apartment for rent you are providing an opportunity for someone you know nothing about to occupy your property. Your risks include potential damage to the property, nonpayment of rent, and the possibility the new tenant will drive the other tenants away. How do you protect yourself against these risks? By getting information, doing some checking, and applying judgment. Your desire, on the one hand, is to get someone to sign on the dotted line and get the task over with. On the other, you should be aware of the risks involved.

When a prospect says, "Yes, we'll take the apartment," you should respond by explaining you would like them to complete the rental application and give you a deposit to hold the apartment. In addition, you will let them know whether they can have it no later than by a specified time. You should not ask for more than 48 hours in which to check out their application. It should be made quite clear that the deposit will be refunded *in full* if they do not qualify. If they do qualify, they should know that a rental agreement or lease will be prepared and signed by both parties.

A sample rental application form is reproduced on pages 156-157. Your form should be as brief as possible and ask for only essential information. Some people may resent what they feel to be an intrusion of their privacy, and you may have to point out diplomatically that they are going to have possession of your property and it only makes good sense for you to learn something about them. You can assure them the information will be kept confidential and is for your use only.

There are two major items: employment and previous landlords. You should plan to verify the information on both. You want to assure yourself that the prospect has the ability to pay the rent and the desire to be a responsible citizen—at least insofar as his activities affect your property. By checking with a previous landlord, you can find out whether he paid his rent and left in good standing. Ask what amount of rent was paid—that will help to determine whether he can afford yours. In checking employment, you can verify that he does in fact have a job and you

LEASE

CALIFORNIA REAL ESTATE ASSOCIATION STANDARD FORM

THIS INDENTURE, made the ....Twenty-fifth.... day of ....August.... .....A.D. 197-....

between ....John A. Investor and Mary B. Investor..

...., hereinafter called the lessor,

and ....Margaret A. Tenant...

...., hereinafter called the lessee.

WITNESSETH, that the lessor does by these presents, lease and demise unto the lessee all of the property

situated in the ....City of Utopia...,

County of ....Glory.., State of California, described as follows, to wit:

Apartment 3, 1234 Wistful Vista, Utopia, CA,
including stove and refrigerator.

for the term of ....Twelve Months ***..

beginning ..September 1......197-...., and ending ..August 31.............197-....

for the total rent or sum of **Twenty-Four Hundred Dollars***

....Dollars, in lawful money of the United States of America, payable as follows, to wit:

Four Hundred Dollars ($400) upon execution of this lease,
$200 of which to be applied to rent for the month of
September, 197- and $200 for the month of August, 197-;
and $200 on the first day of each month, beginning
October 1, 197-.

All of said rent shall be paid at the office of .... 220 Angus Crescent, Utopia, CA 99999........,
XXXXXXXXXXXXXXXXXXXXXXXXXXXXXXXXXXXXXXXXXXXXXXXXXXXXXXXXXXXXXXXXXXXX
XXXXXXX, or at such other place as may be designated by the lessor. mailed to

IN ADDITION THERETO IT IS HEREBY AGREED AS FOLLOWS, TO WIT:

First: That the lessee shall pay the lessor said rent in the manner hereinbefore specified, and shall not let or underlet the whole or any part of said premises, nor sell or assign this lease, either voluntarily or by operation of law, nor allow said properly to be occupied by anyone contrary to the terms hereof, without the written consent of the lessor;

Second: That should said rent be not paid when due or should the lessee default in any of the covenants or conditions contained herein, the lessor, or his representative or agent, may re-enter said premises and remove all persons therefrom;

Third: That the lessee shall occupy said demised premises and shall keep the same in good condition, including such improvements as may be made thereon hereafter, the usual wear and tear and damage by the elements excepted, and shall not make any alterations thereon without the written consent of the lessor and shall not commit or suffer to be committed any waste upon said premises;

Fourth: That said premises shall not be used by the lessee, nor anyone else, during the term hereof or any extension thereof, for the sale of any intoxicating liquors, nor for any illegal or immoral purpose, and that possession of said premises by the lessee or his successors or assigns shall not be construed as conveying any title thereto or ownership thereof;

Fifth: That all Governmental laws and ordinances shall be complied with by the lessee;

Sixth: That the lessee waives all rights under Section 1942 of the Civil Code of California and releases the lessor from any and all damages which may be sustained by the lessee or any other party during the time he may be in possession of said premises;

Seventh: That should the occupancy of said premises, by the lessee, cause the present fire and liability insurance rates applicable thereto to be increased, the lessee shall pay the difference upon the amount of fire and liability insurance now being carried by the lessor and said difference shall be in addition to the amount of rental specified herein and shall be paid to the lessor upon demand;

Eighth: That should the lessor be compelled to commence or sustain an action at law to collect said rent or parts thereof or to dispossess the lessee or to recover possession of said premises, the lessee shall pay all costs in connection therewith including a reasonable fee for the attorney of the lessor;

Ninth: That the waiver, by the lessor, of any covenant or condition herein contained shall not vitiate the same or any other covenant or condition contained herein and that the terms and conditions contained herein shall apply to and bind the heirs, successors and assigns of the respective parties hereto;

Tenth: That should the lessee occupy said premises after the expiration date of this lease, with the consent of the lessor, expressed or implied, such possession shall be construed to be a tenancy from month to month and said lessee shall pay said lessor for said premises the sum of $200.00..................per month for such period as said lessee may remain in possession thereof;

Eleventh: That said premises shall not be used by the lessee during the term of this lease for other than ....residential purposes occupied by..not more than..2 residents...XXXXXX except with the written consent of the lessor;

Twelfth: That at the expiration of said term or the sooner determination thereof, the lessee shall peacefully quit and surrender possession of said premises in as good condition as reasonable use and wear thereof will permit;

Thirteenth: That all words used herein in the singular number shall include the plural and the present tense shall include the future and the masculine gender shall include the feminine and neuter.

Fourteenth: That the tenant shall maintain the garden associated with Apartment #3 at her own expense, in a manner in keeping with the surroundings.

Fifteenth: Receipt is hereby acknowledged of the sum of Fifty Dollars ($50) as a cleaning deposit, to be returned at the end of tenancy and on surrendering the premises in proper order in the judgment of the landlord.

IN WITNESS WHEREOF, the lessor and the lessee have executed this indenture as of the day and year first above written.

Margaret Grant.
Margaret A. Grant (Tenant)

John B. Investor
John B. Investor (Landlord)

Mary B. Investor
Mary B. Investor (Landlord)

FORM # L-14

For these forms address California Real Estate Association,
520 So. Grand Ave. Los Angeles 90017
(Copyright 1928, by California Real Estate Association)

LEASE

TO

Dated

RENTAL APPLICATION

Desired Possession Date:_____

Property Address:_____Apt. No._____

Name of Applicant(s):_____Married_____Age:_____

Name of Spouse:_____Other Occupants:_____

Pets (Number and Type)_____

Present Address:_____

How Long:_____Reason for Leaving:_____

Name of Present Landlord:_____

His Address and Phone No._____

Employment: Social Security #_____Driver's License #_____

Present Employer:_____How Long:_____

Address:_____Phone #_____

Employed as:_____Salary:_____Per:_____

Employment: (Spouse) Social Security #_____Driver's License #_____

Present Employer:_____How Long:_____

Address:_____Phone #_____

Employed as:_____Salary:_____Per:_____

Bank Accounts (Branch)_____Checking____Saving_____

Credit References (Please list three)

Name	Address	Phone #

Auto License #_____State of Registry:_____

Make and Model_____Year_____Color_____

Name of Closest Relative:_____Relationship:_____

Address:_____Phone #_____

I hereby sign this application on the basis of the following:
I declare the foregoing information to be true, under the penalty
of perjury, and I understand that the owner of the property, or
his agent, will rely on this information in entering into a rental
agreement with me.

It is further understood that the deposit of $_____
is for the purpose of reserving the apartment for me until this
application is acted upon. In the event this application is not
accepted I am to receive a full refund of said deposit; otherwise
the deposit will be applied to the rental agreement obligation.
The decision concerning this application is to be made on or before
_____failing which I am entitled to a full
refund of deposit and will have no further obligation.

_____   _____
(Applicant)   (Date)

_____   _____
(Applicant)   (Present Phone #)

should also ask if the job is expected to continue. It is unlikely you can obtain income data and probably should not ask. Other references may be useful in determining how responsible the party is. It may also provide a way to locate the tenant if it is needed after he has departed, especially with an unpaid bill.

After you have had some practice in handling tenants, you may be able to make up your mind about someone on the basis of a conversation. It is still good practice to obtain the information asked for on this form. You never know when you might need it later.

Pricing Policy

At what rent are you going to offer the apartment? When you analyzed this investment opportunity you used the rental income being realized by the seller. If you found the rents were under the market you may have decided to raise them. Unless rents are way out of line, the best time to change them is between tenants. Many successful investors deliberately set their rents just under the current market in order to provide present tenants with an incentive to stay. Of course, if your expenses increase, you have a legitimate reason for passing the increase on to the tenants. Be sure you explain carefully the basis on which the increase is charged. On the other hand, if you raise the rent when a unit becomes vacant, you may find it hard to get a new tenant. As a part of your ongoing education and experience, you should keep in touch with what your competitors are doing. Watch the ads. Go see rental units being offered and compare them with your own. It is not hard to find out what the going rent is for your type of accommodation. Be sure to compare on a proper basis and allow for the cost of utilities or slight differences in facilities. Then decide just what monthly rent you should charge. If you overprice your unit you may have trouble getting a rent-paying tenant. Prospective tenants will ordinarily have a very good idea of what the rent should be.

If you adopt a pricing policy of being just slightly under the market, you probably will have little or no trouble finding tenants and your turnover will likely be at a minimum. You may also avoid some tenant complaints or requests for favors. When the rent is very favorable, you can always turn down a request by saying that the rent is so low you cannot do what is asked without raising it.

Also related to pricing is your policy concerning advance payments and damage deposits. As a newcomer to this business you are hardly in a position to pioneer new practices. By now you should know what other owners do in this regard and you will pretty much have to go along with it. But get the first month's rent *before* the tenant moves in; get the last month's rent, too. You may have to compromise slightly and agree to accept some of this total shortly after the move-in. Be careful, however. An indication of softness or lack of desire to enforce agreements can cost you a lot of money and force you out of this type of investment.

The amount of damage deposit will be governed not only by local custom but also by the prospects of needing it. Your objective is to have some money in hand so that if, at the time the tenant moves out, damage is to be repaired, it can be paid for with the tenant's funds. True, if there is a shortage, you can always sue, but collecting on a judgment can be a tough proposition. When renting to adults who appear to be the kind who will treat the property properly, you may wish to take a modest $25 or $50 deposit. You may stipulate it is for cleaning rather than damage. In either case, the conditions for refund should be stated clearly in the rental or lease agreement. If it is your policy to rent to families with children, you must recognize the possibility of an above-average amount of "wear and tear" on your property. Obtain a deposit large enough to take care of what you expect will be needed. The same holds true for tenants with pets.

From a marketing point of view, you want to be able to offer an apartment that will be more attractive than anything else on the market at the same time. If people with children and/or pets have great difficulty in locating accommodations, you may decide against a restriction, thus tapping that demand.

Marketing

All marketing campaigns considered successful turned out that way because of the careful thought and planning that went into them. You need to decide whether you will advertise the unit to the world at large, or list it with one or more commercial rental agencies. Either way, all of the previously discussed decisions are necessary. If you use a rental agency it will do some screening of prospects, but it is likely it will fall to you to show the apartment. If you want your applicants to be screened before you show them the apartment, you might find it well to use a rental agency. Have a clear understanding of the cost *beforehand.* You may cut yourself off from prospective tenants who either do not know about rental agencies or who do not wish to pay the fee, if it is the tenant who pays the fee. You need to decide whether you want to expose yourself to the world by offering it on the open market. Assuming you are going to handle everything yourself, the next question is: how do you advertise?

The customary place is the classified advertising section of a newspaper circulated in the area where the property is located. Check the "Apartment Wanted" classification. Perhaps you can find a tenant without having to advertise at all. Some prospective tenants want landlords to come to them.

It is also a good idea to contact the personnel departments of large companies, because many assist their employees in finding housing. If there is a college or university nearby, it will have a housing office glad to hear of your vacancy. You may want to put a notice on the supermarket notice board or on the bulletin board at a senior citizens' center.

Study the advertisements placed by other landlords to see how they word their advertising. The newspaper advertising staff will help you with the wording. After you have done this a few times you will know what works and what should be avoided. The following information should be included in any ad, as a minimum: the size of the apartment (number of bedrooms), whether it is furnished, monthly rent, whether a lease is available, utilities included, amount of advance rent and security deposit required, an indication of the area (preferably not the address), and your phone number. If there are some attractions that will help to rent the apartment, they should be mentioned. For instance: near shopping or transportation; in a particular school district; garage;

garden; and so on. Remember: if you were a prospective tenant, what would you want to know without making a phone call and what would you see that would prompt you to call to make an appointment to see the property?

If you want to restrict renting to certain groups, say so and save yourself some time and effort. For example: "1 BR studio ideal for retired person." This should eliminate calls from a mother of six or a newly-liberated teenager with a set of drums.

You should not place an ad for only one insertion in a daily newspaper. Go for the extended run at a discount price. You can always cancel the ad or take the phone off the hook if you rent quickly. Don't be discouraged if the first 50 prospects turn you down. Be alert to why the property is not renting and make changes in policy as indicated. Be patient. Believe that there is a tenant out there somewhere who is destined to rent your apartment. He will come along. Be prepared to show the property at a time convenient for the prospect even if it is not the best time for you. Particularly if you have to travel a distance to meet people at the property, try to line up appointments in sequence to eliminate going back and forth. Some property owners hold an open house and advertise the apartment as being open from, say, 10 A.M. to 5 P.M. Make a plan and be prepared to stick to it.

Handling Prospects

You have obtained a supply of application and agreement forms, you have written and placed the ad, and now you sit by the phone. Be sure to have a good book available; you may have some time on your hands.

What might be involved after you have answered the phone a few times and finally someone says he would like to see what you are offering? You set a time to meet him and go to the apartment early. If the departing tenant has not left yet, you will need to make appropriate arrangements to be sure you are expected. A disgruntled departing tenant can sabotage you more effectively than a Russian spy.

A golden rule: never let a tenant show the property to a prospect. Always show the property yourself, unless you have an agent to handle the whole transaction. Whenever possible, show the property only when the current tenant is not around. That may mean you will have to take precautions with respect to the personal property lying around. Be businesslike and demonstrate you are familiar with the apartment; if you aren't, become so. Don't try a hardsell or be ingratiating, condescending, or apologetic. This is a business proposition. You have an apartment that affords good accommodation and is fairly priced. The prospect is either attracted to it or not. If the prospect indicates that it will not do, don't harass him in your eagerness to rent the unit. This is not a life-or-death proposition—it may only seem so.

At all costs, avoid showing the property to two different prospects at the same time. (If you hold an open house, that is different.) When making appointments to show it, space them to allow prospects to have your undivided attention. If two happen to arrive at the same time, suggest that one be patient until you get back to him.

Suppose you have two prospects on board and they both seem interested. Be careful to deal fairly. Take a deposit from the first one who says he wants to do business, but be sure to get a name and address or phone number from the second in case the first one falls through. Don't rely on the second one to check back with you to see whether the first deal went through. You will not hear from the second prospect, and if the first does not qualify, you will be sorry you passed up the second without a way to contact him.

Discrimination in housing is illegal. No sermon here, just a reminder that if you, as a landlord, discriminate on the basis of race, color, or creed, you are almost certainly violating the law.

Assume now you are about to make a contract with a prospective tenant. During the negotiations you may have made certain commitments. Certainly you will ask the prospect to give you a deposit and complete an application form. If everything checks out, promptly notify him and prepare the rental agreement or lease for signature. Ask the party to bring the balance of the money and set a time for signing the documents. Be sure to include in the agreement whatever commitments you made during the negotiation. Put in writing what you have agreed to.

Don't create problems in the future by failing to have a written record.

The time for occupancy will ordinarily coincide with the date from which rent is being charged. Make a date to meet the new tenant at the apartment.

Turning Over the Keys

Wait until all is settled before celebrating. Inform the present tenant that the apartment is rented. Confirm his departure date and make arrangements to inspect the property and return the cleaning or damage deposit. If personal property is included you will want to check it over against the inventory and make certain all is accounted for. Check the keys to make sure they have been returned and that they operate the locks. Don't find out later the tenant changed the locks and you didn't get the right keys. Get a forwarding address from the departing tenant.

Turning utilities on and off is normally the responsibility of the incoming and outgoing tenants. As an assist to incoming tenants, you might find out where the utility offices are, but you should avoid getting involved in the transaction.

When the new tenant arrives, go through the apartment carefully. When applicable, check off the personal property inventory. Make a note of any damaged areas so they can be repaired, or so you will not blame the new tenant later for the damage. Introduce the new tenant to the neighbors if the opportunity presents itself. Review again with the tenant any special features. For example, perhaps you have included in the agreement that the tenant is responsible for taking care of the garden. Discuss this again at this time. Stress how important it is to make the rent payments on time and confirm that the tenant knows where to send the payments. Be businesslike, not overly familiar. This is not a social enterprise. Accomplish your business and get out. Leave the tenants to enjoy the first moments in their new home. Besides, you may end up agreeing to a new paint job, carpeting, and a new refrigerator. Get out while you are ahead.

When you return home, check your property file to see that you have all the documents for the new tenants in the right place.

Make any notes you think useful as to what you learned so the information will be available the next time you have to get a new tenant. Be sure the money is properly recorded and deposited.

Some Miscellaneous Matters

You are now running a business and will want to pay even more attention than before to income tax matters. You will incur expenses in connection with your investment that are tax-deductible—provided you have records to support them. Make it a practice *always* to ask for a receipt or invoice. Pay all bills by check; deposit all income to a bank account. Keep detailed records. In the next chapter there will be a complete treatment of how to do this.

If you use a portion of your residence regularly and exclusively for the conduct of a business activity you can charge against income the value of that space. The easiest way to compute the charge is to determine the fair rental value of the entire home and the proportion of the space devoted to the office. That fraction multiplied by the rental value will give you the expense.

If you need a safety deposit box to safeguard the documents and records associated with your investment, you can deduct the annual charge.

Travel expenses are deductible. Keep a log of the date and mileage of the trips you take *in connection with the apartment*. At the current rate of 12¢ per mile, for the first 15,000 miles, the total tax deductible allowance can be substantial if you have any amount of running around to do.

Do you need to make any change in your last will and testament? If you do not have a will, better prepare one right away. Sometimes it is important to refer specifically to property and how you wish it to be treated in the event of your death. Now is the time to make whatever adjustment may be needed.

Take another look at your property and casualty insurance program. As a property owner you not only have a greater exposure to loss, but you will be more of a target, and for larger amounts, in the event someone is injured. The potential loss from liability claims is unlimited. Check with your insurance adviser and make sure your liability coverage applies to all the property you own and is written for limits large enough adequately to protect you. The charge for increasing liability coverage amounts is very nominal.

Do you have enough property (fire) insurance to completely cover losses that may occur? Have you done what is necessary to have the benefit of replacement cost coverage? If the property is damaged badly enough that the tenants have to move out, will your policy pay the amount of the lost rents during the time it takes to repair the damage?

Be conscious of the need to avoid and prevent losses even if you have insurance. Money can never make up for the injury or damage.

To summarize: you bought the apartment building to make money. This money-making machine requires management. To maximize return on your investment you need to keep expenses at a minimum but you cannot simply refuse to spend at all. If the property is adequately maintained, its resale value will be better than otherwise. If you keep it repaired the tenants will be more satisfied. You will have to be hard-nosed if tenants get behind in their rents; maximizing rental income is one of your goals. Keeping the property filled with rent-paying people will be one of your most important activities. You may even have to undertake an eviction if there is no other solution to problems that may arise. Finally, you will want to be able to see how your investment is faring. Are you ahead or behind? Is it a good investment? The answers to these questions are in good record-keeping and accounting reports. All of this is covered in detail in the next chapter.

7

Accounting Records

You have put your money to work in a money-making machine. How can you tell if the machine is functioning properly? You certainly must not rely on your memory. Good records provide the answer. Bank records will be useful, but you need more. Best to have a running record of income and expense and then prepare it in a conventional "accounting statement" format such as an earnings or profit-and-loss statement.

There are really two goals to be achieved: accurate records not only to tell you where you are going, but also to support your income tax return. To make it easy to achieve these goals we have some specially designed forms and all you have to do is fill in the blanks.

Banking

Throughout this discussion, we will assume the following banking arrangements: you will process all income and expenditures through a checking account while maintaining a savings account to which you transfer surplus funds each month. The surplus will be simply the difference between income and outgo for the month. From time to time you may have to withdraw funds from the savings account to pay certain expenses—taxes, for instance. You may decide to use your regular personal checking account rather than open a separate one for the investment. The philosophy behind this arrangement is as follows: the assumption is that you have invested cash to generate current income and long-term gain. You do not intend to spend any of the return from the investment; instead, you will let it accumulate. This will allow you to know—when you have ultimately disposed of the property —exactly how much the investment has produced. You will have every last cent tucked away in the savings account—plus the proceeds of the sale.

The suggested accounting procedure will work just as well if you do not follow the banking suggestion. There is nothing in the process that will prevent you from spending the money as soon as you get your hands on it each month. The system is very flexible, as you will see.

As we review how to handle your records, think in terms of depositing all income to your checking account and paying all bills associated with the property from that same account. The records you keep will tell you how much in that account belongs to the investment. The forms will also show you how much should be in the savings account, assuming you have been transferring as you go along.

Accounting Forms

A complete example is reproduced on the following pages. Look at these forms now and then come back to the description of the entries. Recall that the example of the analysis and purchase assumed a midyear transaction date. In order to provide a maximum amount of detail in the accounting forms, we have switched the date to the first of the year. This will serve as a guide no matter when the record-keeping is begun. Note in particular that if you already own property you can set up your accounting records according to the procedure discussed.

Your complete record-keeping consists of the following forms:

Monthly Record of Income/Expense
Depreciation Schedules

Annual Operating Statement
Summary of Investment Results

For a complete record on a piece of property, all you need is a
Monthly Record form for each year you own it and the same
number of Annual Operating Statements, but only one Depreciation Schedule and one Investment Summary. It is assumed you
keep a faithful record in your checkbook of checks written and deposits made and that you reconcile your bank statement each time
you receive it.

Monthly Record of Income/Expense

You can make the entries on this form at the end of each
month, posting the figures from your checkbook and receipt book
or other record of rental income. You would have a separate sheet
for *each* property; don't combine the records for one building
with another. It is assumed you are operating on a cash basis for
accounting and therefore will make the entries according to the
month in which the transaction occurred. For example, the mortgage payments are payable on the first of the month. Even though
you might write the check a few days beforehand, record the expenditure as of the date used on the check. Further, you will
charge as expense the cost of goods or services at the time they are
paid for; do not spread it out over the time to be used. You may
want to do otherwise if, for example, you bought insurance for a
three-year term and paid the premium in advance.

The other accounting basis is called "accrual." It is used by
corporations and other business entities but rarely by individuals.
The accrual basis calls for recording income as of the date it is re-
ceivable, regardless of when you actually get your hands on it, and
expenses as of the date the obligation is incurred, regardless of
when you actually pay it. Further, the expense is charged against
income for the period during which the expenditure applies. For
example, if you bought insurance for one year you would charge
$1/12$th of the amount against income each month. The objective of
accrual accounting is to reflect income and expense more accurately. That accuracy is quite unnecessary for an individual
operating a small apartment building.

MONTHLY RECORD OF INCOME/EXPENSE

Location: 1234 Wistful Vista, Utopia Year Ending 12-31-7-

	JAN	FEB	MAR	APR	MAY	JUN	JUL	AUG	SEP	OCT	NOV	DEC	TOTAL
INCOME													
Rents	1800 -	900 -	700 -	1100 -	900 -	910 -	910 -	910 -	910 -	710 -	710 -	1110 -	11,570
Deposits	200 -		⟨50⟩	50 -						⟨50⟩		50 -	200
INTEREST			18 -			20 -			32 -			40 -	110
TOTAL	2000 -	900 -	668 -	1150 -	900 -	930 -	910 -	910 -	942 -	660 -	710 -	1200 -	11,880
EXPENSES													
Property taxes				1313 -								1350 -	2663
Utilities	22 -	17 -	20 -	20 -	21 -	22 -	25 -	26 -	25 -	24 -	16 -	20 -	258
Insurance	50 -						50 -						100
Maintenance	45 -	15 -	100 -		10 -	5 -	10 -			40 -		120	345
1st Mortgage Payment		452 -	452 -	452 -	452 -	452 -	452 -	452 -	452 -	452 -	452 -	452 -	4972
2nd Mortgage Payment		70	70	70	70	70	70	70	70	70	70	70	770
Interest			15 -						10 -	20 -	15 -		60
ADVERTISING													
TOTAL	117 -	554 -	657 -	1855 -	553 -	549 -	607 -	548 -	557 -	606 -	553 -	2012 -	9168
To Bank	1883 -	346 -	11 -	⟨705⟩	347 -	381 -	303 -	362 -	385 -	54 -	157 -	⟨812⟩	2712
Beginning Balance	0	1883 -	2229 -	2240 -	1535 -	1882 -	2263 -	2566 -	2928 -	3313 -	3367 -	3524 -	
Ending Balance	1883 -	2229 -	2240 -	1535 -	1882 -	2263 -	2566 -	2928 -	3313 -	3367 -	3524 -	2712 -	2712

You will also be guided by the rules and regulations of the Internal Revenue Service. For example, when you collect rent in advance (such as the first and last month's), all of it is to be recorded as income for the month in which you receive it.

Notice that the Monthly Record form is divided into two parts, with columns for each month in the year. First, the Income section.

Recall in the escrow the buyer received credit for the advance rents held by the seller. This is treated as income for the first month of ownership. The tenants, duly notified of the change of ownership and anxious to impress their new landlord, have all paid their rents on time, so now we have $900 from current rents and $900 credit from the seller as rental income for the first month.

The damage or cleaning deposits of $200 were also credited in the escrow and the amount is to be entered. In the future, as changes take place in the deposits, they will be recorded on this line. Later, when looking at the bank balance, it will be important to remember how much is included for tenant deposits so that you are not misled by what appears to be affluence.

The total income for the month is $2,000, but you received only $900 in cash. Recall the admonition in the chapter on closing that, although you did not have to put up as much money as you might have because of these credits, you would need the funds later. The time is now. Be prepared to deposit the $1,100 along with the current rental income.

Now for the expenses.

Your first month may be a light one. As a general rule, mortgage payments start a full month, or even more, after the papers are signed and the loan disbursed. In our example, we have assumed that no mortgage payments are to be made in January. The lender may specify the first loan payment to be made on, say, the first of each month; but with an escrow closing more than a month before that first payment, there will be interest charged. Example: loan disbursed May 20, first mortgage payment due July 1. In the escrow the borrower will be charged interest from May 20 to May 31; the July 1 payment will take care of the interest for the period

June 1 to July 1. In this case you would enter, as an expense item, "interest" on a blank line, and show the amount in the column for May.

Another item from the closing statement to be entered on the Monthly Record is insurance. Recall we were charged a proration in the escrow. We treat this as an operating expense in the first month. The other expense items handled in the escrow are not operational so we do not show them here. They will be recorded later, however.

By the end of the first month we will have paid a utility bill. Here we are paying the cost of water and gas used for the building in general; the tenants have their own meters for their individual consumption. We also found we had to take care of a small plumbing problem and incurred a $45 maintenance expense.

All of these entries can be made at the end of the month. Simply go to your checking account checkbook and post the items as indicated. You will also refer to the escrow closing statement. By subtracting the expenses from the income, we find there is a total of $1,883. Write a check for this amount and open a savings account. The Monthly Record shows clearly the changes in the savings account as you consistently each month transfer funds to or from the savings account. Each month during the ownership period, you repeat the process. No other monthly accounting record is needed—this does it all.

Once you have kept your records in this manner, you will have no trouble seeing how to handle any transaction that may arise. There are, however, some unusual items that will come up; here are some examples:

Refer back to the Income section for the month of March. Here we lost a tenant. During February we were told the tenant was leaving at the end of March. No rent was received because the advance was to apply; here it was $200. The apartment was in satisfactory condition so the damage deposit of $50 was refunded in full. Note we recorded a withdrawal of the deposit. We also found that the savings account earned $18 interest on the funds on deposit since the beginning of the quarter. This is income attributable to the investment and has been added to the account balance, hence the amount is entered. Write in "interest" in the column on the left. In the example you will see how this interest income has been entered at the end of each calendar quarter, the time most savings institutions credit interest, even though compounding is more frequent.

We found a new tenant at the beginning of April and collected two months' rent and a $50 deposit. Note the entries. A similar in-and-out transaction is shown for October and December. There we had more trouble locating a tenant and had a month's vacancy.

Effective in June, we raised the rent on one of the apartments by $10. Because we are renting on a month-to-month basis we had to give a month's notice. Or, here this may reflect a renewal of a lease with an increase in rent. No adjustment in the advance rent has been made, but that would have been a good idea. If you have had a tenant for a while, and raise the rent, remember to obtain an increase in the advance. You may find, when the last month of occupancy has come and gone, you shortchanged yourself for that last month by applying only the original advance, which of course was less than the current rent.

In our previous discussion of tax shelters we pointed out that when there was an operating loss you would have a reduction in the total amount of income tax to be paid. By computing your income tax twice—once including the investment and once without it—you can quickly determine the credit earned by the investment. Take that amount of money and deposit it to your property investment account. In the left-hand column in the Income section of the Monthly Record form, write "tax shelter benefit" and enter the dollar amount under the month in which you make the deposit. This will then be a part of the income from the investment. At the end of the year, of course, you will be taking only the rental income and interest income for tax purposes from the Monthly Record form.

Property taxes are usually payable in two installments—in the example we have used, April and December. By the due date in April we have accumulated more than enough to pay the taxes, but the funds are in the savings account, earning interest. We want to withdraw the minimum amount required, so, after collecting the rents and making the other disbursements for the month, we can calculate how much cash we need to pay the tax bill. Here it comes to $705, the difference between the income for the month and the outgo, including the taxes. This difference is the amount to be withdrawn from the savings account and deposited to the checking account. Now we can cover all the checks to be written. Note the use of brackets to indicate subtraction or withdrawal. If our record-keeping has been accurate and is up-to-date, the Monthly Record bottom line will show the exact balance of the savings account. Here we would reconcile the savings passbook balance to $1,535.

For expenses not specified in the left-hand column, simply write the appropriate designation. Notice how we handled the Advertising item.

You may have some expenses for which you do not issue a check. For example, you use some stamps, or the telephone, or drive your car on business associated with the property. Be certain to keep track of these items and at the end of the year do a tally and compute the amounts involved. You can reimburse yourself for these deductible amounts by showing them on the Monthly Record of Income/Expense and thereby deduct them from the rental income, assuming you are using your regular family checking account to handle apartment funds. If you have a separate checking account for the property, prepare a tabulation of the expenses much like a bill or invoice, write a check payable to yourself for the total, and enter the appropriate amounts on the Monthly Record form. Check with the Internal Revenue Service for the current allowance per mile for car expense.

If the lender has insisted upon collecting for taxes and insurance and maintaining a loan trust fund or impounds account you will not be paying those bills directly. The expense, however, will be included in the monthly payment made to the lender. In this situation, enter on the "mortgage payment" line the part of the payment attributable to principal and interest and apportion the balance to taxes and insurance. That will call for entries every month on those lines. At the end of the year the lender will give you the exact amounts paid out for those items; use them in preparing the income statement. If a surplus has built up in the loan trust fund you can ask the lender to return it to you.

There is virtually no limitation on the different kinds of entries that can be made on these forms. Once you have made the entries for a few months you will see how true that statement is.

At the end of the year, after all entries have been made, we total the form horizontally and vertically and hope for a balance. From this sheet we will get our income and expense totals. The savings account balance should also check out. This will be the amount to enter on the new sheet for the next year. All funds remaining in the checking account should be transferred if you are to achieve the objectives stated. Here we would have $2,712 in the savings account. You should keep in mind, of course, that $200 of it belongs to tenants in the form of damage or cleaning deposits. Also, although we have treated it as income, there is $900 of advance rent—and rental income will be reduced in future months when tenants move. On the other hand, ordinarily the incoming tenant will also be paying an advance, so it all evens out in the long run.

Perhaps you are saying at this point it looks as though we have made a profit of $2,512 for the first year. Be careful. $2,512 is the cash in hand. Profit is computed in another way.

The only worthwhile profit figure to look at is the one *after* income tax, so let's see what has to be done to calculate it.

Depreciation Schedules

As an expert real estate investor by now, you will be quick to point out that there is an expense for which we do not write a check—depreciation. Each year when it is time to prepare a report card for Uncle Sam and his cousin at the State Capitol, you will need to have amounts to show for depreciation. To have those numbers readily available, you will want to prepare the Depreciation Schedule at the time you set up your initial records.

The information needed for this form will come both from the analysis we made before we decided to buy and from the

DEPRECIATION SCHEDULES

Enter here the figures to be used in preparing Income Tax Returns

BUILDING: Date acquired __1-1-7-__   Total Purchase Price $ __77,000__

Remaining useful life __30 years__ Costs not expensed $ __0__

Total $ __77,000__

Depreciation method-

__Straight Line ~ 3 1/3 % per yr__

Less land value $ __17,000__

Basis for Depreciation $ __60,000__

End of Year	Beginning Book Value	Depreciation	Ending Book Value	Total Depreciation
97-	$60,000	$2,000	$58,000	$2,000
9				
9				
9				
9				
9				
9				
9				

EQUIPMENT: Description __Stoves & Refrigerators__ Date acquired __1-1-7-__

Cost $ __2,000__

Salvage $ __200__

Amount to be depreciated $ __1,800__

Estimated useful life __5__

Method __Straight Line__

End of Year	Beginning Book value	Depreciation	Ending Book Value	Total Depreciation
7-	$2,000	$360	$1,640	$360

closing statement. We concluded the building had a remaining useful life of 30 years, so that means the annual depreciation would be 3.3 percent on a straight-line basis. To be conservative and to avoid complications involved in using accelerated depreciation, we have selected the straight-line basis. Always remember it is only the structure that is subject to depreciation. Here we have a $60,000 value, so the first year depreciation will be 3.3 percent of that amount, or $2,000. If you bought the property during the year, you would take only a proportion of the annual amount.

You will use this same form for the time you own the property up to ten years, after which you would simply continue on another copy of the form. Note that you will have the cumulative depreciation figure readily available; this will be needed when you prepare your income tax return.

The example assumes we have lumped all the equipment together. If you choose to depreciate pieces of equipment separately you can see from the form what to do. The choice of estimated remaining useful lifetimes is critical. The shorter the period, the larger the amount of depreciation expense, hence a lower income tax liability. A prudent investor will seek guidance from the Internal Revenue Service and his tax adviser.

From the sample Depreciation Schedule you can see how much total depreciation you have taken and can avoid going beyond the expected salvage value, something you must do to keep out of trouble with income tax examiners.

With depreciation amounts available, we now are prepared to make up the first Annual Operating Statement in a form customarily used by accountants and easily understood by all.

Annual Operating Statement

The address is to be entered because you will have a separate statement for each property. Unless you have chosen otherwise you would prepare your tax return and other records on a calendar-year basis.

Now would be a good time to check the amounts you see in the example with those shown on the Monthly Record of Income/Expense. This will confirm where the numbers come from

ANNUAL OPERATING STATEMENT

r property at _1234 Wistful Vista, Utopia, Calif._ For year ended _12-31-7-_

CASH FLOW BEFORE INCOME TAX

Total Rental Income received	$ 11,570	
Other Income	110	$ 11,680
Less: Property Taxes	$ 2,663	
Utilities	258	
Insurance	100	
Maintenance	345	
ADVERTISING	60	
Total Operating Expenses	$ 3,426	
Mortgage Payments - First	4,972	
- Second	770	
- Third		
Total Cash Outlay		$ 9,168

NET CASH INCOME $ 2,512

INCOME TAX COMPUTATION

Total Income		$ 11,680
Less: Total Operating Expenses	$ 3,426	
Total Mortgage Interest Expenses	4,512	
Depreciation - Building	2,000	
- Equipment	360	
First year special deductions	1,100	
Total Deductible Expense		$ 11,398

NET TAXABLE INCOME $ 282

INCOME TAX LIABILITY: **.40** x Net Taxable Income $ 113
(rate)
(If Net Taxable Income is negative, the Tax Liability
is your Tax Shelter Benefit.)

MORTGAGE REDUCTION

Total of Mortgage Balances at beginning of year $ 61,000
Less ending balances, all mortgages, end of year   59,770

TOTAL MORTGAGE REDUCTION $ 1,230

RECONCILIATION OF CASH GAIN

Net Cash Income $ 2,512
Less Income Tax Liability or Plus Tax Shelter Benefit   113

TOTAL SPENDABLE CASH AFTER INCOME TAX $ 2,399

for the first section, "Cash Flow Before Income Tax." For Section B, "Income Tax Computation," there is some figuring to do. The first item is Mortgage Interest Expense. The $4,512 is the total for both first and second mortgages; these must be computed separately.

Recall that each mortgage payment of $452 for the first and $70 for the second is divided between interest and repayment of principal. At the end of the year the coupon payment book or lender's statement will show the totals needed. It is important to confirm such figures to see that they are correct. For income tax purposes we can deduct only the interest portion. Note that in Section A, the total payment was used, but that was because we were dealing with cash income and outgo.

In Chapter Three we used some of the Tables in the back of the book to compute unpaid mortgage balances and interest expense. Then we were estimating what the situation would be; now it is for real. And we do it the same way as before, using factors for balances due and interest expense. Be sure to note that the second mortgage carries a "stipulated" payment.

There is a small matter to allow for in our example. Because our first mortgage payment comes in February, there are only 11 payments made in the year. As a consequence, the total mortgage interest expense of $4,512 is for 11 months, not a full year. On next year's Annual Operating Statement, a full year's expense will be used. Ordinarily you will be working from data provided by the lender and you have reason to assume it will be correct.

Now for the special first-year deductions. We have elected to treat as expense the title insurance, mortgage loan fees and one-time costs; charges for prorations are not included, as they are recovered in effect out of income. From the title or escrow company closing statement we find that these special expenses total $1,100. When totaled we have $11,398 as the sum of deductible expenses. With a gross income of $11,680, the net taxable income is $282. If the combined federal and state taxes amount to $113, obtained by applying the correct tax rates, you can calculate the total spendable cash after tax as shown in Section D. Here it is $2,399—not bad on a cash investment of just over $17,000.

We passed over Section C, "Mortgage Reduction." Here we

see how much of the mortgage is being paid off by the tenants. To the extent that we can sell the property for at least what we paid for it, the amount of mortgage reduction will be part of our gain. Previously when we calculated the mortgage interest for income tax purposes we had the figures needed to compute the unpaid mortgage balances used in this section in determining the total mortgage reduction for the period. From time to time you will make use of the formula:

total of the mortgage payments = *interest expense* + *mortgage reduction.*

So now we have a picture of our first full year's operation and in a conventional business format. Our "bottom line" is a good healthy figure. And we have all that money in a safe place, a savings account. In April we will be able to prepare our income tax returns quickly because all the calculating has been done.

Each year we do the same thing, using current figures. But we are anxious to know, on a cumulative basis, how the investment is coming out. For that we turn to the final accounting record, the Summary of Investment Results.

Summary of Investment Results

The entries in the top section should be made at the time we are setting up our records. The figures come from the escrow closing statement. Your decision whether to expense or capitalize the closing costs will affect your book value or "basis" for use in calculating long-term capital gain on resale. As a result of deciding to treat costs as expense, we deducted the $1,100 from first-year income. These amounts would still show on the Summary sheet because they are a part of the cash invested. In our example the beginning book value or basis is $77,000. If we had chosen, instead, to capitalize all or part of these costs, we would still make the entries as in the example, to arrive at the amount of cash invested, but we would make a memorandum note of the beginning book value or basis by adding the capitalized amount to the purchase price.

The primary purpose of this Summary is to provide a run-

Property at **1234 Wistful Vista, Utopia, California** Purchased on **1-1-7-** for **$77,000**

Costs:
Mortgage Points/Fees $ **540** Cash Down Payment $ **16,000**
Title Insurance/Escrow fees **449** Total Costs **1,100**
Other one-time fees **111**

TOTAL COSTS $ **1,100** TOTAL CASH INVESTED $ **17,100**

Year	Rental Income	Net Cash Income	Tax or Shelter Benefit	Total Cash Gain	Percent of Cash Invested	Cumulative Cash Recovery	Mortgage Reduction	Total Gain	Percent of Cash Invested	Additional Capital Invested
19	$11,570	2,512	T 113	$2,399	14.02%	$2,399	$1,230	$3,629	21.2%	—
19										
19										
19										
19										
19										
19										
19										
19										
19										

Notes:
Enter data from the Annual Operating Statement. Prepare a Summary form for each separate property. This provides a year-by-year summary of investment returns and performance. The Cumulative Cash Recovery column enables you to see when your total cash investment has been recovered.

Total Gain includes the reduction in the mortgages. This will be realized only if the property is ultimately sold for at least its original cost plus resale expense. Gain on resale may be subject to income tax.

Do not include the prorations part of the closing costs when computing the amount of cash invested.

© Copyright 1972 by Douglas M. Temple

ning record of investment results. With a sheet for each piece of property, one investment can readily be compared with others.

The "Cumulative Cash Recovery" column will show how much actual cash, after taxes, the property has returned, and you can compare it with the total money at risk. Somewhere along the line you will see you have recovered all of your invested capital with more to come, if all is going well and you made a good decision initially. In particular, note that the figures for entering on this form already appear on the other sheets, except for the percentages. A few comments on the entries.

The form calls for both Rental Income and Net Cash Income. The figure in the first column does not include income other than from rents, whereas the second includes earned interest plus any other income you might have—from coin-operated equipment, for example. Identify Income Tax charge or Tax Shelter Benefit by an appropriate letter in the narrow column. The total cash gain is the last figure on the Annual Operating Statement. Mortgage Reduction similarly comes from the Statement. With respect to the Total Gain, notice the qualification stated on the form. The amount is the sum of Total Cash Gain and Mortgage Reduction. If you purchase additional equipment or make capital improvements on the property, you can show the increase in the investment by using the right-hand column. Under those conditions the total cash invested will change and a new value will be used in calculating entries for the two percentage columns.

To summarize: all business activity requires adequate accounting records. When you own a money-making machine you are in business but you do not want to spend a lot of time keeping records. There is no need to employ someone else to do your record-keeping. By bringing together each month a record of the money coming in and the money going out, you will, at the end of the year, be able to obtain totals that can be used in preparing an annual operating statement.

With a very few additional computations you can obtain figures needed to calculate income tax information. By taking the totals for each year and entering them on a summary sheet you can have a complete history of the financial results obtained from the ownership and operation of the property. Perhaps for the first time in your investment experience, you know where you stand: how much is invested, how much has been returned after taxes, and what kind of a yield you are getting.

Once the work has been completed for the year, bring together the receipts and other papers related to the investment and place them with the accounting reports in a folder filed by property address. Put a fresh Monthly Record sheet in a file folder and keep it near your checkbook and savings passbook. That's all there is to it. Your moneymaking machine will hum—and so should you.

8

Disposing of the Investment

WHEN you decided to make an investment in an apartment house, it was your plan to hold on to it for a number of years, to receive an adequate current return, and most importantly, to sell it ultimately to realize a long-term capital gain that was greater than alternative investment opportunities offered. You are now faced with an important decision. Timing can be critical. It is a mistake with any investment to put it out of mind, expecting someday to discover you have made a fortune. Particularly with an investment in income property, you need to keep aware of changing values and conditions and have a plan already formulated to use in the event you need to dispose of the investment. There are many variables and factors to consider in being prepared for this step.

Reasons to Sell

The urgency of the need to liquidate should be carefully measured against the possible gains and losses. Even though there is a great need for cash, which could be obtained if you sold, this might not be the best asset to turn into cash, considering what you might be giving up. You need to know just how you stand with the investment and what its future prospects are.

Because you have been diligently keeping your records according to the procedures and on the forms described in previous chapters, you can readily tell how you stand. The Investment Summary is all-important here.

Some of the questions to ask yourself are: what is my after-tax rate of return and how does it compare with alternatives? Have I received back all of my original cash investment? Can I meet my need for cash out of the funds built up from the investment without selling it? If I have been using accelerated depreciation, will I have a tax penalty if I sell now? How big is my equity and would re-financing rather than selling produce the cash I need? Have the repairs and maintenance become so great that the profit potential is at a minimum?

You should learn how to analyze thoroughly the financial record of the property and use the record to forecast the future. You should always stand prepared to evaluate an opportunity that comes your way against the present investment. Most of the time you will decide to retain the status quo. If you do not make the most of the information you have and the skills you have developed, you will miss opportunities to increase your estate significantly.

At the end of each year it would be a good idea to check to see if the investment is in fact progressing as well as your original analysis suggested it would. Perhaps rents should be increased. It may be economical to undertake some preventive maintenance rather than let things go. You simply can't neglect the money-machine. This does not mean you should always be fussing over it —that would be a mistake. But it will not produce the maximum return if you do not manage it intelligently. Intelligent management includes knowing always where you stand and when you should make a change.

Besides an urgent need for cash for non-investment purposes, there are other perfectly respectable reasons for considering selling. You may have made this investment as part of a plan to provide a retirement income. If that is the case, the way you dispose of the investment will be affected by how you want to use the proceeds. If you cash out you then must find a place for the proceeds. Those funds must not lie idle in a non-interest-bearing checking account. Perhaps putting the money in a savings account is the best plan. Buying government bonds is another possibility. How about leaving a lot of it in the property in the form of a mortgage and earn higher interest than the alternatives would pay? Not as secure, you say, and you are right. But if your retirement is not being financed exclusively by the liquidation, you may be able to assume a modest amount of risk in order to gain a larger return.

A highly successful financier announced long ago that the secret of his success was in liquidating investments only *after* he knew exactly where the proceeds were going. Here we are stressing the need to decide very carefully whether to sell, and before doing so, to decide equally carefully how to employ the proceeds once the sale is made. The timing and manner of sale will be very much affected by how you are going to handle the ensuing cash.

Perhaps you are so enamored of real estate investing that you want to become involved further. You feel prepared to take on a bigger project. The only problem seems to be that all your funds for investing are tied up in the first investment. Is that the end of it? Not necessarily. It may be possible to trade a smaller property in on a larger one. We will treat the matter of exchanging and trading in more detail later. Meanwhile, realize if you do want to go after bigger things, it is quite possible to use your first investment as a steppingstone.

You may have found, on the other hand, that responding to unreasonable demands of unreasonable tenants is just not your cup of tea. What are your choices? You could hire a manager and retain ownership. You could sell for a minimum cash down and continue to receive a return on your investment by way of mortgage interest. Note carefully, of course, that your status as owner or mortgagee seriously affects your income tax situation as long as there are tax benefits arising from charging depreciation and other operating expenses.

You may want not only to retain this property but also to invest in more; but you need cash to do so. The equity in the first property may be tapped by re-financing or by a junior mortgage, thus avoiding the sale. You do not always have to sell in order to get your money out of an investment in real estate. It will cost money to re-finance. There will be loan fees, new title insurance, and other expenses. By now, of course, you are skilled in these matters and also in the evaluation of investment opportunities, so you will be able to determine whether the prospective investment —for which you want the cash—is really worth the cost.

If interest rates have increased, you may want to think twice about replacing a mortgage that has a favorable rate with one that comes at a high price. Of course, the reverse situation may exist, and it will be possible to figure how much a new mortgage would save. Never overlook prepayment penalties, however, if they apply.

You may have observed a strong demand in your area for income property. It is always pleasant to be a seller in a seller's market. A reminder: don't sell just because you have a chance to sell. Where are you going to invest the proceeds? Of course, you may have been thinking it would be a good idea to unload and all you have been waiting for is a strong market. It is important to keep in touch with the market all the time—even when you are reasonably content with your investment. Observing the strong demand may spark your interest in finding another property or investment alternative, and once you do you then can proceed to liquidate. This does not mean you should stay wedded to your apartment building, come what may. Instead, try to stay alert and be prepared to make intelligent moves.

It may be that changes are taking place in the area and the value of your property is not appreciating the way you had expected. Perhaps if you wait, things will get even worse. Selling, even at a loss, may be necessary to prevent an even greater loss. Again, you simply must keep your eyes and ears open.

Perhaps you bought the property in an "as-is" condition. This is sometimes the case when the seller carries all the financing and there is no lender insisting that the property be brought up to a higher standard. You may have had some idea of doing the work yourself, to increase the value of the investment and enhance your return. Then perhaps you didn't get around to making the repairs. To have it done commercially would be uneconomical. What do you do now?

If the present mortgagee is agreeable to a new borrower, perhaps you can find a buyer who will take it over on an "as-is" basis and assume the present loan. You may realize only part of your equity in cash; but if the buyer is responsible the balance will be paid ultimately by way of a second mortgage or sales contract. The technical aspects of that will be described later.

The basic problem you face is this: you made the investment as a long-term proposition. We have emphasized the idea that real estate is not a short-term, in-and-out investment vehicle. Under these conditions there is a tendency to sit tight, collect the rents, do the bookkeeping, and ignore the possibility of getting rid of the property. That may lull you into a false sense of security. You may have made a mistake; the investment may not be a good one. You need to know as soon as possible whether that is the case, and cut loose promptly. If it is a good investment, and you can tell as you look at your records, you still do not want to ignore the market place, because the conditions making it good may change and you will want to be among the first to know. The solution to the problem lies in being aware, all the time, of the investment and real estate world around you. And one way to ensure that is to do an evaluation of your investment from time to time.

Interim Evaluation

You made an evaluation, of course, at the beginning. The only difference is, now you are the owner, not a prospective purchaser. And you still need information. This time, however, you have the benefit of the actual past history of the property. Regardless of whether you need cash, want to make another investment, or are very content, you should take a set of analysis forms and prepare an evaluation of your money-machine.

When you have completed the analysis you will be in a better position than otherwise to decide whether you should continue to own and operate the property or to see about liquidating it even at a loss. If you do decide to put the property on the market you will have an extremely useful sales tool in the form of your set of completed analysis forms.

You will now be looking at this procedure from a different point of view, so we should discuss some of the angles. You may want to refer again to the example in Chapter Three, the one we prepared at the outset. This time you will be using an estimated sales price based—at first—on what you would like to sell it for, but you will also be facing up to the justification of that price. If the amount you use can be justified you can proceed to offer the property for sale, full of confidence. You will also be able to calculate where you will be if in fact you do sell it. The amount of cash to be realized, what you plan to do with it, the income tax picture, all will materially assist you in knowing in advance the terms on which you prefer to sell—and also, to what extent you can meet the terms a prospective purchaser might offer.

Just how much is your money-making machine worth today? Gather the facts and complete the forms, then you will know.

We need to look at the Fact Sheet in some detail. Much of the information required is available right in your own files. Current rents? This may be the time to face up to the fact you have not increased rents when you should have. Some sellers say to a prospect that the rents are low and can be increased. Astute buyers know the only rent you can count on is the rent the tenant pays—and after the check has cleared. If there is room for an increase, make it. This may make it necessary for you to go into the marketplace and find out what other comparable apartments are bringing. If you have done that, you can speak authoritatively to your prospects.

How about the cost of building new today? Perhaps you have become acquainted with contractors who are building apartments in the area. In very recent times there have been some dramatic increases in construction costs. Who is to say this will not be true in the future? You should find out, in one way or another, current costs.

You may have replaced the equipment or added some. From your records you will be able to estimate accurately its current value. Tax and other expense data is for real—you have been paying the bills and you *know* what they are. If you have notice of the assessed value for the next year and have some way of estimating a tax rate, compute the prospective property tax figures rather than use past (and undoubtedly lower) amounts.

Now for the investment assumptions. You have no way of knowing what a prospect may have in mind, but you can use figures you know from experience to be reasonable. If you have done your homework you will know what the past appreciation rate has been and can reasonably estimate it for the future. If you analyzed several properties in the past, and kept the data, it would be worthwhile now to see if they are for sale again and at what prices. It is not impossible to find out at what rate property has been appreciating (or depreciating).

Financing

As a seller, you must assume the responsibility for lining up the financing. Check your loan(s) to see about prepayment penalties and assumption privileges. Perhaps you should discuss the matter with the present lender. Times and conditions change. Above all, learn what new financing might be available; watch your prepayment penalty. If possible and useful, try to obtain a loan commitment. Remember, your prospective buyer may have no ability to arrange for a loan and unless he has help he will not be able to make the purchase.

Depending upon your objectives for making the sale you may not want to take back a second mortgage unless there is no other way to make the sale. On the other hand, you may be anxious to minimize the amount of equity you realize and so you will want to sell for a minimum down payment. Have a plan for financing, including your participation, if any.

Closing Costs

You should estimate what the closing costs will be. The amount of proration cost will be governed by the time of year the sale is made. To make it easier on the buyer, you will want to minimize as much as you can the amount of cash required. For example, don't pay any expenses any further in advance than is absolutely necessary.

You may want to obtain a termite inspection report in an effort to anticipate what costs you will have if you have to pay for repairs called for by such a report. Regardless of the sales aspect, you may find it desirable to have that information about the property. A small amount of work done in time can save a larger expense later. The report may satisfy the buyer and, particularly if it gives the property a clean bill of health, could swing the sale to a nervous buyer. Reports calling for substantial repair should not scare anyone. Sometimes recommended work is "cosmetic" in nature, and, if done, would not materially affect either the structure or earning power of the property. That expense should be avoided.

If you know there is a termite problem and want to keep it quiet, you may not succeed. In some states, such as California, there is a state law requiring that reports of inspection by pest-control organizations be filed with a state regulatory agency. Persons interested in the property can obtain, for a small fee, a copy of the report of any inspection made during the previous few years. Some owners, when they discover—usually by way of a report—they have a serious problem, attempt to do the work themselves and cover up the difficulty. They then arrange for a new report to be prepared by a "friendly" inspector or by one who does not look very closely. This is not intended as a slander of inspectors or control companies. Not every inspector would write the same report on a given piece of property. A buyer would do well to get copies of previously made inspections and compare. Some inspectors recommend work to be done that is not really necessary, and others may be rushed and issue a report that is not as complete as it might be. As a seller, you should learn all you can about the property; the buyer should do likewise.

All of the foregoing came up because we got involved in closing costs, one of which is the cost of a termite inspection report. If you, the seller, obtain a report, you may be able to pass the cost to the buyer if it is customary in your area for the buyer to pay for it. You may want to throw it in as a selling point.

Expenses

A word about any and all expenses. Money spent in connection with the property will be tax-deductible for you. Be sure, as always, to obtain and retain receipts and notes to explain. This is especially true if you fix up the property to be put on the market. Also, keep track of your travel and other marketing expenses, including advertising.

Mortgages

If the present financing is to be assumed, you already know what the monthly payments are. If you are tentatively arranging new financing, calculate the payments. Remember, there are tables in the back of the book to be used for this purpose. If you are going to take back a second mortgage, you will have to decide on interest rate, monthly payment, and due date, if any. As for the payment, you can simply stipulate it to be 1 percent of the amount borrowed, as we did in our example. An alternative is to compute the payment for an amortization period such as 15, 20, or 25 years and find the amount accordingly, using the tables. Then include in the loan papers the provision that on such and such a date the unpaid balance is due and payable in full. This gives you a due date, usually set five to ten years hence, yet a monthly payment less than 1 percent.

Depreciation

Here you are making a judgment as to what a buyer might use. What you have done in the past is in no way binding on him. It is usually helpful to a buyer to learn what the seller says he has been doing here, but that does not mean the buyer will continue the practice. The shorter the estimated useful life, the larger the depreciation and the smaller the taxable income. There is also the question of whether to use an accelerated basis. This has been covered previously, and you may wish to review it in order to be prepared to answer questions during your selling episode.

At this point you should have all the information needed to complete the analysis. Much of the remaining work to be done is simply making computations with the figures recorded in the Fact Sheet. As you prepare this analysis, remember that if you intend to show it to a prospective buyer—a very good reason for preparing it

—you will need to be able to justify the conclusions it shows.

Asking Price

You have some idea of what your asking price should be. How about returning to your original estimate of the appreciation rate and applying it? Certainly you would want to compare your property with those already on the market at this time. At any rate, you will have to pick a number and start to work with it.

Indicated Economic Value

Next comes one of the most important steps—computing the Indicated Economic Value.

First, the cost approach. Here is where you give real meaning to square-foot cost figures obtained from building contractors, lenders, appraisers, or evaluation services. You will have to be careful in judging past depreciation. At this point you may want to reconsider whatever decision you reached previously about fixing up the property. So now you have an estimated reproduction cost.

Now for the gross multiplier, an important tool used in applying what appraisers call the "market approach." Again, from your experience and current research in the marketplace, you should know what competing properties have as gross multipliers. Do your homework and learn.

From an investment point of view, the capitalization of income approach is most important. You may get some argument from the purists when you want to apply it to small apartments but be brave, it works! Here is where you can see, graphically, what even a modest increase in rent or reduction in operating expense can do to the resulting value. Be realistic, too, in selecting the desired yield. You should know even more about this than you did when you bought the property and used this form the first time.

Now you have some results. If you like, find the average of the three figures. Compare it with your asking price. Any adjustment needed? If your figures are out of line you won't fool a prospect for very long. (He may have a copy of this book, too.) Just think of the confidence you can have in your asking price and terms if they are backed up by a sound analysis and evaluation.

If at this point you still have some doubts about setting the asking price, perhaps you should consider employing a professional appraiser. This could be well worth the cost, which may run as much as a few hundred dollars. There is always the chance that such an appraisal could result in your obtaining a higher price that more than covers the cost of the appraisal.

Sales Strategy

We have covered before the cash flows, yields, and estimated returns. You should have no difficulty preparing these now for presentation to a prospect to show him why he should buy. These results may also raise the question: "If they are so good, why am I selling?" You may even reconsider your decision to offer the property. In fact, you should never make such a decision before you have plotted out just what this investment will do for you if you keep it. Of course, you may be able to show yourself conclusively that you should sell and sell fast.

Just because this is not a good investment for you does not mean it is not good for someone else. Each person has varying investment opportunities available. You may have chances others don't have, and it makes good sense to upgrade your portfolio. Your property, when compared with their opportunities, may present a good investment for them. Always be prepared to answer, convincingly, the prospects' query as to why you are selling. Especially if you tell him what an extremely good investment this is!

Be sure to consider carefully what first-year deductions the buyer might have. This is of particular interest to investors seeking a tax shelter. If the present financing is being assumed there will be less here than if prepaid interest is going to be charged. You do not know what tax rate your buyer may be using —you have not met the buyer yet. If you review this analysis with him, be sure to point out the tax rates at which the amounts have been figured. He will then know whether his prospective return will be larger or smaller than your example.

Your Own Position

After you have prepared the estimated results from the resale for a prospective buyer, better take your own present situation and calculate just how you will stand if you make the sale at the asking price indicated. This is an extremely important step to take, whether you simply have to sell or can use some discretion. You should determine what your income tax picture will be according to the options you take. The manner in which you make the sale will have an impact on your tax liability. Figure out the most beneficial alternative and push for it when selling.

If you have been using accelerated depreciation—unless you have held the property long enough (currently, 100 months)—some of the depreciation expense will have to be recaptured as ordinary income, thus increasing the amount of income tax you will pay. You must have owned the property long enough for the gain to be classified as "long-term." This varies from one state to another for state income tax rules; for federal, currently, it is over · six months.

If you have owned the property for a very long time, or if it is very old and worn-out, you may have fully depreciated it, so there is no relief. The sooner you sell, the sooner you may be able to reduce your income taxes.

The tax rate to be applied to your gain from the sale is dependent upon your other income. Perhaps you are approaching retirement and soon will have a minimum taxable income from other sources. Waiting another year or so to sell may make a dramatic difference in the amount of income tax payable on the profit from this investment.

By all means, expend the effort to calculate just how many dollars you will have left over after all bills are paid once the sale is complete. Then, don't resist the temptation to see how good an investment analyst you are. Compare these results with what you forecast when you made the original analysis and bought the property. You may have the world's greatest record and now is the time to find out. Just think what that realization would do for your self-confidence when dealing with prospective purchasers.

So now you know how you will stand if you make the sale under the conditions assumed. You have had a chance to consider seriously whether in fact you should even sell at all. Given that the decision is still to go ahead and sell, look now at the various ways in which you could finance the sales transaction, because some will be more to your advantage than others and you should know which are which before you go to the market.

Financial Alternatives

Many sellers seem to prefer all cash. If you have a large equity, or if financing has become difficult, asking for all cash for your equity will probably create problems that will interfere with making a sale. More buyers have less cash, so the more cash it takes, the fewer prospects there may be. If the buyer has to obtain new financing, that could be troublesome. There may be loan fees to pay and restrictions on qualification. The selling price will be very much affected by the lender's appraisal.

If the equity is not too large, the seller could offer to take all cash and arrange for the buyer to assume the existing loans, providing the current financing can be assumed.

But there may be good reasons either for not requesting all cash or for agreeing to terms that do not entirely liquidate the seller's position. If the buyer is short on cash he may want the seller to take back a second mortgage or trust deed. There are other potential second mortgagees but a seller is a prime candidate. If the seller does not absolutely have to have all cash he might welcome the opportunity to earn some interest on a second mortgage. He has some risk, of course, as described before. He may wish to sell the mortgage, but that would be at a discount, as a general rule. Perhaps more importantly, there is the income tax consideration.

Assuming the seller has held the property long enough to qualify for the gain to be treated as long-term, the maximum amount of income tax will be payable if he cashes out his equity.

Installment Sales

A rule currently applicable to long-term capital gains when

calculating federal income tax liability—state laws may vary—is taxation of installment sales. You will want to consult with the Internal Revenue Service and your tax adviser if you expect to elect this option. The following is not intended to be a complete treatment of the regulations.

The idea behind the rule is to assess equitably tax on profits from the sale of capital assets when the seller does not receive all of the purchase price at the time of sale or within the tax year. Many sales, particularly of real estate, are made on the basis of the purchaser paying a relatively small amount down and the balance over an extended period. If the seller had to pay tax right away on the total profit, regardless of how the purchase price is ultimately paid, it would be inequitable. Uncle Sam has rules to ease the burden. When the sale qualifies as an "installment" sale, to minimize the tax the seller should receive not more than 30 percent of the contract price during the tax year in which the sale is made. Some examples:

Assume the property is free and clear and sells at a profit for $100,000 with $25,000 down and the balance in monthly payments applied to a mortgage of $75,000. Assume, further, that the principal portion of the mortgage payments received in that year aggregate $4,000. So we see the seller has received a total of $29,000 of the contract price. He also has received mortgage interest which will be treated as ordinary income. The amount (excluding interest) received in the first year is less than 30 percent of the contract or sales price; income tax is assessed on the profit portion. That is the next step. Note first, however, the importance of that 30 percent provision. Tax on the entire profit would be assessed if more than 30 percent was paid. This will explain what is behind those ads you have seen offering property for sale for 29 percent down.

How do you compute the profit? Carefully. If we assume we bought the property for $75,000 and sell it several years later for $100,000, our profit rate is 25 percent. Once we compute this rate we apply it in each tax year after the sale to the portion of the contract price received during the year, provided it is not more than 30 percent of the original amount. In our example, we apply the 25 percent to the $29,000 received for a taxable gain of $7,250.

This will be taxed on the favorable long-term capital gain basis.

If in our desire to cash out we received more than $29,000 during the first tax year we would have had to pay income tax on the entire long-term gain of $25,000 in our next tax return.

Now, another example where there is a mortgage and it is assumed by the buyer: a sales price of $60,000 and a $45,000 mortgage to be taken over by the purchaser. In this case we have sold $15,000 worth of property. If we receive no more than 30 percent of this during the first year we can treat the sale on the installment basis for income tax purposes. The profit rate would be the percentage of the equity that is represented by the profit. For example: assume original cost was $50,000. (This is greater than the mortgage being assumed—that is a requirement, too.) Selling for $60,000 gives a profit or long-term gain of $10,000. The rate of profit would then be $10,000/$15,000 = 66 2/3 percent.

To qualify for the minimum income tax and the use of the installment sale rule, the seller must not receive in the tax year more than 30 percent of the $15,000—which here would be a maximum of $4,500. Whether the seller would choose to sell for as little as $4,500 down is another matter. Perhaps you have observed that the most likely situation for which the installment sale rule would be used is where the property is free and clear of mortgages.

The taxable gain, on a long-term capital gain basis, in the first year would be 66 2/3 percent of $4,500. The $4,500 would be the total of cash down payment and principal payments on the debt owed the seller. A way this might be handled is as follows: sales price, $60,000. Buyer assumes $45,000 mortgage, pays $4,500 in cash and executes a second mortgage or trust deed to the seller for $10,500 with no principal payments to be made until the following tax year. That is, the seller's tax year.

Astute taxpayers have chosen to use 29 percent instead of 30 percent to avoid any argument with Uncle Sam.

So now you can see if you are to minimize income taxes, you will want to take care in how you finance the sale of real estate.

Land Contracts

One of the fears a seller may have if he does not get all cash for his equity is the risk he will not collect all that is coming to him. It is true that he can take a mortgage—first, second, or third —but he has been warned about the risk inherent there, too. Perhaps he would rest easier if he could hang on to the title to the property until the debt is fully satisfied. And indeed he can. All he has to do is sell on a sales or land contract. Let's see how that works.

Assume you are the owner and there is a first mortgage on the property. Your buyer does not have enough cash to cover your equity and you think it unwise to take a second mortgage for the deficiency. Instead, you offer to sell on a sales or land contract. You may even find printed blank forms for this purpose in your local stationery store. You are doing this to avoid giving the buyer a deed to the property until the property is paid for.

You draw up the agreement in which the buyer contracts to pay you the purchase price, less the cash down payment, in monthly installments including interest. Upon receiving his monthly payment, you will in turn make the mortgage payment and retain the difference (be sure your arithmetic is good, so there *is* a difference) as payment of interest and principal on your remaining equity. Now you control the situation. If the buyer defaults you do not have to foreclose because you still have title. Of course, to allay the buyer's concern, the land contract was recorded. Also, the buyer knows full well of the existence of the first mortgage. What are the problems?

The buyer may find that the seller somehow never got around to making payments on the first mortgage and then there will be a default and a foreclosure. The buyer may find himself out in the cold. His recorded land contract might provide some protection, but if the foreclosure sale brought only enough to pay off the first mortgage, our contract purchaser has trouble.

The buyer may find, after he has paid off the contract, that he cannot get a deed from the seller. The latter may have inconveniently died or disappeared.

The seller may find the buyer is slow in making the payments, and now the seller has to make the first mortgage payments himself to avoid foreclosure. That really is not what he bargained for. But then he takes comfort in the fact he still has that all-important title. But is it that important?

Before the seller could legally contract with another, presumably more reliable, buyer, he would have to do something to clear the record of the original land contract. This could be done by bringing a "quiet title" action. An attorney would be needed. If the contract purchaser showed up and contested the matter, he would have to be reckoned with. Further, a considerable period of time is required for the quiet title action, so the seller will be held up.

Even after the contract purchaser has defaulted he has a right to redeem the property by making up the back payments. This right would gum up any possible sale to a new buyer. Meanwhile the original seller still retains the title to the property. By this time he probably wishes he had taken a second mortgage, deeded the property to the buyer, and then sold the second to someone at a discount and banked the cash proceeds.

The foregoing has been written with the basic provisions of California real estate law in mind; it may not be quite the same in other jurisdictions. For whatever reasons, if you have trouble collecting on a land contract or a first, second, or third mortgage, see your lawyer, and quickly.

"Wrap-Around" Mortgages

A new development in some areas is the "wrap-around" mortgage. In a sense, it takes the place of the sales or land contract just described. Example: your equity is too large for the buyer, so you have him execute a mortgage to you for the difference between the sales price and the down payment. The buyer takes title subject to the mortgages. Of course, the first mortgage is still unpaid and is a prior lien on the title. The amount of the wrap-around is larger than the first mortgage but it is a junior lien. Nothing can disturb the rights of the first mortgagee. The agreement between the buyer and seller provides for the payment of the first mortgage obligation. If the second or wrap-around mortgage is handled by a mortgage servicing agency, the purchaser is probably well protected, and can assume the first mortgage payments will be made. The holder of the second mortgage or trust deed is still faced with the potential default of the buyer. The buyer may prefer this wrap-around arrangement to a sales or land contract, because he should have no trouble getting a clear title when all the debts are paid.

The wrap-around mortgage has a place in fairly large transactions and is not likely to be widely used by individual buyers and sellers of small apartment properties. An imaginative private seller, however, might well find this to be a way to accomplish his objectives.

Income taxes are usually uppermost in the minds of investors. Is there a way to avoid—or at least to defer, preferably forever—paying up? Yes. There are tax-free or tax-deferred "exchanges." Let's see what is involved.

Tax-Deferred Exchanges

Once again, you will need to know more about the intricate details of the Internal Revenue Service rules than you can learn from what is written here. That is why there are attorneys and tax accountants. But here is a brief description of what the law provides.

If you can find someone else who owns an apartment house, as you do, exchange properties; whatever profit one or the other or both realizes will not be taxed at the time of the exchange. The properties do not have to be identical, of course. The rules require that they be of the same general nature or "like kind." The exchange of an apartment building for an office building or a building rented for commercial purposes would be eligible. Exchanging real estate for a car would not qualify.

The persons involved in the exchange must not be related. Also, you cannot exchange on the preferential basis with a corporation you control.

Be certain to notice that even though you use the proceeds of the sale of real estate to make another investment in real estate, even of the same kind, you have *not* made a non-taxable exchange. The two property owners must in fact *exchange* property.

The net effect of a qualified exchange is to eliminate an income tax on the transaction at the time. When, subsequently, an exchanged asset is sold, the gain—if any—will be taxable and the basis will be governed by the terms of the previously executed exchange.

If, in the exchange, one party winds up with a cash payment in hand, there will be tax on the gain realized; but the taxable gain will not exceed the amount of cash received.

Properties of quite different values can be exchanged successfully without being subject to income tax at the time if the owners simply trade equities. For example, assume property A with a market value of $100,000 and a mortgage of $75,000. Property B has a market value of $150,000 and a mortgage of $125,000. The owners could effect an exchange and defer the income tax. Why is this important to us at this point? Perhaps you have heard the expressions "trading up" and "trading down." There are Horatio Alger-type stories of real estate investors who made millions by starting with one small piece of property and then trading. Of course, here you can sell a property and use the proceeds to buy a larger piece of property and accomplish what you want. By making nontaxable trades, however, you avoid losing the buying power of your equity by having to share profits with a tax man.

If you own a fourplex and have a present equity of, say, $20,000, you may look around for the owner of an eight-unit property who would like to trade down and have fewer responsibilities. You persuade him to take your fourplex and apply your $20,000 equity to his property. If it is clear, the equity might simply be treated as a down payment, without any cash changing hands. You now have a larger property and are on your way to increased fame and fortune. (You may be trying to trade down to a fourplex some day yourself.) You have traded up and he has traded down. You both have realized a profit if the market prices used in the exchange are greater than cost or basis; but you do not have to pay tax now—only later when you ultimately sell. Remember, the tax is only deferred, not eliminated. It is a misnomer to call these exchanges "tax-free." But you may well be in a lower tax bracket at some future time and would benefit by paying the tax later.

So perhaps you should be looking for an exchange rather than a sale and purchase, now that you have decided to dispose of the property. Your *reason* for getting rid of the property will largely determine how you will go about selling it. If you want more income property, consider trying for a tax-deferred exchange.

Now that we have covered many of the financial alternatives

facing you, let's move on to the marketing plan. There are more choices to be made.

Marketing Alternatives

There is the basic choice: employ a real estate agent or do it yourself. If you go the latter route, you expect to save the amount of the commission. Any prospective buyer coming to you will also expect to save the commission because he is dealing direct. But only one of you can save the commission, and if you are particularly anxious to sell, it will be the buyer, not you.

The decision here should be based on a frank appraisal of your own abilities. Can you deal effectively with strangers, especially if they severely criticize the property and perhaps even you? Can you arrange the financing? Can you find prospects to consider the offering? Can you afford the time it takes to show the property to many, many people before a buyer arrives? Although we will shortly discuss what you will have to do if you do it yourself, that choice is not necessarily recommended. As a broad general rule, if you choose a competent real estate agent, he will be well worth the cost and will probably earn it for you—so you should not feel you came out less than whole by not handling the deal on your own.

As stressed before, you must decide *how* the property is to be sold *before* you put it on the market. That is, on what terms: all cash? take a second? size of down payment? In trying to make up your mind, you may want to consider some of the potential marketing problems and suggested solutions.

You may have built up a substantial equity and now you find liberal financing hard to come by. There are always fewer buyers with large amounts of cash. Taking back a second mortgage may not appeal to you, perhaps because you have investment plans for the entire equity. Just how do you spring that pot of gold that has accumulated? How about the condominium?

Not all condominiums are created by building a new structure. It is quite feasible to take an existing apartment building (or other type of property too, for that matter) and convert it into a condominium. Although a fourplex is a little small to justify the trouble and expense, you may want at least to explore the idea. Once you have made the conversion, you then have four units to sell, instead of one, and although you might prefer to find and deal with only one buyer instead of four, it may just be easier to find four. Why?

An apartment tenant knows he cannot take a deduction on his income tax for rent. He has no mortgage interest or property taxes to use to reduce the tax bite. But if he were an owner, the situation would change. If he buys an apartment unit that is a condominium, he then has all the rights and privileges of home ownership—but not some of the disadvantages. It is possible you may find it easier to locate a buyer than a tenant for the same apartment. A condominium buyer can obtain financing comparable to that for a single-family home; and when financing is favorable, the down payment can be very attractive. The major advantage over the private home is that usually the exterior maintenance of the property is taken care of, and charged to the condominium owners. There is more time for golf and no need to spend the weekend mowing the lawn.

Converting property to condominium ownership is not a job for amateurs. You can obtain guidance by talking to your banker, escrow agency, legal counselors, or real estate adviser. Larger properties are being converted every day, currently. This technique might just provide the solution to your marketing problem.

Once you have decided to sell, why not see if one of your tenants would like to buy? You may have a live prospect right on your doorstep. Or, the tenant may know of someone who would buy. Tenants may jump at the chance to choose their landlord. Speak also to your friends and acquaintances in the financial world. A lending officer might know of someone who is anxious to make an investment in income property.

Seek out managers of real estate syndicates. Usually a syndicate is looking for large properties, but not always. Your property might fit in well with their plans.

During the time you have owned the property you must have told your friends about the virtues of owning income property. Be sure to let them know you might be interested in selling your little gem, perhaps because you are going on to bigger and better things. Here is their chance to get started too.

There are some other decisions to make in preparing your marketing plan. What can be done to make the property even more attractive? The obvious has to do with physical appearance. Would a coat of paint speed up the sale? How about the garden? Be careful to spend money only if you are sure it will help. A return is required. But there are other things.

We have stressed the importance of income in the determination of the value of income property. Should rents be increased? We have discussed this before. You do not want to drive tenants out. A vacant unit is not necessarily attractive to a buyer, because it is unlikely the buyer is looking for living accommodations. (That may not be so for a duplex, of course.) An owner should not live on the property, anyway. But perhaps there is another way to increase the income without pricing yourself out of the market.

Some structures lend themselves to remodeling. If you have one, consider seriously increasing the number of rental units by making some structural changes. True, you may reduce the size of a unit when you change it into two, for example, but the combined rent for the two smaller units will exceed what you were able to charge for one. And your expenses, including property taxes, will not ordinarily eliminate the advantage. You can increase the value of your property by having as many living units as are legal and possible. Some investors have systematically bought, converted, and sold their way to millions of dollars of profits. You might have such an opportunity right in your hands.

Let's assume you have decided to offer the property yourself. What do you have to do now that you have cleaned it up, not found a buyer despite all the things suggested, and now must enter the wide-open marketplace?

The Do-it-Yourself Seller

You have to find ways to let prospective buyers know you want to sell. This will mean advertising. When you were a buyer, where did you look? The local newspaper is one place. Another is the *Wall Street Journal*. Each week the Journal has a "Real Estate Corner"; other days they run real estate ads too. Investors read this advertising carefully. Take a look yourself and get some ideas on how you might put an ad together. Do the same for the local newspaper. There will probably be a separate column for Income Property. Be sure your ad appears in it and not among the much more numerous single-family houses for sale.

In writing the ad, give the reader a reason for being attracted to your property and encourage him to respond. State a price and an indication of the financing; describe the return in one of the conventional ways, such as net or gross multiplier. Don't be secretive. Most investors do not have time for sellers who try to be coy. This is a business proposition. State what you have and what you want. The negotiating can come only after a prospect has made contact. Include in the ad an offer to show the financial analysis you have prepared; that ought to bring many responses. Remember how useful it was to you in deciding to buy in the first place?

Keep in mind you are not trying to sell a home. The prospect will be interested primarily in the financial aspect and ways to determine investment values. You will want to be able to show the inside of at least one apartment. Make appropriate arrangements with a friendly tenant (if there is one). Try to qualify your prospect before you trouble the tenant. A serious buyer will understand.

As someone who has bought a piece of income property, you know what a prospective buyer wants to know. How about preparing an information sheet to give to prospects? When you were looking, wouldn't it have been useful if sellers had stated the pertinent information on a piece of paper and handed it to you?

A prospect indicates he is interested. What do you do? Your goal will be to have him put up a deposit and sign a purchase agreement. To get ready for this activity, you should make contact with a title company or escrow agency so that you and your buyer can open an escrow. The buyer, of course, may be sophisticated and have plans of his own. No need to suggest otherwise if the buyer wants to do business with a reputable organization. It is his money. If you have any doubts about protecting yourself, hire an attorney.

As a minimum, you should have a supply of deposit receipts

or purchase agreement forms. These are provided on a compli-
mentary basis by title companies and escrow agencies. If the buyer
does not demonstrate an ability to prepare such an agreement, do
it yourself. After all, you have samples to use for guidance—the
one used when you purchased the property and the one illustrated
and discussed back in Chapter Four. If you are hesitant about
doing this yourself, and are not using a real estate broker, then
hire an attorney who is skilled in these matters.

There are many points to watch out for and they have been
touched on previously. A few need some emphasis at this time as
you prepare to become a seller.

Getting your price is important, of course. But that is not all
there is to selling. You must avoid being tied to a prospective
purchaser for a long time, only to find the deal falls through.
Basically, the prospect is making an offer to you and there should
be a fairly short time period in which you will make up your
mind. If you want to reject his offer, make a counter-offer. Tell
him the terms that would be satisfactory. The best way to accomplish this is to make out a new set of forms containing the new
terms and then give him a short time in which to decide. This sort
of thing can bounce back and forth and consume a lot of time if
you are not careful. But now there are the qualifications in the
purchaser's offer.

He offers to buy "subject to obtaining financing, . . . etc."
Do not agree to too long a period here. Before you accept this type
of qualification, have a good idea as to whether the proposal is reasonable. For example, if current interest rates are 9 percent and he
offers to buy subject to getting a loan at 6 percent, he is dreaming
and you are wasting time accepting such an offer. You may also
want to get some idea as to whether the buyer is likely to qualify
for the financing. If he is elderly and expects to get a loan from a
financial institution, again he may be wasting his time trying.

Watch also for qualifications with respect to inspections for
termites, earth movement, and other soils problems. Do not accept
an offer that provides that it is "subject to obtaining a satisfactory
report from a soils engineer." Who is to be the judge of whether
the report is "satisfactory"? Regardless of the nature of the report,
a buyer who wanted to back out for other reasons could easily

claim the report was not satisfactory, claim a return of his deposit, and there you would sit.

Preferable language might be: "subject to property being inspected by a licensed soils engineer who certifies that the building site meets current standards set by the City of _____"—or words to that effect. The provision needs to be clear and unambiguous so that no one has any difficulty determining whether the property meets the standards. A buyer who cannot make up his mind, or who tries to play one seller against another, will try to include loopholes in the offer to give him an opportunity to simply back out of the deal without having a good reason, from the seller's point of view. Read all offers with this in mind.

Remember, after you accept an offer, you are not able to continue, on any practical basis, to offer the property to others; and if the deal falls through, you have to start all over. Reactivating the marketing momentum may be a very difficult thing to do.

Who should sign the purchase contract? In many states, when the parties involved are husband and wife, it is best to have both sign all documents. In some situations, technically, if a wife did not sign the offer to buy, you might not be very successful in obtaining damages for breach of contract when suing the husband, the only party you could sue. While being able to sue both husband and wife will not guarantee your success by any means, you ordinarily will be better off if both sign. When both parties feel committed because they signed the contract, you probably will have a stronger position.

Many buyers are unfamiliar with the purchasing process, are apprehensive, and are concerned they might be swindled. This feeling can be minimized if you avoid asking for the deposit or earnest money to be given to you directly. Have the buyer make out his check to a title company or escrow agent. Be sure the purchase agreement is clear on the terms for the return or forfeiture of the deposit so that future arguments will be avoided. The buyer should know that if he does everything he has agreed to do, but you fail to fulfill your obligation (such as providing clear title subject only to the liens and encumbrances agreed to), then he will get his money back. In turn, the buyer should understand that if he fails to do his part he is going to lose his deposit. All of that is the essence of any purchase agreement with respect to the deposit. And time is of the essence, too.

Assume you have found a buyer. An agreement has been reached, an escrow opened, and the buyer is busy arranging the financing. To conclude the transaction you will need to execute the instructions to the escrow agent. All of the details of this are covered in Chapter Five and you may want to review them at this time.

One final matter in your marketing plan and its execution. What do you do if you cannot find a buyer? There are several choices. Perhaps the best thing to do is take the property off the market and return to being a landlord and property manager. If a prospective buyer learns that the property has been "on the market" for many, many months, he becomes suspicious. Perhaps there is something wrong with the property that he has not seen. He shies away. The real reason for its not selling may simply be that the timing was wrong. If you pursue the selling activity vigorously and cannot make a sale within 90 days, and you have a choice, it may be best to stop, take it off the market, and do nothing more for, say, six months or a year. Of course, if during the time you have discussed the property with prospects who did not buy, and you can find out why they are not buying, you may be able to rectify the situation and go from there. Either the property is at fault, or the buyer is deficient. It is not always possible either to correct the problem with the property or change the situation for a given buyer. Finding out as best you can what is preventing the sale is important.

Depending on the motivation for trying to dispose of the property, you may find a solution in another direction. One way to get out from under the management problems—and, to some extent, the responsibility—is to lease the entire building to someone. This will require there be a financial advantage to the lessee and hence a sacrifice on your part. But if you are to give up some of the troubles, you will have to pay for the privilege. Similarly, you may want to arrange for a property management firm to take it over.

You do have some alternatives to selling, provided you do not have to liquidate the investment. Be sure to consider all options and avoid a hasty decision that may not prove to be the best.

Finally, have you fully considered potential future developments? Is it possible there is some plan for change in the area that could affect favorably your investment? There is a risk on the other side too, of course. Maybe the neighborhood is about to change for the worse and you had better sell out now, even at a loss, before the loss increases. But more on the positive side. Check with local building authorities, planning commission and zoning staffs, real estate people, and bankers. What is the outlook for the area? You may just be trying to sell at the wrong time. Real estate is a *long-term* investment proposition. Has your term of ownership been long enough to produce the maximum return?

The cycle is complete. You have been told about the virtues of an investment in real estate income property, how to determine values to minimize the price to pay, and how to compute cash flows and potential long-term gains. Once you have chosen a piece of property, you know how to make an offer on it and how to close the deal. You even know how to be a successful property manager. You could offer to do accounting for all the property investors you could find. We have discussed how to consider properly whether you should sell the property and how to go about disposing of it. And to make it easy to see the whole picture, we have assembled a complete example in this book. Also, to help you with needed computations, there are tables.

Now, put down this book, grab your checkbook, and go out to look for some income property to buy. You can't make any money just sitting there.

Appendix

Table I   Payment Amortizes Loan

Term: 10 to 30 years
Rates: 6% to 10%, ½% intervals

MORTGAGE OF $1000. FOR   10   YEARS AT   6.00   PERCENT

MONTHLY PAYMENT :$ 11.10394

END OF YEAR	BALANCE DUE	INTEREST	MTGE. REDUCT.
1	924.7029	57.95016	75.29712
2	844.762	53.30637	79.94092
3	759.8904	48.3757	84.87158
4	669.7834	43.14035	90.10693
5	574.1199	37.58371	95.66357
6	472.5554	31.68283	101.56445
7	364.7273	25.41916	107.828
8	250.2478	18.76782	114.4795
9	128.7091	11.70859	121.5387
10	0.0	4.212372	129.0349

MORTGAGE OF $1000. FOR   10   YEARS AT   6.50   PERCENT

MONTHLY PAYMENT :$ 11.35639

END OF YEAR	BALANCE DUE	INTEREST	MTGE. REDUCT.
1	926.5596	62.8363	73.44043
2	848.2009	57.91809	78.35864
3	764.5945	52.67029	83.60645
4	675.3884	47.07068	89.20605
5	580.2083	41.09656	95.18018
6	478.6538	34.72229	101.55444
7	370.2979	27.92078	108.356
8	254.6853	20.66418	115.6125
9	131.3311	12.92255	123.3542
10	0.0	4.661331	131.6154

MORTGAGE OF $1000. FOR   10   YEARS AT   7.00   PERCENT

MONTHLY PAYMENT :$ 11.61219

END OF YEAR	BALANCE DUE	INTEREST	MTGE. REDUCT.
1	928.3835	67.72986	71.61646
2	851.5896	62.55237	76.79395
3	769.2446	57.00134	82.34497
4	680.947	51.04871	88.29761
5	586.2666	44.66589	94.68042
6	484.7415	37.82117	101.52515
7	375.8767	30.48157	108.8647
8	259.1426	22.61218	116.7341
9	133.9708	14.17458	125.1717
10	0.0	5.125946	134.2204

MORTGAGE OF $1000. FOR 10 YEARS AT 7.50 PERCENT

MONTHLY PAYMENT :$ 11.87136

END OF YEAR	BALANCE DUE	INTEREST	MTGE. REDUCT.
1	930.1743	72.63062	69.82568
2	854.9287	67.21069	75.24561
3	773.8413	61.3689	81.0874
4	686.4585	55.07349	87.38281
5	592.2922	48.29004	94.16626
6	490.8154	40.97949	101.47681
7	381.4602	33.10107	109.3552
8	263.6165	24.61255	117.8438
9	136.6249	15.46472	126.9916
10	0.0	5.606094	136.8502

MORTGAGE OF $1000. FOR 10 YEARS AT 8.00 PERCENT

MONTHLY PAYMENT :$ 12.13371

END OF YEAR	BALANCE DUE	INTEREST	MTGE. REDUCT.
1	931.9343	77.53888	68.06567
2	858.2192	71.88947	73.71509
3	778.3857	65.77106	79.8335
4	691.926	59.14484	86.45972
5	598.2903	51.96881	93.63574
6	496.8828	44.19708	101.40747
7	387.0588	35.78058	109.824
8	268.1194	26.6651	118.9395
9	139.3091	16.79424	128.8103
10	0.0	6.103241	139.5013

MORTGAGE OF $1000. FOR 10 YEARS AT 8.50 PERCENT

MONTHLY PAYMENT :$ 12.39934

END OF YEAR	BALANCE DUE	INTEREST	MTGE. REDUCT.
1	933.6616	82.45369	66.33838
2	861.4595	76.58992	72.20215
3	782.8755	70.20808	78.58398
4	697.3455	63.26204	85.53003
5	604.2551	55.70174	93.09033
6	502.9368	47.47371	101.31836
7	392.6624	38.51765	110.2744
8	272.6406	28.77034	120.0217
9	142.0115	18.16298	130.6291
10	0.0	6.616684	142.1754

MORTGAGE OF $1000. FOR 10 YEARS AT 9.00 PERCENT

MONTHLY PAYMENT :$ 12.66822

END OF YEAR	BALANCE DUE	INTEREST	MTGE. REDUCT.
1	935.3572	87.37581	64.64282
2	864.6497	81.31111	70.70752
3	787.3096	74.67854	77.34009
4	702.7144	67.42342	84.59521
5	610.1836	59.48787	92.53076
6	508.9731	50.80818	101.21045
7	398.2678	41.31331	110.7053
8	277.1777	30.92854	121.0901
9	144.7297	19.57063	132.448
10	0.0	7.146393	144.8722

MORTGAGE OF $1000. FOR 10 YEARS AT 9.50 PERCENT

MONTHLY PAYMENT :$ 12.94025

END OF YEAR	BALANCE. DUE	INTEREST	MTGE. REDUCT.
1	937.0203	92.30331	62.97974
2	867.79	86.05283	69.23022
3	791.6892	79.18222	76.10083
4	708.0352	71.629	83.65405
5	616.0784	63.32626	91.95679
6	514.9954	54.20004	101.08301
7	403.8801	44.16782	111.1152
8	281.7368	33.13974	122.1433
9	147.4723	21.01849	134.2646
10	0.0	7.693268	147.5898

MORTGAGE OF $1000. FOR 10 YEARS AT 10.00 PERCENT

MONTHLY PAYMENT :$ 13.21545

END OF YEAR	BALANCE DUE	INTEREST	MTGE. REDUCT.
1	938.6519	97.2372	61.34814
2	870.8799	90.81337	67.77197
3	796.0112	83.71669	74.86865
4	713.3032	75.87733	82.70801
5	621.9343	67.21645	91.3689
6	520.998	57.64906	100.93628
7	409.4922	47.07948	111.5059
8	286.3101	35.40321	123.1821
9	150.2306	22.50589	136.0795
10	0.0	8.25679	150.3286

MORTGAGE OF $1000. FOR 11 YEARS AT 6.00 PERCENT

MONTHLY PAYMENT :$ 10.368733

END OF YEAR	BALANCE DUE	INTEREST	MTGE. REDUCT.
1	933.7725	58.19725	66.22754
2	863.4597	54.11205	70.31274
3	788.8103	49.77538	74.64941
4	709.5569	45.17137	79.25342
5	625.415	40.28294	84.14185
6	536.084	35.09373	89.33105
7	441.2429	29.58372	94.84106
8	340.5525	23.73436	100.69043
9	233.6518	17.52409	106.9007
10	120.1587	10.93166	113.4931

MORTGAGE OF $1000. FOR 11 YEARS AT 6.50 PERCENT

MONTHLY PAYMENT :$ 10.62519

END OF YEAR	BALANCE DUE	INTEREST	MTGE. REDUCT.
1	935.6001	63.10243	64.3999
2	866.8872	58.78944	68.71289
3	793.5725	54.18764	73.3147
4	715.3477	49.27748	78.22485
5	631.884	44.03871	83.46362
6	542.8306	38.44887	89.05347
7	447.813	32.48476	95.01758
8	346.4324	26.12172	101.38062
9	238.2621	19.33209	108.1702
10	122.8486	12.08885	115.4135

MORTGAGE OF $1000. FOR 11 YEARS AT 7.00 PERCENT

MONTHLY PAYMENT :$ 10.8853

END OF YEAR	BALANCE DUE	INTEREST	MTGE. REDUCT.
1	937.3918	68.01549	62.60815
2	870.2576	63.48936	67.13428
3	798.2705	58.63658	71.98706
4	721.0793	53.43248	77.19116
5	638.3076	47.85191	82.77173
6	549.5525	41.86852	88.75513
7	454.3813	35.4525	95.17114
8	352.3296	28.57188	102.05176
9	242.9012	21.19528	109.4284
10	125.5634	13.28584	117.3378

MORTGAGE OF $1000. FOR 11 YEARS AT 7.50 PERCENT

MONTHLY PAYMENT :$ 11.14906

END OF YEAR	BALANCE DUE	INTEREST	MTGE. REDUCT.
1	939.1462	72.93494	60.85376
2	873.5681	68.21057	65.57813
3	802.8992	63.11975	70.66895
4	726.7441	57.63367	76.15503
5	644.6772	51.7218	82.06689
6	556.2393	45.35071	88.43799
7	460.9355	38.48499	95.30371
8	358.2327	31.08582	102.70288
9	247.5577	23.11371	110.675
10	128.2913	14.52228	119.2664

MORTGAGE OF $1000. FOR 11 YEARS AT 8.00 PERCENT

MONTHLY PAYMENT :$ 11.41629

END OF YEAR	BALANCE DUE	INTEREST	MTGE. REDUCT.
1	940.866	77.86143	59.13403
2	876.824	72.95348	64.04199
3	807.4663	67.6378	69.35767
4	732.3525	61.8817	75.11377
5	651.0042	55.64708	81.34839
6	562.9036	48.89488	88.10059
7	467.491	41.58287	95.4126
8	364.1587	33.66319	103.33228
9	252.2505	25.08728	111.9082
10	131.0551	15.80006	121.1954

MORTGAGE OF $1000. FOR 11 YEARS AT 8.50 PERCENT

MONTHLY PAYMENT :$ 11.68708

END OF YEAR	BALANCE DUE	INTEREST	MTGE. REDUCT.
1	942.5503	82.7952	57.44971
2	880.0225	77.71707	62.52783
3	811.9673	72.18973	68.05518
4	737.897	66.17459	74.07031
5	657.2795	59.62747	80.61743
6	569.5359	52.50125	87.74365
7	474.0366	44.74564	95.49927
8	370.0967	36.30496	103.93994
9	256.9688	27.11697	113.1279
10	133.8427	17.1188	123.1261

MORTGAGE OF $1000. FOR 11 YEARS AT 9.00 PERCENT

MONTHLY PAYMENT :$ 11.96137

END OF YEAR	BALANCE DUE	INTEREST	MTGE. REDUCT.
1	944.198	87.73442	55.802
2	883.1611	82.49956	61.03687
3	816.3984	76.77373	66.7627
4	743.3726	70.51054	73.02588
5	663.4968	63.66069	79.87573
6	576.1279	56.16753	87.3689
7	480.5632	47.97173	95.5647
8	376.0344	39.00761	104.52881
9	261.7002	29.20219	114.3342
10	136.6415	18.47777	125.0587

MORTGAGE OF $1000. FOR 11 YEARS AT 9.50 PERCENT

MONTHLY PAYMENT :$ 12.23908

END OF YEAR	BALANCE DUE	INTEREST	MTGE. REDUCT.
1	945.8105	92.6795	54.18945
2	886.2427	87.30109	59.56787
3	820.7634	81.38971	65.47925
4	748.7849	74.89044	71.97852
5	669.6628	67.74689	79.12207
6	582.688	59.8941	86.97485
7	487.0811	51.26202	95.60693
8	381.9856	41.7735	105.0955
9	266.46	31.34332	115.5256
10	139.4697	19.87868	126.9903

MORTGAGE OF $1000. FOR 11 YEARS AT 10.00 PERCENT

MONTHLY PAYMENT :$ 12.5202

END OF YEAR	BALANCE DUE	INTEREST	MTGE. REDUCT.
1	947.3882	97.63054	52.61182
2	889.2671	92.12126	58.12109
3	825.0601	86.03532	64.20703
4	754.1296	79.31194	70.93042
5	675.7722	71.88493	78.35742
6	589.2097	63.67986	86.5625
7	493.583	54.61565	95.62671
8	387.9426	44.60197	105.6404
9	271.2407	33.54045	116.7019
10	142.3195	21.32117	128.9212

MORTGAGE OF $1000. FOR   12   YEARS AT   6.00 PERCENT

MONTHLY PAYMENT :$ 9.760048

END OF YEAR	BALANCE DUE	INTEREST	MTGE. REDUCT.
1	941.2808	58.40134	58.71924
2	878.9395	54.77927	62.34131
3	812.7532	50.9343	66.18628
4	742.4851	46.85251	70.26807
5	667.8826	42.51804	74.60254
6	588.6792	37.91721	79.20337
7	504.5913	33.03268	84.08789
8	415.3162	27.84543	89.27515
9	320.5352	22.33957	94.78101
10	219.9086	16.494	100.62657

MORTGAGE OF $1000. FOR   12   YEARS AT   6.50 PERCENT

MONTHLY PAYMENT :$ 10.020503

END OF YEAR	BALANCE DUE	INTEREST	MTGE. REDUCT.
1	943.0764	63.32245	56.92358
2	882.3406	59.51019	60.73584
3	817.5374	55.44281	64.80322
4	748.3943	51.10297	69.14307
5	674.6206	46.47235	73.77368
6	595.9063	41.53168	78.71436
7	511.9199	36.2597	83.98633
8	422.3088	30.63495	89.61108
9	326.6965	24.63373	95.6123
10	224.6816	18.23114	102.01489

MORTGAGE OF $1000. FOR   12   YEARS AT   7.00 PERCENT

MONTHLY PAYMENT :$ 10.284891

END OF YEAR	BALANCE DUE	INTEREST	MTGE. REDUCT.
1	944.8323	68.25096	55.16772
2	885.6768	64.26317	59.15552
3	822.2446	59.98656	63.43213
4	754.2271	55.40111	68.01758
5	681.2925	50.48412	72.93457
6	603.0857	45.2119	78.20679
7	519.2249	39.55785	83.86084
8	429.302	33.49583	89.92285
9	332.8782	26.99486	96.42383
10	229.4846	20.0251	103.39359

MORTGAGE OF $1000. FOR   12 YEARS AT   7.50 PERCENT

MONTHLY PAYMENT :$ 10.5532

END OF YEAR	BALANCE DUE	INTEREST	MTGE. REDUCT.
1	946.5476	73.18605	53.45239
2	888.9456	69.03639	57.60205
3	826.8718	64.56471	62.07373
4	759.979	59.74562	66.89282
5	687.8933	54.55275	72.08569
6	610.2112	48.95631	77.68213
7	526.4985	42.9258	83.71265
8	436.2874	36.42726	90.21118
9	339.073	29.42409	97.21436
10	234.3115	21.87695	104.76149

MORTGAGE OF $1000. FOR   12 YEARS AT   8.00 PERCENT

MONTHLY PAYMENT :$ 10.82527

END OF YEAR	BALANCE DUE	INTEREST	MTGE. REDUCT.
1	948.2241	78.12735	51.77588
2	892.1511	73.83023	56.073
3	831.4243	69.17642	60.72681
4	765.657	64.13589	65.76733
5	694.4312	58.6774	71.22583
6	617.2935	52.76553	77.1377
7	533.7532	46.36295	83.54028
8	443.2793	39.42935	90.47388
9	345.2961	31.92007	97.98315
10	239.1805	23.78758	106.1156

MORTGAGE OF $1000. FOR   12 YEARS AT   8.50 PERCENT

MONTHLY PAYMENT :$ 11.10116

END OF YEAR	BALANCE DUE	INTEREST	MTGE. REDUCT.
1	949.8613	83.07529	50.13867
2	895.2908	78.6434	54.57056
3	835.8965	73.81967	59.39429
4	771.2527	68.57016	64.6438
5	700.8945	62.8558	70.35815
6	624.3174	56.63681	76.57715
7	540.9714	49.86801	83.34595
8	450.2588	42.50131	90.71265
9	351.5281	34.48325	98.73071
10	244.0703	25.75618	107.4578

MORTGAGE OF $1000. FOR 12 YEARS AT 9.00 PERCENT

MONTHLY PAYMENT :$ 11.3808

END OF YEAR	BALANCE DUE	INTEREST	MTGE. REDUCT.
1	951.4592	88.02885	48.54077
2	898.365	83.47539	53.09424
3	840.2903	78.49492	58.07471
4	776.7671	73.04643	63.52319
5	707.2852	67.08769	69.48193
6	631.2854	60.56987	75.99976
7	548.157	53.44121	83.12842
8	457.2302	45.64287	90.92676
9	357.7742	37.11357	99.45605
10	248.9881	27.78355	108.7861

MORTGAGE OF $1000. FOR 12 YEARS AT 9.50 PERCENT

MONTHLY PAYMENT :$ 11.66411

END OF YEAR	BALANCE DUE	INTEREST	MTGE. REDUCT.
1	953.0186	92.9879	46.98145
2	901.3748	88.32555	51.6438
3	844.605	83.19957	56.76978
4	782.2009	77.56529	62.40405
5	713.6038	71.37218	68.59717
6	638.1982	64.56383	75.40552
7	555.3091	57.08018	82.88916
8	464.1936	48.85387	91.11548
9	364.0349	39.81065	100.15869
10	253.9355	29.8699	110.0994

MORTGAGE OF $1000. FOR 12 YEARS AT 10.00 PERCENT

MONTHLY PAYMENT :$ 11.95107

END OF YEAR	BALANCE DUE	INTEREST	MTGE. REDUCT.
1	954.5396	97.95233	45.46045
2	904.3191	93.19232	50.22046
3	848.8401	87.93378	55.479
4	787.551	82.12372	61.28906
5	719.8447	75.70648	67.7063
6	645.0488	68.61688	74.7959
7	562.4211	60.7851	82.62769
8	471.1406	52.13226	91.28052
9	370.302	42.57416	100.83862
10	258.9045	32.01532	111.3975

MORTGAGE OF $1000. FOR 13 YEARS AT 6.00 PERCENT

MONTHLY PAYMENT :$ 9.248644

END OF YEAR	BALANCE DUE	INTEREST	MTGE. REDUCT.
1	947.5894	58.57307	52.41064
2	891.9458	55.34016	55.64355
3	832.8706	51.90852	59.0752
4	770.1516	48.26472	62.71899
5	703.5645	44.39656	66.58716
6	632.8701	40.28938	70.69434
7	557.8157	35.92928	75.05444
8	478.1316	31.29964	79.68408
9	393.5334	26.38557	84.59814
10	303.7178	21.16805	89.81567

MORTGAGE OF $1000. FOR 13 YEARS AT 6.50 PERCENT

MONTHLY PAYMENT :$ 9.513081

END OF YEAR	BALANCE DUE	INTEREST	MTGE. REDUCT.
1	949.3503	63.50731	50.64966
2	895.3086	60.11522	54.04175
3	837.6477	56.49608	57.66089
4	776.125	52.63426	61.52271
5	710.4822	48.51414	65.64282
6	640.4429	44.11766	70.03931
7	565.7129	39.42699	74.72998
8	485.978	34.4221	79.73486
9	400.9041	29.08299	85.07397
10	310.1323	23.38524	90.77173

MORTGAGE OF $1000. FOR 13 YEARS AT 7.00 PERCENT

MONTHLY PAYMENT :$ 9.781722

END OF YEAR	BALANCE DUE	INTEREST	MTGE. REDUCT.
1	951.0681	68.44878	48.93188
2	898.5991	64.91167	52.46899
3	842.3364	61.11797	56.2627
4	782.0068	57.05107	60.32959
5	717.3159	52.68974	64.69092
6	647.9487	48.01347	69.36719
7	573.5671	42.99907	74.38159
8	493.8081	37.62163	79.75903
9	408.2832	31.85576	85.5249
10	316.5754	25.6729	91.70776

MORTGAGE OF $1000. FOR 13 YEARS AT 7.50 PERCENT

MONTHLY PAYMENT :$ 10.054543

END OF YEAR	BALANCE DUE	INTEREST	MTGE. REDUCT.
1	952.7417	73.39621	47.2583
2	901.8147	69.72751	50.927
3	846.9341	65.7739	54.88062
4	787.7932	61.51364	59.14087
5	724.0608	56.92209	63.73242
6	655.3804	51.97409	68.68042
7	581.3684	46.64255	74.01196
8	501.6101	40.89621	79.7583
9	415.6606	34.70505	85.94946
10	323.0383	28.0322	92.62231

MORTGAGE OF $1000. FOR 13 YEARS AT 8.00 PERCENT

MONTHLY PAYMENT :$ 10.331413

END OF YEAR	BALANCE DUE	INTEREST	MTGE. REDUCT.
1	954.3728	78.34976	45.6272
2	904.9585	74.56265	49.41431
3	851.4424	70.46085	53.51611
4	793.4849	66.01944	57.95752
5	730.7173	61.20938	62.76758
6	662.7397	55.99942	67.97754
7	589.1201	50.35733	73.61963
8	509.3899	44.24673	79.73022
9	423.0422	37.6293	86.34766
10	329.5278	30.46255	93.5144

MORTGAGE OF $1000. FOR 13 YEARS AT 8.50 PERCENT

MONTHLY PAYMENT :$ 10.61233

END OF YEAR	BALANCE DUE	INTEREST	MTGE. REDUCT.
1	955.9614	83.3094	44.03857
2	908.0298	79.41634	47.93164
3	855.8616	75.17976	52.16821
4	799.0823	70.56868	56.7793
5	737.2842	65.54988	61.7981
6	670.0237	60.08748	67.2605
7	596.8181	54.14241	73.20557
8	517.1416	47.67146	79.67651
9	430.4226	40.62898	86.71899
10	336.0383	32.9637	94.38428

MORTGAGE OF $1000. FOR 13 YEARS AT 9.00 PERCENT

MONTHLY PAYMENT :$ 10.89725

END OF YEAR	BALANCE DUE	INTEREST	MTGE. REDUCT.
1	957.5068	88.2738	42.49316
2	911.0278	84.28796	46.479
3	860.189	79.9281	50.83887
4	804.5811	75.15906	55.60791
5	743.7571	69.94299	60.82397
6	677.2273	64.23718	66.52979
7	604.4563	57.99597	72.771
8	524.8586	51.16931	79.59766
9	437.7947	43.703	87.06396
10	342.5632	35.53552	95.23145

MORTGAGE OF $1000. FOR 13 YEARS AT 9.50 PERCENT

MONTHLY PAYMENT :$ 11.18606

END OF YEAR	BALANCE DUE	INTEREST	MTGE. REDUCT.
1	959.0117	93.24443	40.98828
2	913.9553	89.17632	45.0564
3	864.4275	84.70488	49.52783
4	809.9839	79.78911	54.4436
5	750.137	74.38579	59.84692
6	684.3499	68.4456	65.78711
7	612.0344	61.91728	72.31543
8	532.5413	54.73955	79.49316
9	445.1592	46.85063	87.38208
10	349.1042	38.17778	96.05493

MORTGAGE OF $1000. FOR 13 YEARS AT 10.00 PERCENT

MONTHLY PAYMENT :$ 11.47873

END OF YEAR	BALANCE DUE	INTEREST	MTGE. REDUCT.
1	960.4749	98.21957	39.52515
2	916.8108	94.08066	43.66406
3	868.5745	89.50839	48.23633
4	815.2874	84.45761	53.28711
5	756.4199	78.87729	58.86743
6	691.3892	72.71396	65.03076
7	619.5488	65.90439	71.84033
8	540.1855	58.38144	79.36328
9	452.512	50.07114	87.67358
10	355.658	40.89072	96.854

MORTGAGE OF $1000. FOR 14 YEARS AT 6.00 PERCENT

MONTHLY PAYMENT :$ 8.813645

END OF YEAR	BALANCE DUE	INTEREST	MTGE. REDUCT.
1	952.9551	58.71881	47.04492
2	903.0083	55.81696	49.94678
3	849.9812	52.73663	53.0271
4	793.6833	49.46588	56.29785
5	733.9133	45.99371	59.77002
6	670.4568	42.30719	63.45654
7	603.0867	38.39362	67.37012
8	531.5613	34.23834	71.52539
9	455.624	29.82648	75.93726
10	375.0032	25.14288	80.62085

MORTGAGE OF $1000. FOR 14 YEARS AT 6.50 PERCENT

MONTHLY PAYMENT :$ 9.082035

END OF YEAR	BALANCE DUE	INTEREST	MTGE. REDUCT.
1	954.6799	63.66435	45.32007
2	906.325	60.62944	48.35498
3	854.7312	57.39067	51.59375
4	799.6821	53.93535	55.04907
5	740.9463	50.24858	58.73584
6	678.2769	46.31499	62.66943
7	611.4104	42.11797	66.86646
8	540.0662	37.64018	71.34424
9	463.9434	32.86162	76.1228
10	382.7224	27.76347	81.22095

MORTGAGE OF $1000. FOR 14 YEARS AT 7.00 PERCENT

MONTHLY PAYMENT :$ 9.354897

END OF YEAR	BALANCE DUE	INTEREST	MTGE. REDUCT.
1	956.3572	68.61594	43.64282
2	909.5591	65.46066	46.7981
3	859.3782	62.07785	50.18091
4	805.5698	58.45041	53.80835
5	747.8721	54.561	57.69775
6	686.0032	50.38986	61.8689
7	619.6619	45.91745	66.34131
8	548.5251	41.12204	71.13672
9	472.2454	35.97897	76.27979
10	390.4514	30.46481	81.79395

MORTGAGE OF $1000. FOR 14 YEARS AT 7.50 PERCENT

MONTHLY PAYMENT :$ 9.632198

END OF YEAR	BALANCE DUE	INTEREST	MTGE. REDUCT.
1	957.9871	73.57344	42.01294
2	912.7131	70.31245	45.27393
3	863.9246	66.79781	48.78857
4	811.3484	63.01021	52.57617
5	754.6904	58.92842	56.65796
6	693.634	54.52998	61.0564
7	627.8379	49.79024	65.79614
8	556.9341	44.68257	70.90381
9	480.5254	39.17769	76.40869
10	398.1846	33.24556	82.34082

MORTGAGE OF $1000. FOR 14 YEARS AT 8.00 PERCENT

MONTHLY PAYMENT :$ 9.913792

END OF YEAR	BALANCE DUE	INTEREST	MTGE. REDUCT.
1	959.5723	78.53777	40.42773
2	915.7888	75.18205	43.78345
3	868.3716	71.54826	47.41724
4	817.0188	67.61272	51.35278
5	761.4041	63.35075	55.61475
6	701.1729	58.7343	60.2312
7	635.9421	53.73479	65.23071
8	565.2976	48.32097	70.64453
9	488.7896	42.45744	76.50806
10	405.9316	36.10759	82.85791

MORTGAGE OF $1000. FOR 14 YEARS AT 8.50 PERCENT

MONTHLY PAYMENT :$ 10.199673

END OF YEAR	BALANCE DUE	INTEREST	MTGE. REDUCT.
1	961.1104	83.50642	38.88965
2	918.7837	80.06941	42.32666
3	872.7161	76.32845	46.06763
4	822.5762	72.25618	50.13989
5	768.0039	67.82381	54.57227
6	708.6086	63.00081	59.39526
7	643.9631	57.75056	64.64551
8	573.6038	52.0367	70.35938
9	497.0249	45.81721	76.57886
10	413.6772	39.04842	83.34766

MORTGAGE OF $1000. FOR 14 YEARS AT 9.00 PERCENT

MONTHLY PAYMENT :$ 10.48977

END OF YEAR	BALANCE DUE	INTEREST	MTGE. REDUCT.
1	962.6038	88.48103	37.39624
2	921.6992	84.97273	40.90454
3	876.9575	81.13557	44.7417
4	828.0188	76.93855	48.93872
5	774.4893	72.34773	53.52954
6	715.9387	67.32674	58.55054
7	651.8955	61.83406	64.04321
8	581.8452	55.82698	70.05029
9	505.2231	49.2552	76.62207
10	421.4136	42.0677	83.20957

MORTGAGE OF $1000. FOR 14 YEARS AT 9.50 PERCENT

MONTHLY PAYMENT :$ 10.78398

END OF YEAR	BALANCE DUE	INTEREST	MTGE. REDUCT.
1	964.0522	93.46001	35.94775
2	924.5369	89.89238	39.51538
3	881.0996	85.9705	43.43726
4	833.3516	81.65971	47.74805
5	780.8647	76.92094	52.48682
6	723.1687	71.71172	57.69604
7	659.7458	65.98491	63.42285
8	590.0288	59.69072	69.71704
9	513.3928	52.77177	76.63599
10	429.1506	45.16557	84.24219

MORTGAGE OF $1000. FOR 14 YEARS AT 10.00 PERCENT

MONTHLY PAYMENT :$ 11.08224

END OF YEAR	BALANCE DUE	INTEREST	MTGE. REDUCT.
1	965.4573	98.44417	34.54272
2	927.2971	94.82674	38.16016
3	885.1411	90.83089	42.15601
4	838.5703	86.41609	46.5708
5	787.1235	81.54012	51.44678
6	730.2898	76.15315	56.83374
7	667.5046	70.20174	62.78516
8	598.1455	63.62776	69.35913
9	521.5225	56.36385	76.62305
10	436.8765	48.3409	84.646

MORTGAGE OF $1000. FOR 15 YEARS AT 6.00 PERCENT

MONTHLY PAYMENT :$ 8.439751

END OF YEAR	BALANCE DUE	INTEREST	MTGE. REDUCT.
1	957.5674	58.84439	42.43262
2	912.5178	56.22745	45.04956
3	864.6895	53.44864	47.82837
4	813.9109	50.49844	50.77856
5	760.0007	47.36685	53.91016
6	702.7656	44.0419	57.23511
7	642.0002	40.51163	60.76538
8	577.4873	36.76407	64.51294
9	508.9946	32.78433	68.49268
10	436.2783	28.5607	72.71631

MORTGAGE OF $1000. FOR 15 YEARS AT 6.50 PERCENT

MONTHLY PAYMENT :$ 8.712062

END OF YEAR	BALANCE DUE	INTEREST	MTGE. REDUCT.
1	959.2539	63.79865	40.74609
2	915.7795	61.07037	43.47437
3	869.3931	58.15826	46.38647
4	819.9006	55.05231	49.49243
5	767.0935	51.73761	52.80713
6	710.749	48.20026	56.34448
7	650.6321	44.4278	60.11694
8	586.4883	40.40094	64.1438
9	518.0488	36.10529	68.43945
10	445.0259	31.52179	73.02295

MORTGAGE OF $1000. FOR 15 YEARS AT 7.00 PERCENT

MONTHLY PAYMENT :$ 8.9891

END OF YEAR	BALANCE DUE	INTEREST	MTGE. REDUCT.
1	960.8901	68.75932	39.10986
2	918.9534	65.93242	41.93677
3	873.9844	62.90019	44.96899
4	825.7651	59.64995	48.21924
5	774.0601	56.16411	51.70508
6	718.6174	52.42656	55.44263
7	659.1667	48.4185	59.45068
8	595.4185	44.1209	63.74829
9	527.062	39.51274	68.35645
10	453.7639	34.57109	73.2981

227

MORTGAGE OF $1000. FOR 15 YEARS AT 7.50 PERCENT

MONTHLY PAYMENT :$ 9.270818

END OF YEAR	BALANCE DUE	INTEREST	MTGE. REDUCT.
1	962.4768	73.72661	37.52319
2	922.04	70.81303	40.43677
3	878.4644	67.67412	43.57568
4	831.5056	64.29106	46.95874
5	780.9016	60.6458	50.604
6	726.3687	56.71684	54.53296
7	667.6023	52.48344	58.76636
8	604.2734	47.92094	63.32886
9	536.0288	43.00517	68.24463
10	462.4863	37.70732	73.54248

MORTGAGE OF $1000. FOR 15 YEARS AT 8.00 PERCENT

MONTHLY PAYMENT :$ 9.557072

END OF YEAR	BALANCE DUE	INTEREST	MTGE. REDUCT.
1	964.0137	78.69853	35.98633
2	925.0403	75.71147	38.97339
3	882.8323	72.47685	42.20801
4	837.1208	68.97343	45.71143
5	787.6155	65.17949	49.50537
6	734.001	61.07036	53.6145
7	675.9363	56.62016	58.0647
8	613.0522	51.80083	62.88403
9	544.9487	46.58134	68.10352
10	471.1934	40.92949	73.75537

MORTGAGE OF $1000. FOR 15 YEARS AT 8.50 PERCENT

MONTHLY PAYMENT :$ 9.847835

END OF YEAR	BALANCE DUE	INTEREST	MTGE. REDUCT.
1	965.501	83.67499	34.49902
2	927.9524	80.62543	37.54858
3	887.0857	77.30731	40.8667
4	842.6067	73.69501	44.479
5	794.1963	69.76361	48.4104
6	741.5063	65.48407	52.68994
7	684.1592	60.82684	57.34717
8	621.7427	55.75751	62.4165
9	553.8093	50.24066	67.93335
10	479.8716	44.23627	73.93774

MORTGAGE OF $1000. FOR 15 YEARS AT 9.00 PERCENT

MONTHLY PAYMENT :$ 10.143026

END OF YEAR	BALANCE DUE	INTEREST	MTGE. REDUCT.
1	966.9409	88.65723	33.05908
2	930.7803	85.55566	36.16064
3	891.2273	82.16333	39.55298
4	847.9644	78.45337	43.26294
5	800.6433	74.39526	47.32104
6	748.8821	69.95508	51.76123
7	692.2661	65.10034	56.61597
8	630.3391	59.78931	61.927
9	562.6035	53.98071	67.7356
10	488.5134	47.62622	74.09009

MORTGAGE OF $1000. FOR 15 YEARS AT 9.50 PERCENT

MONTHLY PAYMENT :$ 10.442515

END OF YEAR	BALANCE DUE	INTEREST	MTGE. REDUCT.
1	968.3335	93.64368	31.6665
2	933.5237	90.50037	34.80981
3	895.259	87.04553	38.26465
4	853.1968	83.24792	42.06226
5	806.96	79.07336	46.23682
6	756.1348	74.48499	50.8252
7	700.2649	69.44031	55.86987
8	638.8499	63.89514	61.41504
9	571.3398	57.80017	67.51001
10	497.1299	51.10022	74.20996

MORTGAGE OF $1000. FOR 15 YEARS AT 10.00 PERCENT

MONTHLY PAYMENT :$ 10.74624

END OF YEAR	BALANCE DUE	INTEREST	MTGE. REDUCT.
1	969.6794	98.63435	30.32056
2	936.1838	95.4593	33.49561
3	899.1804	91.95149	37.00342
4	858.3022	88.07674	40.87817
5	813.1438	83.79646	45.15845
6	763.2563	79.06746	49.88745
7	708.145	73.84358	55.11133
8	647.2625	68.07234	60.88257
9	580.0049	61.69734	67.25757
10	505.7048	54.65486	74.30005

MORTGAGE OF $1000.   FOR   16   YEARS AT   6.00   PERCENT

MONTHLY PAYMENT :$ 8.11547

END OF YEAR	BALANCE DUE	INTEREST	MTGE. REDUCT.
1	961.5676	58.95326	38.43237
2	920.7644	56.58241	40.80322
3	877.4451	54.0663	43.31934
4	831.4539	51.39442	45.99121
5	782.6257	48.55751	48.82813
6	730.7859	45.54579	51.83984
7	675.7493	42.34901	55.03662
8	617.3179	38.95424	58.4314
9	555.2827	35.35048	62.03516
10	489.4211	31.52406	65.86157

MORTGAGE OF $1000.   FOR   16   YEARS AT   6.50   PERCENT

MONTHLY PAYMENT :$ 8.391663

END OF YEAR	BALANCE DUE	INTEREST	MTGE. REDUCT.
1	963.2161	63.91602	36.78394
2	923.9685	61.45239	39.24756
3	882.0918	58.82324	41.87671
4	837.4111	56.01929	44.68066
5	789.738	53.02686	47.6731
6	738.8726	49.83447	50.86548
7	684.6001	46.42749	54.27246
8	626.6926	42.79248	57.90747
9	564.9072	38.91455	61.7854
10	498.9839	34.77661	65.92334

MORTGAGE OF $1000.   FOR   16   YEARS AT   7.00   PERCENT

MONTHLY PAYMENT :$ 8.672828

END OF YEAR	BALANCE DUE	INTEREST	MTGE. REDUCT.
1	964.8101	68.88399	35.18994
2	927.0759	66.3398	37.73413
3	886.6147	63.61275	40.46118
4	843.228	60.68721	43.38672
5	796.7046	57.55049	46.52344
6	746.8179	54.18721	49.88672
7	693.325	50.58101	53.49292
8	635.9653	46.71431	57.35962
9	574.4587	42.56734	61.50659
10	508.5061	38.12129	65.95264

MORTGAGE OF $1000. FOR 16 YEARS AT 7.50 PERCENT

MONTHLY PAYMENT :$ 8.958911

END OF YEAR	BALANCE DUE	INTEREST	MTGE. REDUCT.
1	966.3513	73.85825	33.64868
2	930.0898	71.24545	36.26147
3	891.0134	68.43051	39.07642
4	848.9033	65.39682	42.11011
5	803.5239	62.12753	45.37939
6	754.6216	58.60458	48.90234
7	701.9226	54.80795	52.69897
8	645.1326	50.71689	56.79004
9	583.9341	46.30844	61.19849
10	517.9844	41.55722	65.94971

MORTGAGE OF $1000. FOR 16 YEARS AT 8.00 PERCENT

MONTHLY PAYMENT :$ 9.249755

END OF YEAR	BALANCE DUE	INTEREST	MTGE. REDUCT.
1	967.8394	78.83641	32.16064
2	933.0093	76.16698	34.83008
3	895.2883	73.27611	37.72095
4	854.4368	70.14549	40.85156
5	810.1941	66.75438	44.24268
6	762.2798	63.08275	47.91431
7	710.3884	59.1057	51.89136
8	654.1909	54.79955	56.19751
9	593.3281	50.13426	60.86279
10	527.4138	45.08275	65.91431

MORTGAGE OF $1000. FOR 16 YEARS AT 8.50 PERCENT

MONTHLY PAYMENT :$ 9.545314

END OF YEAR	BALANCE DUE	INTEREST	MTGE. REDUCT.
1	969.2759	83.81964	30.72412
2	935.8367	81.10455	33.43921
3	899.4419	78.14899	36.39478
4	859.8296	74.93146	39.6123
5	816.7156	71.42975	43.11401
6	769.791	67.6192	46.92456
7	718.7188	63.4715	51.07227
8	663.1321	58.95709	55.58667
9	602.6323	54.04401	60.49976
10	536.7849	48.69635	65.84741

MORTGAGE OF $1000. FOR 16 YEARS AT 9.00 PERCENT

MONTHLY PAYMENT :$ 9.845481

END OF YEAR	BALANCE DUE	INTEREST	MTGE. REDUCT.
1	970.6624	88.80812	29.33765
2	938.5723	86.05568	32.09009
3	903.4722	83.04567	35.1001
4	865.0801	79.75368	38.39209
5	823.0862	76.15187	41.9939
6	777.1528	72.21242	45.93335
7	726.9104	67.90334	50.24243
8	671.9548	63.1902	54.95557
9	611.8447	58.03566	60.11011
10	546.0955	52.3965	65.74927

MORTGAGE OF $1000. FOR 16 YEARS AT 9.50 PERCENT

MONTHLY PAYMENT :$ 10.150138

END OF YEAR	BALANCE DUE	INTEREST	MTGE. REDUCT.
1	971.9985	93.80019	28.00146
2	941.2183	91.02138	30.78027
3	907.3831	87.96645	33.83521
4	870.1897	84.60829	37.19336
5	829.3052	80.91713	40.88452
6	784.363	76.85951	44.94214
7	734.9604	72.39906	49.40259
8	680.6543	67.4955	54.30615
9	620.959	62.10634	59.69531
10	555.3379	56.18056	65.62109

MORTGAGE OF $1000. FOR 16 YEARS AT 10.00 PERCENT

MONTHLY PAYMENT :$ 10.459189

END OF YEAR	BALANCE DUE	INTEREST	MTGE. REDUCT.
1	973.2859	98.79616	26.71411
2	943.7749	95.99928	29.51099
3	911.1731	92.90846	32.60181
4	875.158	89.49513	36.01514
5	835.3718	85.72414	39.78613
6	791.4192	81.55763	43.95264
7	742.864	76.95509	48.55518
8	689.2239	71.87013	53.64014
9	629.9673	66.25368	59.25659
10	564.5061	60.04909	65.46118

MORTGAGE OF $1000. FOR   17 YEARS AT   6.00 PERCENT

MONTHLY PAYMENT :$ 7.832021

END OF YEAR	BALANCE DUE	INTEREST	MTGE. REDUCT.
1	965.064	59.0482	34.93604
2	927.9736	56.89391	37.09033
3	888.5947	54.60533	39.37891
4	846.7876	52.17711	41.80713
5	802.4021	49.59874	44.3855
6	755.2788	46.86095	47.12329
7	705.2488	43.95421	50.03003
8	652.1328	40.86827	53.11597
9	595.7412	37.59264	56.3916
10	535.8713	34.11436	59.86987

MORTGAGE OF $1000. FOR   17 YEARS AT   6.50 PERCENT

MONTHLY PAYMENT :$ 8.112048

END OF YEAR	BALANCE DUE	INTEREST	MTGE. REDUCT.
1	966.6726	64.01718	33.32739
2	931.1138	61.78574	35.55884
3	893.1733	59.40414	37.94043
4	852.6917	56.86288	40.48169
5	809.499	54.15195	43.19263
6	763.4136	51.25912	46.08545
7	714.2417	48.1727	49.17188
8	661.7766	44.87949	52.46509
9	605.7979	41.36581	55.97876
10	546.0701	37.61679	59.72778

MORTGAGE OF $1000. FOR   17 YEARS AT   7.00 PERCENT

MONTHLY PAYMENT :$ 8.397294

END OF YEAR	BALANCE DUE	INTEREST	MTGE. REDUCT.
1	968.2249	68.99237	31.77515
2	934.1521	66.69476	34.07275
3	897.6162	64.23163	36.53589
4	858.4392	61.59052	39.177
5	816.4302	58.75848	42.00903
6	771.3843	55.72162	45.0459
7	723.0818	52.46503	48.30249
8	671.2881	48.97382	51.7937
9	615.75	45.22943	55.53809
10	556.1975	41.21503	59.55249

MORTGAGE OF $1000. FOR 17 YEARS AT 7.50 PERCENT

MONTHLY PAYMENT :$ 8.687677

END OF YEAR	BALANCE DUE	INTEREST	MTGE. REDUCT.
1	969.7197	73.97185	30.28027
2	937.0889	71.62126	32.63086
3	901.9248	69.08806	35.16406
4	864.0305	66.35783	37.89429
5	823.1946	63.41618	40.83594
6	779.1887	60.24626	44.00586
7	731.7661	56.82951	47.42261
8	680.6626	53.14861	51.10352
9	625.5913	49.18083	55.07129
10	566.2454	44.90617	59.34595

MORTGAGE OF $1000. FOR 17 YEARS AT 8.00 PERCENT

MONTHLY PAYMENT :$ 8.983029

END OF YEAR	BALANCE DUE	INTEREST	MTGE. REDUCT.
1	971.1602	78.9565	28.83984
2	939.9263	76.56245	31.23389
3	906.1001	73.97017	33.82617
4	869.4666	71.1628	36.63354
5	829.7925	68.12227	39.67407
6	786.8254	64.8293	42.96704
7	740.2922	61.26314	46.5332
8	689.8967	57.40083	50.39551
9	635.3184	53.21797	54.57837
10	576.2102	48.68819	59.10815

MORTGAGE OF $1000. FOR 17 YEARS AT 8.50 PERCENT

MONTHLY PAYMENT :$ 9.283286

END OF YEAR	BALANCE DUE	INTEREST	MTGE. REDUCT.
1	972.5461	83.94557	27.45386
2	942.6658	81.51906	29.88037
3	910.1436	78.87721	32.52222
4	874.7471	76.00294	35.39648
5	836.2219	72.87428	38.52515
6	794.2913	69.46877	41.93066
7	748.6545	65.76271	45.63672
8	698.9839	61.72878	49.67065
9	644.9224	57.33791	54.06152
10	586.083	52.56007	58.83936

MORTGAGE OF $1000. FOR 17 YEARS AT 9.00 PERCENT

MONTHLY PAYMENT :$ 9.58833

END OF YEAR	BALANCE DUE	INTEREST	MTGE. REDUCT.
1	973.8789	88.93886	26.12109
2	945.3066	86.48769	28.57227
3	914.0549	83.80824	31.25171
4	879.8716	80.8766	34.18335
5	842.4812	77.66957	37.39038
6	801.5835	74.16225	40.89771
7	756.8494	70.32582	44.73413
8	707.9187	66.12929	48.93066
9	654.3982	61.53944	53.52051
10	595.8569	56.51869	58.54126

MORTGAGE OF $1000. FOR 17 YEARS AT 9.50 PERCENT

MONTHLY PAYMENT :$ 9.898024

END OF YEAR	BALANCE DUE	INTEREST	MTGE. REDUCT.
1	975.1594	93.9357	24.84058
2	947.8533	91.47012	27.30615
3	917.8369	88.75992	30.01636
4	884.8418	85.78116	32.99512
5	848.5718	82.50626	36.27002
6	808.7021	78.90665	39.86963
7	764.8755	74.94962	43.82666
8	716.6992	70.60001	48.17627
9	663.7415	65.81851	52.95776
10	605.5283	60.56314	58.21313

MORTGAGE OF $1000. FOR 17 YEARS AT 10.00 PERCENT

MONTHLY PAYMENT :$ 10.212257

END OF YEAR	BALANCE DUE	INTEREST	MTGE. REDUCT.
1	976.3887	98.93576	23.61133
2	950.3052	96.46359	26.0835
3	921.4897	93.73166	28.81543
4	889.6575	90.71481	31.83228
5	854.4915	87.38107	35.16602
6	815.6436	83.69919	38.8479
7	772.7283	79.63181	42.91528
8	725.3186	75.13742	47.40967
9	672.9446	70.17307	52.37402
10	615.0862	64.68869	57.8584

MORTGAGE OF $1000. FOR 18 YEARS AT 6.00 PERCENT

MONTHLY PAYMENT :$ 7.582563

END OF YEAR	BALANCE DUE	INTEREST	MTGE. REDUCT.
1	968.1411	59.13187	31.85889
2	934.3179	57.16751	33.82324
3	898.4082	55.08109	35.90967
4	860.2834	52.866	38.12476
5	819.8074	50.51468	40.47607
6	776.835	48.01834	42.97241
7	731.2119	45.36771	45.62305
8	682.7749	42.55374	48.43701
9	631.3506	39.56644	51.42432
10	576.7542	36.39432	54.59644

MORTGAGE OF $1000. FOR 18 YEARS AT 6.50 PERCENT

MONTHLY PAYMENT :$ 7.866391

END OF YEAR	BALANCE DUE	INTEREST	MTGE. REDUCT.
1	969.7102	64.10689	30.28979
2	937.3918	62.07832	32.31836
3	902.9089	59.91377	34.48291
4	866.1167	57.60445	36.79224
5	826.8608	55.14082	39.25586
6	784.9753	52.51118	41.8855
7	740.2847	49.70601	44.69067
8	692.6011	46.71309	47.68359
9	641.7241	43.51973	50.87695
10	587.4399	40.1125	54.28418

MORTGAGE OF $1000. FOR 18 YEARS AT 7.00 PERCENT

MONTHLY PAYMENT :$ 8.155659

END OF YEAR	BALANCE DUE	INTEREST	MTGE. REDUCT.
1	971.219	69.0869	28.78101
2	940.3577	67.00658	30.86133
3	907.2649	64.77513	33.09277
4	871.7798	62.3828	35.48511
5	833.7302	59.81834	38.04956
6	792.9299	57.06761	40.80029
7	749.1799	54.1179	43.75
8	702.2671	50.95506	46.91284
9	651.9631	47.56395	50.30396
10	598.0227	43.92747	53.94043

MORTGAGE OF $1000. FOR 18 YEARS AT 7.50 PERCENT

MONTHLY PAYMENT :$ 8.450269

END OF YEAR	BALANCE DUE	INTEREST	MTGE. REDUCT.
1	972.6685	74.07167	27.33154
2	943.2153	71.95009	29.45313
3	911.4756	69.66347	31.73975
4	877.2717	67.19936	34.20386
5	840.4124	64.54384	36.85938
6	800.6919	61.68275	39.72046
7	757.8882	58.5995	42.80371
8	711.7607	55.27577	46.12744
9	662.0532	51.69569	49.70752
10	608.4861	47.83607	53.56714

MORTGAGE OF $1000. FOR 18 YEARS AT 8.00 PERCENT

MONTHLY PAYMENT :$ 8.750051

END OF YEAR	BALANCE DUE	INTEREST	MTGE. REDUCT.
1	974.0608	79.0614	25.93921
2	945.9688	76.90857	28.09204
3	915.5449	74.57678	30.42383
4	882.5964	72.05212	32.94849
5	846.9131	69.31726	35.68335
6	808.2678	66.35535	38.64526
7	766.4146	63.14734	41.85327
8	721.0879	59.67395	45.32666
9	671.999	55.91174	49.08887
10	618.8359	51.83752	53.16309

MORTGAGE OF $1000. FOR 18 YEARS AT 8.50 PERCENT

MONTHLY PAYMENT :$ 9.054909

END OF YEAR	BALANCE DUE	INTEREST	MTGE. REDUCT.
1	975.396	84.0549	24.604
2	948.6169	81.87985	26.77905
3	919.4709	79.51291	29.146
4	887.7493	76.93723	31.72168
5	853.2231	74.13278	34.52612
6	815.6453	71.08102	37.57788
7	774.7454	67.759	40.8999
8	730.2312	64.14474	44.51416
9	681.782	60.20969	48.44922
10	629.0505	55.92746	52.73145

MORTGAGE OF $1000. FOR   18   YEARS AT   9.00   PERCENT

MONTHLY PAYMENT :$ 9.364715

END OF YEAR	BALANCE DUE	INTEREST	MTGE. REDUCT.
1	976.6755	89.05211	23.32446
2	951.1628	86.86388	25.5127
3	923.2571	84.47081	27.90576
4	892.7339	81.85338	30.52319
5	859.3469	78.98961	33.38696
6	822.8284	75.85802	36.51855
7	782.8838	72.43199	39.94458
8	739.1929	68.68565	43.69092
9	691.4028	64.58653	47.79004
10	639.1299	60.10362	52.27295

MORTGAGE OF $1000. FOR   18   YEARS AT   9.50   PERCENT

MONTHLY PAYMENT :$ 9.679314

END OF YEAR	BALANCE DUE	INTEREST	MTGE. REDUCT.
1	977.9011	94.05289	22.09888
2	953.6089	91.85953	24.29224
3	926.906	89.44888	26.70288
4	897.553	86.79874	29.35303
5	865.2861	83.88492	32.26685
6	829.8171	80.68277	35.46899
7	790.8276	77.16226	38.9895
8	747.9688	73.29288	42.85889
9	700.8562	69.03922	47.11255
10	649.0681	64.36368	51.78809

MORTGAGE OF $1000. FOR   18   YEARS AT   10.00   PERCENT

MONTHLY PAYMENT :$ 9.998572

END OF YEAR	BALANCE DUE	INTEREST	MTGE. REDUCT.
1	979.074	99.05684	20.92603
2	955.9563	96.86519	23.11768
3	930.4182	94.44478	25.53809
4	902.2061	91.77071	28.21216
5	871.04	88.81685	31.16602
6	836.6101	85.55293	34.42993
7	798.575	81.94771	38.03516
8	756.5564	77.96431	42.01855
9	710.1387	73.56514	46.41772
10	658.8604	68.70454	51.27832

MORTGAGE OF $1000. FOR 19 YEARS AT 6.00 PERCENT

MONTHLY PAYMENT :$ 7.361706

END OF YEAR	BALANCE DUE	INTEREST	MTGE. REDUCT.
1	970.8655	59.20595	29.13452
2	939.9336	57.40858	30.93188
3	907.0945	55.50136	32.83911
4	872.2297	53.47572	34.86475
5	835.2151	51.32582	37.01465
6.	795.917	49.04237	39.2981
7	754.1953	46.61879	41.72168
8	709.9001	44.0453	44.29517
9	662.8728	41.31313	47.02734
10	612.9458	38.41347	49.927

MORTGAGE OF $1000. FOR 19 YEARS AT 6.50 PERCENT

MONTHLY PAYMENT :$ 7.649282

END OF YEAR	BALANCE DUE	INTEREST	MTGE. REDUCT.
1	972.394	64.18542	27.60596
2	942.9395	62.33679	29.45459
3	911.5127	60.36462	31.42676
4	877.981	58.25964	33.53174
5	842.2039	56.01428	35.7771
6	804.0305	53.61804	38.17334
7	763.3005	51.0614	40.72998
8	719.8428	48.33362	43.45776
9	673.4746	45.42322	46.36816
10	624.001	42.31775	49.47363

MORTGAGE OF $1000. FOR 19 YEARS AT 7.00 PERCENT

MONTHLY PAYMENT :$ 7.942516

END OF YEAR	BALANCE DUE	INTEREST	MTGE. REDUCT.
1	973.8599	69.17006	26.14014
2	945.8311	67.28139	28.02881
3	915.7754	65.25453	30.05566
4	883.5471	63.08192	32.22827
5	848.989'	60.75209	34.55811
6	811.9331	58.25429	37.05591
7	772.198	55.57509	39.73511
8	729.5908	52.70302	42.60718
9	683.9036	49.62294	45.68726
10	634.9138	46.32045	48.98975

MORTGAGE OF $1000. FOR   19 YEARS AT   7.50 PERCENT

MONTHLY PAYMENT :$ 8.241282

END OF YEAR	BALANCE DUE	INTEREST	MTGE. REDUCT.
1	975.2644	74.15979	24.7356
2	948.6084	72.23938	26.65601
3	919.8835	70.17053	28.72485
4	888.9282	67.94006	30.95532
5	855.5698	65.53699	33.3584
6	819.6218	62.94739	35.948
7	780.8831	60.15662	38.73877
8	739.1365	57.1488	41.74658
9	694.1494	53.90833	44.98706
10	645.6699	50.41589	48.47949

MORTGAGE OF $1000. FOR   19 YEARS AT   8.00 PERCENT

MONTHLY PAYMENT :$ 8.545401

END OF YEAR	BALANCE DUE	INTEREST	MTGE. REDUCT.
1	976.6084	79.1532	23.3916
2	951.2761	77.21252	25.33228
3	923.8411	75.10974	27.43506
4	894.1282	72.83191	29.71289
5	861.9495	70.36609	32.17871
6	827.1001	67.69543	34.84937
7	789.3579	64.80261	37.74219
8	748.4832	61.67004	40.87476
9	704.2161	58.27771	44.26709
10	656.2744	54.60315	47.94165

MORTGAGE OF $1000. FOR   19 YEARS AT   8.50 PERCENT

MONTHLY PAYMENT :$ 8.854764

END OF YEAR	BALANCE DUE	INTEREST	MTGE. REDUCT.
1	977.8933	84.15047	22.10669
2	953.8325	82.19637	24.06079
3	927.645	80.06966	26.1875
4	899.1431	77.7552	28.50195
5	868.1218	75.23592	31.02124
6	834.3584	72.49373	33.76343
7	797.6108	69.5096	36.74756
8	757.6152	66.26155	39.99561
9	714.0837	62.72566	43.53149
10	666.7048	58.87825	47.37891

MORTGAGE OF $1000. FOR 19 YEARS AT 9.00 PERCENT

MONTHLY PAYMENT :$ 9.169208

END OF YEAR	BALANCE DUE	INTEREST	MTGE. REDUCT.
1	979.1206	89.15109	20.87939
2	956.2825	87.19235	22.83813
3	931.302	85.05002	24.98047
4	903.9788	82.70724	27.32324
5	874.092	80.14377	29.88672
6	841.4021	77.34055	32.68994
7	805.6455	74.2739	35.75659
8	766.5347	70.91965	39.11084
9	723.7544	67.25021	42.78027
10	676.9609	·63.23703	46.79346

MORTGAGE OF $1000. FOR 19 YEARS AT 9.50 PERCENT

MONTHLY PAYMENT :$ 9.488575

END OF YEAR	BALANCE DUE	INTEREST	MTGE. REDUCT.
1	980.2927	94.15562	19.70728
2	958.6289	92.19908	21.66382
3	934.8152	90.04918	23.81372
4	908.6379	87.68565	26.17725
5	879.8625	85.08751	28.77539
6	848.2314	82.2318	31.6311
7	813.4614	79.09288	34.77002
8	775.2402	75.64171	38.22119
9	733.2261	71.84874	42.01416
10	687.0417	67.67857	46.18433

MORTGAGE OF $1000. FOR 19 YEARS AT 10.00 PERCENT

MONTHLY PAYMENT :$ 9.812711

END OF YEAR	BALANCE DUE	INTEREST	MTGE. REDUCT.
1	981.4097	99.16219	18.59033
2	960.8726	97.21541	20.53711
3	938.1851	95.06502	22.6875
4	913.1211	92.68855	25.06396
5	885.4333	90.06477	27.68774
6	854.8457	87.16487	30.58765
7	821.0557	83.96248	33.79004
8	783.7271	80.4239	37.32861
9	742.4897	76.51521	41.2373
10	696.9343	72.1971	45.55542

MORTGAGE OF $1000. FOR   20 YEARS AT   6.00 PERCENT

MONTHLY PAYMENT :$ 7.165128

END OF YEAR	BALANCE DUE	INTEREST	MTGE. REDUCT.
1	973.2903	59.2718	26.70972
2	944.9333	57.62459	28.35693
3	914.8271	55.87532	30.1062
4	882.8645	54.01888	31.96265
5	848.9304	52.04744	33.93408
6	812.9031	49.95418	36.02734
7	774.6538	47.73225	38.24927
8	734.0457	45.37337	40.60815
9	690.9329	42.86873	43.11279
10	645.1609	40.20955	45.77197

MORTGAGE OF $1000. FOR   20 YEARS AT   6.50 PERCENT

MONTHLY PAYMENT :$ 7.456405

END OF YEAR	BALANCE DUE	INTEREST	MTGE. REDUCT.
1	974.7795	64.25639	25.22046
2	947.8696	62.56694	26.90991
3	919.1577	60.76494	28.71191
4	888.5227	58.84184	30.63501
5	855.8362	56.79033	32.68652
6	820.9609	54.60161	34.87524
7	783.7495	52.26543	37.21143
8	744.0466	49.77397	39.70288
9	701.6843	47.11455	42.3623
10	656.4849	44.27739	45.19946

MORTGAGE OF $1000. FOR   20 YEARS AT   7.00 PERCENT

MONTHLY PAYMENT :$ 7.753537

END OF YEAR	BALANCE DUE	INTEREST	MTGE. REDUCT.
1	976.2024	69.24483	23.79761
2	950.6846	67.52461	25.51782
3	923.3215	65.6794	27.36304
4	893.981	63.70186	29.34058
5	862.5188	61.58028	31.46216
6	828.7825	59.30611	33.73633
7	792.6077	56.86763	36.1748
8	753.8171	54.25191	38.79053
9	712.2227	51.44795	41.59448
10	667.6211	48.44087	44.60156

MORTGAGE OF $1000. FOR 20 YEARS AT 7.50 PERCENT

MONTHLY PAYMENT :$ 8.05639

END OF YEAR	BALANCE DUE	INTEREST	MTGE. REDUCT.
1	977.5613	74.23795	22.43872
2	953.3804	72.49576	24.18091
3	927.322	70.61832	26.05835
4	899.2407	68.59537	28.0813
5	868.9795	66.41544	30.26123
6	836.3691	64.06631	32.61035
7	801.2271	61.53458	35.14209
8	763.3567	58.8063	37.87036
9	722.5469	55.86685	40.80981
10	678.5684	52.69815	43.97852

MORTGAGE OF $1000. FOR 20 YEARS AT 8.00 PERCENT

MONTHLY PAYMENT :$ 8.364758

END OF YEAR	BALANCE DUE	INTEREST	MTGE. REDUCT.
1	978.8574	79.23451	21.14258
2	955.9602	77.47987	22.89722
3	931.1624	75.57924	24.79785
4	904.3062	73.52089	26.8562
5	875.2207	71.29164	29.08545
6	843.7214	68.87782	31.49927
7	809.6082	66.26381	34.11328
8	772.6636	63.43251	36.94458
9	732.6523	60.36586	40.01123
10	689.3201	57.04482	43.33228

MORTGAGE OF $1000. FOR 20 YEARS AT 8.50 PERCENT

MONTHLY PAYMENT :$ 8.678515

END OF YEAR	BALANCE DUE	INTEREST	MTGE. REDUCT.
1	980.093	84.2352	19.90698
2	958.4263	82.47543	21.66675
3	934.8442	80.56015	23.58203
4	909.1782	78.47617	25.66602
5	881.2429	76.20688	27.9353
6	850.8384	73.73764	30.40454
7	817.7471	71.05087	33.09131
8	781.73	68.12509	36.01709
9	742.5295	64.94174	39.20044
10	699.8645	61.47714	42.66504

MORTGAGE OF $1000. FOR 20 YEARS AT 9.00 PERCENT

MONTHLY PAYMENT :$ 8.997478

END OF YEAR	BALANCE DUE	INTEREST	MTGE. REDUCT.
1	981.269	89.23878	18.73096
2	960.7805	87.48122	20.48853
3	938.3706	85.55983	22.40991
4	913.8584	83.45753	24.51221
5	887.0464	81.15773	26.81201
6	857.7192	78.64259	29.32715
7	825.6409	75.89137	32.07837
8	790.5537	72.88258	35.08716
9	752.1746	69.59059	38.37915
10	710.1958	65.99098	41.97876

MORTGAGE OF $1000. FOR 20 YEARS AT 9.50 PERCENT

MONTHLY PAYMENT :$ 9.321475

END OF YEAR	BALANCE DUE	INTEREST	MTGE. REDUCT.
1	982.3872	94.2449	17.61279
2	963.0261	92.49661	19.36108
3	941.7439	90.57547	21.28223
4	918.3491	88.46292	23.39478
5	892.6328	86.14139	25.71631
6	864.364	83.5889	28.2688
7	833.2896	80.78323	31.07446
8	799.1311	77.69925	34.15845
9	761.5828	74.30936	37.54834
10	720.3076	70.58255	41.27515

MORTGAGE OF $1000. FOR 20 YEARS AT 10.00 PERCENT

MONTHLY PAYMENT :$ 9.650328

END OF YEAR	BALANCE DUE	INTEREST	MTGE. REDUCT.
1	983.4497	99.25363	16.55029
2	965.1667	97.52097	18.28296
3	944.9688	95.60593	20.198
4	922.656	93.49118	22.31274
5	898.0073	91.15524	24.64868
6	870.7771	88.5737	27.23022
7	840.6956	85.72238	30.08154
8	807.4644	82.57272	33.2312
9	770.7529	79.0925	36.71143
10	730.1975	75.2485	40.55542

MORTGAGE OF $1000. FOR 21 YEARS AT 6.00 PERCENT

MONTHLY PAYMENT :$ 6.989336

END OF YEAR	BALANCE DUE	INTEREST	MTGE. REDUCT.
1	975.4592	59.33125	24.54077
2	949.4043	57.81709	26.05493
3	921.7427	56.2104	27.66162
4	892.3755	54.50484	29.36719
5	861.1965	52.69307	31.17896
6	828.0947	50.77022	33.10181
7	792.9514	48.72871	35.14331
8	755.6404	46.56099	37.31104
9	716.0278	44.25948	39.61255
10	673.9717	41.81587	42.05615

MORTGAGE OF $1000. FOR 21 YEARS AT 6.50 PERCENT

MONTHLY PAYMENT :$ 7.284255

END OF YEAR	BALANCE DUE	INTEREST	MTGE. REDUCT.
1	976.9077	64.31877	23.09229
2	952.269	62.77238	24.63867
3	925.9802	61.12224	26.28882
4	897.9312	59.36198	28.04907
5	868.0029	57.48283	29.92822
6	836.0703	55.47844	31.93262
7	801.9993	53.34001	34.07104
8	765.6465	51.05827	36.35278
9	726.8591	48.6237	38.78735
10	685.4739	46.0258	41.38525

MORTGAGE OF $1000. FOR 21 YEARS AT 7.00 PERCENT

MONTHLY PAYMENT :$ 7.585225

END OF YEAR	BALANCE DUE	INTEREST	MTGE. REDUCT.
1	978.2883	69.31102	21.71167
2	955.0073	67.74168	23.28101
3	930.0435	66.05882	24.96387
4	903.2747	64.25389	26.7688
5	874.5708	62.31883	28.70386
6	843.792	60.24388	30.77881
7	810.7878	58.01854	33.00415
8	775.3979	55.6328	35.38909
9	737.4497	53.07445	37.94824
10	696.7583	50.33128	40.69141

245

MORTGAGE OF $1000. FOR 21 YEARS AT 7.50 PERCENT

MONTHLY PAYMENT :$ 7.892083

END OF YEAR	BALANCE DUE	INTEREST	MTGE. REDUCT.
1	979.6023	74.30728	20.39771
2	957.6204	72.72305	21.98193
3	933.9321	71.01675	23.68823
4	908.4053	69.17813	25.52686
5	880.8967	67.19644	27.50854
6	851.2524	65.0607	29.64429
7	819.3066	62.75919	31.9458
8	784.8811	60.27945	34.42554
9	747.783	57.60684	37.09814
10	707.8047	54.72672	39.97827

MORTGAGE OF $1000. FOR 21 YEARS AT 8.00 PERCENT

MONTHLY PAYMENT :$ 8.20461

END OF YEAR	BALANCE DUE	INTEREST	MTGE. REDUCT.
1	980.8508	79.30614	19.14917
2	960.1128	77.71727	20.73804
3	937.6536	75.99608	22.45923
4	913.3306	74.13231	24.323
5	886.9883	72.11302	26.34229
6	858.4595	69.9265	28.52881
7	827.5627	67.55858	30.89673
8	794.1018	64.99437	33.46094
9	757.864	62.21751	36.23779
10	718.6177	59.20897	39.24634

MORTGAGE OF $1000. FOR 21 YEARS AT 8.50 PERCENT

MONTHLY PAYMENT :$ 8.522651

END OF YEAR	BALANCE DUE	INTEREST	MTGE. REDUCT.
1	982.0374	84.30916	17.96265
2	962.4873	82.72176	19.55005
3	941.2095	80.99397	21.27783
4	918.0508	79.11311	23.15869
5	892.845	77.06599	25.20581
6	865.4111	74.83797	27.43384
7	835.5522	72.41292	29.85889
8	803.0542	69.77376	32.49805
9	767.6843	66.90193	35.36987
10	729.1875	63.77498	38.49683

MORTGAGE OF $1000. FOR 21 YEARS AT 9.00 PERCENT

MONTHLY PAYMENT :$ 8.84601

END OF YEAR	BALANCE DUE	INTEREST	MTGE. REDUCT.
1	983.1631	89.3152	16.83691
2	964.7468	87.73586	18.41626
3	944.603	86.00832	20.1438
4	922.5698	84.11891	22.0332
5	898.4697	82.05202	24.1001
6	872.1091	79.79152	26.3606
7	843.2754	77.31837	28.83374
8	811.7366	74.6133	31.53882
9	777.2395	71.65504	34.49707
10	739.5063	68.41896	37.73315

MORTGAGE OF $1000. FOR 21 YEARS AT 9.50 PERCENT

MONTHLY PAYMENT :$ 9.17449

END OF YEAR	BALANCE DUE	INTEREST	MTGE. REDUCT.
1	984.23	94.32385	15.77002
2	966.8948	92.75867	17.33521
3	947.8391	91.03821	19.05566
4	926.8923	89.14709	20.94678
5	903.8665	87.06799	23.02588
6	878.5557	84.78308	25.31079
7	850.7327	82.27087	27.823
8	820.1477	79.50891	30.58496
9	786.5278	76.474	33.61987
10	749.5708	73.13684	36.95703

MORTGAGE OF $1000. FOR 21 YEARS AT 10.00 PERCENT

MONTHLY PAYMENT :$ 9.507899

END OF YEAR	BALANCE DUE	INTEREST	MTGE. REDUCT.
1	985.2395	99.33429	14.7605
2	968.9338	97.78912	16.30566
3	950.9202	96.08112	18.01367
4	931.02	94.19464	19.90015
5	909.0359	92.11066	21.98413
6	884.7502	89.80914	24.28564
7	857.9214	87.26593	26.82886
8	828.2834	84.45685	29.63794
9	795.542	81.35333	32.74146
10	759.3716	77.92438	36.17041

247

MORTGAGE OF $1000. FOR 22 YEARS AT 6.00 PERCENT

MONTHLY PAYMENT :$ 6.831462

END OF YEAR	BALANCE DUE	INTEREST	MTGE. REDUCT.
1	977.4063	59.38379	22.59375
2	953.4189	57.99023	23.9873
3	927.9524	56.51099	25.46655
4	900.9148	54.93994	27.0376
5	872.2102	53.27295	28.70459
6	841.7346	51.50195	30.47559
7	809.3796	49.62256	32.35498
8	775.0293	47.6272	34.35034
9	738.5603	45.50854	36.46899
10	699.842	43.25928	38.71826

MORTGAGE OF $1000. FOR 22 YEARS AT 6.50 PERCENT

MONTHLY PAYMENT :$ 7.129975

END OF YEAR	BALANCE DUE	INTEREST	MTGE. REDUCT.
1	978.8154	64.37512	21.18457
2	956.2114	62.95569	22.604
3	932.094	61.44226	24.11743
4	906.3616	59.82727	25.73242
5	878.9058	58.10388	27.45581
6	849.6111	56.26501	29.20468
7	818.3542	54.30286	31.25684
8	785.0042	52.20959	33.3501
9	749.4204	49.97595	35.58374
10	711.4541	47.59338	37.96631

MORTGAGE OF $1000. FOR 22 YEARS AT 7.00 PERCENT

MONTHLY PAYMENT :$ 7.434718

END OF YEAR	BALANCE DUE	INTEREST	MTGE. REDUCT.
1	980.1536	69.37018	19.84644
2	958.8723	67.93536	21.28125
3	936.0525	66.39679	22.81982
4	911.583	64.74713	24.46948
5	885.345	62.97858	26.23804
6	857.21	61.0816	28.13501
7	827.041	59.04767	30.16895
8	794.6909	56.86652	32.3501
9	760.0027	54.52838	34.68823
10	722.8066	52.02057	37.19604

MORTGAGE OF $1000. FOR 22 YEARS AT 7.50 PERCENT

MONTHLY PAYMENT :$ 7.745494

END OF YEAR	BALANCE DUE	INTEREST	MTGE. REDUCT.
1	981.4226	74.36853	18.57739
2	961.4033	72.92664	20.01929
3	939.8298	71.37244	21.57349
4	916.5818	69.69788	23.24805
5	891.5286	67.8927	25.05322
6	864.5303	65.94763	26.99829
7	835.4363	63.85193	29.09399
8	804.0837	61.59338	31.35254
9	770.2969	59.15906	33.78687
10	733.8875	56.5365	36.40942

MORTGAGE OF $1000. FOR 22 YEARS AT 8.00 PERCENT

MONTHLY PAYMENT :$ 8.062087

END OF YEAR	BALANCE DUE	INTEREST	MTGE. REDUCT.
1	982.6257	79.37077	17.37427
2	963.8096	77.92888	18.81616
3	943.4316	76.36711	20.37793
4	921.3625	74.67595	22.06909
5	897.4612	72.84367	23.90137
6	871.5762	70.86003	25.88501
7	843.5432	68.71208	28.03296
8	813.1829	66.38469	30.36035
9	780.303	63.86516	32.87988
10	744.6941	61.13615	35.60889

MORTGAGE OF $1000. FOR 22 YEARS AT 8.50 PERCENT

MONTHLY PAYMENT :$ 8.384299

END OF YEAR	BALANCE DUE	INTEREST	MTGE. REDUCT.
1	983.7642	84.37575	16.23584
2	966.0935	82.94093	17.67065
3	946.8601	81.37819	19.2334
4	925.927	79.67848	20.93311
5	903.144	77.82863	22.78296
6	878.3472	75.81471	24.79688
7	851.3584	73.62282	26.98877
8	821.9841	71.23732	29.37427
9	790.0132	68.64064	31.97095
10	755.2161	65.81447	34.79712

MORTGAGE OF $1000. FOR   22 YEARS AT   9.00 PERCENT

MONTHLY PAYMENT :$ 8.711926

END OF YEAR	BALANCE DUE	INTEREST	MTGE. REDUCT.
1	984.8403	89.38344	15.15967
2	968.2585	87.96132	16.58179
3	950.1213	86.4059	18.13721
4	930.2822	84.70399	19.83911
5	908.5823	82.84315	21.69995
6	884.8467	80.80751	23.7356
7	858.8845	78.58095	25.96216
8	830.4873	76.14589	28.39722
9	799.426	73.48183	31.06128
10	765.4509	70.56801	33.9751

MORTGAGE OF $1000. FOR   22 YEARS AT   9.50 PERCENT

MONTHLY PAYMENT :$ 9.044742

END OF YEAR	BALANCE DUE	INTEREST	MTGE. REDUCT.
1	985.8562	94.3931	14.1438
2	970.3093	92.99002	15.54688
3	953.2192	91.44681	17.09009
4	934.4326	89.75027	18.78662
5	913.7815	87.88577	20.65112
6	891.0808	85.83621	22.70068
7	866.127	83.58304	24.95386
8	838.6968	81.10672	27.43018
9	808.5442	78.38431	30.15259
10	775.3992	75.39188	33.14502

MORTGAGE OF $1000. FOR   22 YEARS AT   10.00 PERCENT

MONTHLY PAYMENT :$ 9.382546

END OF YEAR	BALANCE DUE	INTEREST	MTGE. REDUCT.
1	986.8149	99.40549	13.18506
2	972.249	98.02463	14.56592
3	956.1582	96.49973	16.09082
4	938.3821	94.81442	17.77612
5	918.7446	92.95309	19.63745
6	897.0508	90.8967	21.69385
7	873.0852	88.62497	23.96558
8	846.6104	86.11569	26.47485
9	817.363	83.34323	29.24731
10	785.053	80.28049	32.31006

MORTGAGE OF $1000. FOR   23 YEARS AT   6.00   PERCENT

MONTHLY PAYMENT :$ 6.689147

END OF YEAR	BALANCE DUE	INTEREST	MTGE. REDUCT.
1	979.1619	59.43163	20.83813
2	957.0386	58.14647	22.12329
3	933.5508	56.78197	23.48779
4	908.6145	55.33348	24.93628
5	882.1399	53.79515	26.47461
6	854.0325	52.16234	28.10742
7	824.1914	50.4287	29.84106
8	792.51	48.58836	31.6814
9	758.8745	46.63426	33.6355
10	723.1646	44.5598	35.70996

MORTGAGE OF $1000. FOR   23 YEARS AT   6.50   PERCENT

MONTHLY PAYMENT :$ 6.991196

END OF YEAR	BALANCE DUE	INTEREST	MTGE. REDUCT.
1	980.5308	64.42511	19.46924
2	959.7578	63.1214	20.77295
3	937.5938	61.73029	22.16406
4	913.9458	60.2464	23.64795
5	888.7136	58.66217	25.23218
6	861.791	56.97174	26.92261
7	833.0659	55.16925	28.7251
8	802.4175	53.24591	30.64844
9	769.7163	51.19318	32.70117
10	734.8247	49.00275	34.8916

MORTGAGE OF $1000. FOR   23 YEARS AT   7.00   PERCENT

MONTHLY PAYMENT :$ 7.299636

END OF YEAR	BALANCE DUE	INTEREST	MTGE. REDUCT.
1	981.8274	69.42302	18.17261
2	962.3413	68.10954	19.48608
3	941.4463	66.70061	20.88502
4	919.041	65.19035	22.40527
5	895.0156	63.57024	24.02539
6	869.2539	61.83391	25.76172
7	841.6296	59.97136	27.62427
8	812.0083	57.97429	29.62134
9	780.2461	55.83342	31.76221
10	746.1875	53.53703	34.05859

MORTGAGE OF $1000. FOR 23 YEARS AT 7.50 PERCENT

MONTHLY PAYMENT :$ 7.614258

END OF YEAR	BALANCE DUE	INTEREST	MTGE. REDUCT.
1	983.053	74.42407	16.94702
2	964.79	73.10815	18.26294
3	945.1096	71.69067	19.68042
4	923.9014	70.16284	21.20825
5	901.0461	68.51587	22.85522
6	876.4165	66.74146	24.62964
7	849.8755	64.83008	26.54102
8	821.2732	62.7688	28.60229
9	790.4514	60.54932	30.82178
10	757.2366	58.15625	33.21484

MORTGAGE OF $1000. FOR 23 YEARS AT 8.00 PERCENT

MONTHLY PAYMENT :$ 7.934811

END OF YEAR	BALANCE DUE	INTEREST	MTGE. REDUCT.
1	984.2104	79.42818	15.78955
2	967.1104	78.11763	17.1001
3	948.5908	76.6982	18.51953
4	928.5342	75.16109	20.05664
5	906.8127	73.49629	21.72144
6	883.2888	71.6938	23.52303
7	857.8118	69.74068	25.47705
8	830.2205	67.62642	27.59131
9	800.3391	65.33638	29.88135
10	767.9775	62.85610	32.36157

MORTGAGE OF $1000. FOR 23 YEARS AT 8.50 PERCENT

MONTHLY PAYMENT :$ 8.261086

END OF YEAR	BALANCE DUE	INTEREST	MTGE. REDUCT.
1	985.3015	84.43454	14.69849
2	969.3042	83.13571	15.99731
3	951.8928	81.72165	17.41138
4	932.9429	80.18307	18.94995
5	912.3176	78.50778	20.62524
6	889.8694	76.68478	22.44824
7	865.4365	74.70016	24.43286
8	838.8442	72.54074	26.59229
9	809.9019	70.19064	28.94238
10	778.4006	67.63181	31.50122

MORTGAGE OF $1000. FOR   23   YEARS AT   9.00   PERCENT

MONTHLY PAYMENT :$ 8.592849

END OF YEAR	BALANCE DUE	INTEREST	MTGE. REDUCT.
1	986.3298	89.44402	13.67017
2	971.3774	88.16179	14.95239
3	955.0217	86.75847	16.35571
4	937.1326	85.22502	17.88910
5	917.5649	83.54655	19.56763
6	896.1611	81.71037	21.40381
7	872.7505	79.70354	23.41064
8	847.1438	77.50749	25.60669
9	819.1343	75.10466	28.00952
10	788.4978	72.47771	30.63647

MORTGAGE OF $1000. FOR   23   YEARS AT   9.50   PERCENT

MONTHLY PAYMENT :$ 8.92986

END OF YEAR	BALANCE DUE	INTEREST	MTGE. REDUCT.
1	987.2969	94.45518	12.70313
2	973.3325	93.19395	13.96436
3	957.9824	91.80821	15.3501
4	941.1086	90.28453	16.87378
5	922.5608	88.61046	18.54785
6	902.1721	86.76964	20.38867
7	879.7595	84.74571	22.4126
8	855.123	82.52184	24.63647
9	828.0413	80.07652	27.08179
10	798.271	77.38805	29.77026

MORTGAGE OF $1000. FOR   23   YEARS AT   10.00   PERCENT

MONTHLY PAYMENT :$ 9.271894

END OF YEAR	BALANCE DUE	INTEREST	MTGE. REDUCT.
1	988.2046	99.4673	11.79541
2	975.1748	98.23293	13.02979
3	960.7803	96.86818	14.39453
4	944.8787	95.3611	15.90161
5	927.3115	93.69557	17.56714
6	907.9053	91.85646	19.40625
7	886.4673	89.82472	21.43799
8	862.7839	87.57936	23.68335
9	836.6206	85.09938	26.16333
10	807.718	82.36012	28.90259

MORTGAGE OF $1000. FOR   24   YEARS AT   6.00   PERCENT

MONTHLY PAYMENT :$ 6.560417

END OF YEAR	BALANCE DUE	INTEREST	MTGE. REDUCT.
1	980.7502	59.47525	19.24976
2	960.3132	58.28799	20.43701
3	938.6152	57.02701	21.698
4	915.5798	55.68961	23.0354
5	891.1233	54.26846	24.45654
6	865.1577	52.75943	25.96558
7	837.5908	51.15811	27.56689
8	808.324	49.45816	29.26685
9	777.2522	47.65323	31.07178
10	744.2629	45.73575	32.98926

MORTGAGE OF $1000. FOR   24   YEARS AT   6.50   PERCENT

MONTHLY PAYMENT :$ 6.865941

END OF YEAR	BALANCE DUE	INTEREST	MTGE. REDUCT.
1	982.0801	64.47136	17.91992
2	962.9595	63.27068	19.12061
3	942.5586	61.9904	20.40088
4	920.7913	60.62395	21.76733
5	897.5659	59.16594	23.22534
6	872.7854	57.61076	24.78052
7	846.3455	55.95134	26.43994
8	818.1345	54.18034	28.21094
9	788.0344	52.29118	30.1001
10	755.9185	50.27531	32.11597

MORTGAGE OF $1000. FOR   24   YEARS AT   7.00   PERCENT

MONTHLY PAYMENT :$ 7.17801

END OF YEAR	BALANCE DUE	INTEREST	MTGE. REDUCT.
1	983.3347	69.47083	16.66528
2	965.4646	68.26599	17.87012
3	946.3027	66.97424	19.16187
4	925.7556	65.58899	20.54712
5	903.7231	64.10364	22.03247
6	880.0979	62.51086	23.62524
7	854.7651	60.80334	25.33276
8	827.6011	58.97205	27.16406
9	798.4729	57.00793	29.12817
10	767.2395	54.90271	31.2334

MORTGAGE OF $1000. FOR 24 YEARS AT 7.50 PERCENT

MONTHLY PAYMENT :$ 7.496387

END OF YEAR	BALANCE DUE	INTEREST	MTGE. REDUCT.
1	984.5166	74.47325	15.4834
2	967.8318	73.27184	16.68481
3	949.8516	71.97643	17.98022
4	930.4753	70.58043	19.37622
5	909.5952	69.07652	20.88013
6	887.094	67.45543	22.50122
7	862.8457	65.70836	24.24829
8	836.7151	63.82603	26.13062
9	808.5559	61.79747	28.15918
10	778.2107	59.61143	30.34521

MORTGAGE OF $1000. FOR 24 YEARS AT 8.00 PERCENT

MONTHLY PAYMENT :$ 7.820804

END OF YEAR	BALANCE DUE	INTEREST	MTGE. REDUCT.
1	985.6296	79.47928	14.37036
2	970.0669	78.2869	15.56274
3	953.2122	76.9949	16.85474
4	934.959	75.59647	18.25317
5	915.1899	74.0806	19.76904
6	893.7803	72.43997	21.40967
7	870.594	70.66336	23.18628
8	845.4829	68.73856	25.11108
9	818.2876	66.65433	27.19531
10	788.8352	64.39725	29.45239

MORTGAGE OF $1000. FOR 24 YEARS AT 8.50 PERCENT

MONTHLY PAYMENT :$ 8.151026

END OF YEAR	BALANCE DUE	INTEREST	MTGE. REDUCT.
1	986.6748	84.48711	13.3252
2	972.1724	83.30986	14.50244
3	956.3879	82.02788	15.78442
4	939.208	80.63237	17.17993
5	920.51	79.1143	18.698
6	900.1592	77.46147	20.35083
7	878.0093	75.6624	22.1499
8	853.9016	73.70464	24.10767
9	827.6628	71.57353	26.23877
10	799.105	69.25444	28.55786

MORTGAGE OF $1000. FOR 24 YEARS AT 9.00 PERCENT

MONTHLY PAYMENT :$ 8.486793

END OF YEAR	BALANCE DUE	INTEREST	MTGE. REDUCT.
1	987.6563	89.49776	12.34375
2	974.1543	88.33955	13.50195
3	959.386	87.0732	14.76831
4	943.2322	85.6877	16.15381
5	925.563	84.17232	17.66919
6	906.2366	82.51509	19.32642
7	885.0972	80.7021	21.1394
8	861.9746	78.71895	23.12256
9	836.6831	76.55	25.2915
10	809.0193	74.17769	27.66382

MORTGAGE OF $1000. FOR 24 YEARS AT 9.50 PERCENT

MONTHLY PAYMENT :$ 8.827859

END OF YEAR	BALANCE DUE	INTEREST	MTGE. REDUCT.
1	988.5752	94.50949	11.4248
2	976.0168	93.37595	12.55835
3	962.2124	92.12985	13.80444
4	947.0376	90.75949	15.1748
5	930.3567	89.25339	16.68091
6	912.0203	87.59787	18.33643
7	891.864	85.77805	20.15625
8	869.7075	83.7778	22.15649
9	845.3513	81.57809	24.3562
10	818.5784	79.16135	26.77295

MORTGAGE OF $1000. FOR 24 YEARS AT 10.00 PERCENT

MONTHLY PAYMENT :$ 9.173957

END OF YEAR	BALANCE DUE	INTEREST	MTGE. REDUCT.
1	989.4355	99.52303	10.56445
2	977.7654	98.41731	11.67017
3	964.8726	97.19466	12.89282
4	950.6304	95.84529	14.24219
5	934.8958	94.35286	15.73462
6	917.5142	92.70589	17.38159
7	898.3125	90.88582	19.20166
8	877.0999	88.87483	21.21265
9	853.6663	86.65388	23.43359
10	827.7788	84.20003	25.88745

MORTGAGE OF $1000. FOR 25 YEARS AT 6.00 PERCENT

MONTHLY PAYMENT :$ 6.44361

END OF YEAR	BALANCE DUE	INTEREST	MTGE. REDUCT.
1	982.1907	59.51399	17.80933
2	963.2832	58.41585	18.90747
3	943.2097	57.24983	20.07349
4	921.8979	56.01155	21.31177
5	899.2717	54.6971	22.62622
6	875.25	53.30159	24.02173
7	849.7468	51.82014	25.50317
8	822.6702	50.24666	27.07666
9	793.9241	48.57722	28.74609
10	763.4045	46.80379	30.51953

MORTGAGE OF $1000. FOR 25 YEARS AT 6.50 PERCENT

MONTHLY PAYMENT :$ 6.752553

END OF YEAR	BALANCE DUE	INTEREST	MTGE. REDUCT.
1	983.4814	64.51207	16.51855
2	965.8567	63.40587	17.62476
3	947.0515	62.22545	18.80518
4	926.9871	60.96617	20.06445
5	905.5793	59.62291	21.40771
6	882.738	58.18932	22.84131
7	858.3665	56.65904	24.37158
8	832.3628	55.02696	26.00366
9	804.6179	53.28575	27.74487
10	775.0146	51.42735	29.60327

MORTGAGE OF $1000. FOR 25 YEARS AT 7.00 PERCENT

MONTHLY PAYMENT :$ 7.068182

END OF YEAR	BALANCE DUE	INTEREST	MTGE. REDUCT.
1	984.6958	69.51398	15.3042
2	968.2849	68.40729	16.41089
3	950.688	67.22125	17.59692
4	931.8186	65.94879	18.86938
5	911.5857	64.58527	20.23291
6	889.8896	63.12213	21.69604
7	866.6255	61.55402	23.26416
8	841.6797	59.87238	24.9458
9	814.9304	58.06891	26.74927
10	786.2476	56.13531	28.68286

MORTGAGE OF $1000. FOR 25 YEARS AT 7.50 PERCENT

MONTHLY PAYMENT :$ 7.390228

END OF YEAR	BALANCE DUE	INTEREST	MTGE. REDUCT.
1	985.8354	74.51819	14.16455
2	970.5713	73.41858	15.26416
3	954.1223	72.23376	16.44897
4	936.3962	70.95667	17.72607
5	917.2944	69.58093	19.10181
6	896.7092	68.09753	20.58521
7	874.5259	66.49939	22.18335
8	850.6206	64.77747	23.90527
9	824.8594	62.92151	25.76123
10	797.0986	60.922	27.76074

MORTGAGE OF $1000. FOR 25 YEARS AT 8.00 PERCENT

MONTHLY PAYMENT :$ 7.718408

END OF YEAR	BALANCE DUE	INTEREST	MTGE. REDUCT.
1	986.9045	79.52542	13.09546
2	972.7217	78.43802	14.18286
3	957.3623	77.26151	15.35938
4	940.7278	75.98636	16.63452
5	922.7131	74.60623	18.01465
6	903.2026	73.11038	19.5105
7	882.0728	71.491	21.12988
8	859.1892	69.73734	22.88354
9	834.406	67.83768	24.7832
10	807.5667	65.78152	26.83936

MORTGAGE OF $1000. FOR 25 YEARS AT 8.50 PERCENT

MONTHLY PAYMENT :$ 8.052459

END OF YEAR	BALANCE DUE	INTEREST	MTGE. REDUCT.
1	987.905	84.53453	12.09497
2	974.741	83.46544	13.16406
3	960.4133	82.30186	14.32764
4	944.8193	81.03551	15.59399
5	927.8474	79.65758	16.97192
6	909.375	78.15709	18.47241
7	889.2698	76.52428	20.10522
8	867.3872	74.74693	21.88257
9	843.5706	72.81285	23.81665
10	817.6487	70.70763	25.92188

MORTGAGE OF $1000. FOR 25 YEARS AT 9.00 PERCENT

MONTHLY PAYMENT :$ 8.392105

END OF YEAR	BALANCE DUE	INTEREST	MTGE. REDUCT.
1	988.8401	89.54535	11.15991
2	976.6335	88.49872	12.20654
3	963.2822	87.35394	13.35132
4	948.6785	86.1015	14.60376
5	932.7048	84.73163	15.97363
6	915.2324	83.23285	17.47241
7	896.1208	81.59369	19.11157
8	875.2168	79.80121	20.90405
9	852.3516	77.84003	22.86523
10	827.3413	75.69501	25.01025

MORTGAGE OF $1000. FOR 25 YEARS AT 9.50 PERCENT

MONTHLY PAYMENT :$ 8.737063

END OF YEAR	BALANCE DUE	INTEREST	MTGE. REDUCT.
1	989.7136	94.55838	10.286377
2	978.4065	93.53763	11.30713
3	965.9773	92.41556	12.4292
4	952.3145	91.18192	13.66284
5	937.2952	89.82547	15.01929
6	920.7856	88.33524	16.50952
7	902.6375	86.69656	18.14819
8	882.6877	84.89505	19.94971
9	860.7585	82.91556	21.9292
10	836.6528	80.73904	24.10571

MORTGAGE OF $1000. FOR 25 YEARS AT 10.00 PERCENT

MONTHLY PAYMENT :$ 9.087071

END OF YEAR	BALANCE DUE	INTEREST	MTGE. REDUCT.
1	990.5273	99.57219	9.472656
2	980.063	98.58049	10.464355
3	968.5029	97.48479	11.56006
4	955.7319	96.27385	12.771
5	941.6238	94.93669	14.10815
6	926.0386	93.45964	15.58521
7	908.821	91.82732	17.21753
8	889.8003	90.02409	19.02075
9	868.7888	88.03337	21.01147
10	845.5769	85.83293	23.21191

MORTGAGE OF $1000. FOR 26 YEARS AT 6.00 PERCENT

MONTHLY PAYMENT :$ 6.337332

END OF YEAR	BALANCE DUE	INTEREST	MTGE. REDUCT.
1	983.5017	59.54968	16.49829
2	965.9861	58.53235	17.51563
3	947.3899	57.45178	18.59619
4	927.647	56.30505	19.74292
5	906.6865	55.08752	20.96045
6	884.4331	53.79456	22.25342
7	860.8074	52.42224	23.62573
8	835.7241	50.96472	25.08325
9	809.0938	49.4176	26.63037
10	780.8213	47.77551	28.27246

MORTGAGE OF $1000. FOR 26 YEARS AT 6.50 PERCENT

MONTHLY PAYMENT :$ 6.649632

END OF YEAR	BALANCE DUE	INTEREST	MTGE. REDUCT.
1	984.7542	64.54973	15.24585
2	968.4875	63.52898	16.2666
3	951.1316	62.43962	17.35596
4	932.6128	61.27678	18.5188
5	912.8538	60.03654	19.75903
6	891.7717	58.71355	21.08203
7	869.2776	57.30144	22.49414
8	845.2771	55.79509	24.00049
9	819.6694	54.18791	25.60767
10	792.3467	52.47282	27.32275

MORTGAGE OF $1000. FOR 26 YEARS AT 7.00 PERCENT

MONTHLY PAYMENT :$ 6.968741

END OF YEAR	BALANCE DUE	INTEREST	MTGE. REDUCT.
1	985.9282	69.55312	14.07178
2	970.8391	68.53578	15.08911
3	954.6589	67.44472	16.18018
4	937.3091	66.27504	17.34985
5	918.7056	65.02138	18.60352
6	898.7566	63.67592	19.94897
7	877.3655	62.23378	21.39111
8	854.4285	60.68788	22.93701
9	829.8335	59.02992	24.59497
10	803.4604	57.25185	26.37305

MORTGAGE OF $1000. FOR 26 YEARS AT 7.50 PERCENT

MONTHLY PAYMENT :$ 7.294369

END OF YEAR	BALANCE DUE	INTEREST	MTGE. REDUCT.
1	987.0261	74.55855	12.97388
2	973.0454	73.55171	13.98071
3	957.979	72.46602	15.06641
4	941.7429	71.29634	16.23608
5	924.2468	70.03633	17.49609
6	905.3926	68.67818	18.85425
7	885.0742	67.21407	20.31836
8	863.179	65.63716	21.89526
9	839.5835	63.93697	23.59546
10	814.1565	62.10542	25.427

MORTGAGE OF $1000. FOR 26 YEARS AT 8.00 PERCENT

MONTHLY PAYMENT :$ 7.626208

END OF YEAR	BALANCE DUE	INTEREST	MTGE. REDUCT.
1	988.052	79.5665	11.948
2	975.1128	78.57529	12.93921
3	961.0999	77.50156	14.01294
4	945.9233	76.33798	15.17651
5	929.4875	75.0787	16.43579
6	911.6875	73.71445	17.80005
7	892.4099	72.23691	19.27759
8	871.5317	70.63632	20.87817
9	848.9214	68.90414	22.61035
10	824.4343	67.02744	24.48706

MORTGAGE OF $1000. FOR 26 YEARS AT 8.50 PERCENT

MONTHLY PAYMENT :$ 7.963972

END OF YEAR	BALANCE DUE	INTEREST	MTGE. REDUCT.
1	989.0093	84.57693	10.99072
2	977.0476	83.60599	11.96167
3	964.0283	82.54837	13.01929
4	949.8586	81.39798	14.16968
5	934.4363	80.14529	15.42236
6	917.6499	78.78128	16.78638
7	899.3804	77.29813	18.26953
8	879.4958	75.68314	19.88452
9	857.8538	73.92557	21.64209
10	834.2988	72.01273	23.55493

MORTGAGE OF $1000. FOR 26 YEARS AT 9.00 PERCENT

MONTHLY PAYMENT :$ 8.307362

END OF YEAR	BALANCE DUE	INTEREST	MTGE. REDUCT.
1	989.9009	89.58922	10.099121
2	978.8538	88.64122	11.04712
3	966.7703	87.60484	12.0835
4	953.5535	86.47154	13.2168
5	939.0967	85.23155	14.45679
6	923.2844	83.87608	15.81226
7	905.9883	82.3922	17.29614
8	887.0701	80.77013	18.91821
9	866.3772	78.99547	20.69287
10	843.7434	77.05455	22.63379

MORTGAGE OF $1000. FOR 26 YEARS AT 9.50 PERCENT

MONTHLY PAYMENT :$ 8.656078

END OF YEAR	BALANCE DUE	INTEREST	MTGE. REDUCT.
1	990.7288	94.6017	9.27124
2	980.5374	93.68153	10.191406
3	969.335	92.67055	11.20239
4	957.021	91.55898	12.31396
5	943.4839	90.33583	13.53711
6	928.6038	88.99281	14.88013
7	912.2471	87.51625	16.35669
8	894.2666	85.89247	17.98047
9	874.5015	84.1078	19.76514
10	852.7747	82.14613	21.72681

MORTGAGE OF $1000. FOR 26 YEARS AT 10.00 PERCENT

MONTHLY PAYMENT :$ 9.009828

END OF YEAR	BALANCE DUE	INTEREST	MTGE. REDUCT.
1	991.4983	99.61621	8.501709
2	982.106	98.72559	9.392334
3	971.731	97.74292	10.375
4	960.269	96.65601	11.46191
5	947.6064	95.45532	12.6626
6	933.6179	94.12939	13.98853
7	918.1648	92.66479	15.45313
8	901.0933	91.04639	17.07153
9	882.2349	89.25952	18.8584
10	861.4014	87.28442	20.8335

MORTGAGE OF $1000. FOR   27 YEARS AT   6.00 PERCENT

MONTHLY PAYMENT :$ 6.240383

END OF YEAR	BALANCE DUE	INTEREST	MTGE. REDUCT.
1	984.698	59.5826	15.302
2	968.4521	58.63875	16.24585
3	951.2041	57.63655	17.24805
4	932.8926	56.57307	18.31152
5	913.4514	55.44344	19.44116
6	892.8108	54.24307	20.64063
7	870.8977	52.97151	21.91309
8	847.6321	51.61897	23.26563
9	822.9319	50.1844	24.7002
10	796.7085	48.06121	26.22339

MORTGAGE OF $1000. FOR   27 YEARS AT   6.50 PERCENT

MONTHLY PAYMENT :$ 6.555978

END OF YEAR	BALANCE DUE	INTEREST	MTGE. REDUCT.
1	985.9121	64.58383	14.08789
2	970.8801	63.63974	15.03198
3	954.842	62.63364	16.03809
4	937.7297	61.55942	17.1123
5	919.4717	60.41367	18.25806
6	899.9907	59.19077	19.48096
7	879.2053	57.88632	20.7854
8	857.0276	56.49399	22.17773
9	833.365	55.00912	23.6626
10	808.1174	53.42416	25.24756

MORTGAGE OF $1000. FOR   27 YEARS AT   7.00 PERCENT

MONTHLY PAYMENT :$ 6.878491

END OF YEAR	BALANCE DUE	INTEREST	MTGE. REDUCT.
1	987.0466	69.58852	12.95337
2	973.1563	68.6515	13.89038
3	958.2622	67.64784	14.89404
4	942.2917	66.57143	15.97046
5	925.1672	65.41737	17.12451
6	906.804	64.1786	18.36328
7	887.1135	62.85146	19.69043
8	865.9993	61.42763	21.11426
9	843.3586	59.90126	22.64063
10	819.0815	58.26479	24.2771

263

MORTGAGE OF $1000. FOR 27 YEARS AT 7.50 PERCENT

MONTHLY PAYMENT :$ 7.207613

END OF YEAR	BALANCE DUE	INTEREST	MTGE. REDUCT.
1	988.104	74.59535	11.896
2	975.2849	73.67226	12.81909
3	961.47	72.67641	13.81494
4	946.5828	71.60414	14.88721
5	930.5398	70.44838	16.04297
6	913.2512	69.20277	17.28857
7	894.6201	67.86024	18.6311
8	874.543	66.4142	20.07715
9	852.9072	64.85561	21.63574
10	829.5923	63.17641	23.31494

MORTGAGE OF $1000. FOR 27 YEARS AT 8.00 PERCENT

MONTHLY PAYMENT :$ 7.54301

END OF YEAR	BALANCE DUE	INTEREST	MTGE. REDUCT.
1	989.0881	79.60425	10.91187
2	977.2705	78.69849	11.81763
3	964.4722	77.71777	12.79834
4	950.6118	76.65576	13.86035
5	935.6006	75.50488	15.01123
6	919.344	74.25952	16.25659
7	901.738	72.91016	17.60596
8	882.6707	71.44873	19.06738
9	862.0205	69.86597	20.65015
10	839.6565	68.1521	22.36401

MORTGAGE OF $1000. FOR 27 YEARS AT 8.50 PERCENT

MONTHLY PAYMENT :$ 7.884368

END OF YEAR	BALANCE DUE	INTEREST	MTGE. REDUCT.
1	990.0032	84.61559	9.996826
2	979.1221	83.73131	10.8811
3	967.2795	82.76988	11.84253
4	954.3901	81.72301	12.8894
5	940.3613	80.5836	14.02881
6	925.0925	79.34361	15.2688
7	908.4739	77.99376	16.61865
8	890.3867	76.52525	18.08716
9	870.7004	74.92613	19.68628
10	849.2744	73.18639	21.42603

MORTGAGE OF $1000.   FOR   27   YEARS AT   9.00   PERCENT

MONTHLY PAYMENT :$ 8.231372

END OF YEAR	BALANCE DUE	INTEREST	MTGE. REDUCT.
1	990.8506	89.62704	9.149414
2	980.843	88.76889	10.007568
3	969.8967	87.83017	10.94629
4	957.9238	86.80356	11.9729
5	944.8279	85.68051	13.09595
6	930.5034	84.452	14.32446
7	914.8352	83.10825	15.66821
8	897.6968	81.63803	17.13843
9	878.9509	80.03061	18.74585
10	858.4465	78.27206	20.50439

MORTGAGE OF $1000.   FOR   27   YEARS AT   9.50   PERCENT

MONTHLY PAYMENT :$ 8.583693

END OF YEAR	BALANCE DUE	INTEREST	MTGE. REDUCT.
1	991.6362	94.64053	8.36377
2	982.4424	93.81046	9.193848
3	972.3362	92.8981	10.106201
4	961.2266	91.89468	11.10962
5	949.0154	90.79312	12.21118
6	935.5918	89.58072	13.42358
7	920.8354	88.24796	14.75635
8	904.615	86.78384	16.22046
9	886.7847	85.17398	17.83032
10	867.1848	83.40445	19.59985

MORTGAGE OF $1000.   FOR   27   YEARS AT   10.00   PERCENT

MONTHLY PAYMENT :$ 8.94103

END OF YEAR	BALANCE DUE	INTEREST	MTGE. REDUCT.
1	992.3625	99.65489	7.637451
2	983.9253	98.85509	8.437256
3	974.6045	97.97154	9.320801
4	964.3076	96.99547	10.296875
5	952.9329	95.91759	11.37476
6	940.3669	94.72643	12.56592
7	926.4846	93.41002	13.88232
8	911.1487	91.95641	15.33594
9	894.2075	90.35118	16.94116
10	875.4919	88.57677	18.71558

MORTGAGE OF $1000. FOR 28 YEARS AT 6.00 PERCENT

MONTHLY PAYMENT :$ 6.151742

END OF YEAR	BALANCE DUE	INTEREST	MTGE. REDUCT.
1	985.7913	59.61215	14.20874
2	970.7065	58.73618	15.08472
3	954.6912	57.80551	16.01538
4	937.6877	56.81747	17.00342
5	919.6362	55.76938	18.05151
6	900.4705	54.65512	19.16577
7	880.1233	53.47372	20.34717
8	858.5208	52.21835	21.60254
9	835.5859	50.88608	22.93481
10	811.2368	49.47177	24.34912

MORTGAGE OF $1000. FOR 28 YEARS AT 6.50 PERCENT

MONTHLY PAYMENT :$ 6.470564

END OF YEAR	BALANCE DUE	INTEREST	MTGE. REDUCT.
1	986.968	64.61478	13.03198
2	973.0637	63.74246	13.9043
3	958.228	62.81107	14.83569
4	942.3984	61.81717	15.82959
5	925.5088	60.75711	16.88965
6	907.4885	59.6265	18.02026
7	888.261	58.41922	19.22754
8	867.7463	57.13211	20.51465
9	845.8574	55.75784	21.88892
10	822.5022	54.29153	23.35522

MORTGAGE OF $1000. FOR 28 YEARS AT 7.00 PERCENT

MONTHLY PAYMENT :$ 6.796407

END OF YEAR	BALANCE DUE	INTEREST	MTGE. REDUCT.
1	988.064	69.62083	11.93604
2	975.2646	68.75755	12.79932
3	961.5403	67.8325	13.72437
4	946.8232	66.83983	14.71704
5	931.0425	65.77611	15.78076
6	914.1218	64.63622	16.92065
7	895.9778	63.41283	18.14404
8	876.5215	62.10057	19.4563
9	855.6589	60.69432	20.86255
10	833.2883	59.18626	22.37061

MORTGAGE OF $1000. FOR 28 YEARS AT 7.50 PERCENT

MONTHLY PAYMENT :$ 7.128932

END OF YEAR	BALANCE DUE	INTEREST	MTGE. REDUCT.
1	989.0813	74.62848	10.9187
2	977.3149	73.78082	11.76635
3	964.635	72.86725	12.67993
4	950.9705	71.88263	13.66455
5	936.2454	70.82208	14.7251
6	920.3774	69.67926	15.86792
7	903.2776	68.44733	17.09985
8	884.8499	67.11945	18.42773
9	864.9917	65.68903	19.85815
10	843.592	64.14752	21.39966

MORTGAGE OF $1000. FOR 28 YEARS AT 8.00 PERCENT

MONTHLY PAYMENT :$ 7.467782

END OF YEAR	BALANCE DUE	INTEREST	MTGE. REDUCT.
1	990.0247	79.63803	9.975342
2	979.2217	78.81039	10.80298
3	967.522	77.91367	11.69971
4	954.8511	76.94247	12.6709
5	941.1284	75.89072	13.72266
6	926.2671	74.75204	14.86133
7	910.1719	73.51816	16.09521
8	892.741	72.18246	17.43091
9	873.8633	70.73569	18.87769
10	853.4192	69.16928	20.44409

MORTGAGE OF $1000. FOR 28 YEARS AT 8.50 PERCENT

MONTHLY PAYMENT :$ 7.812618

END OF YEAR	BALANCE DUE	INTEREST	MTGE. REDUCT.
1	990.8977	84.64912	9.102295
2	980.991	83.84468	9.906738
3	970.2092	82.96968	10.78174
4	958.4739	82.01607	11.73535
5	945.7017	80.9792	12.77222
6	931.8003	79.85005	13.90137
7	916.6699	78.62105	15.13037
8	900.2024	77.28389	16.46753
9	882.2791	75.82808	17.92334
10	862.7722	74.24458	19.50684

MORTGAGE OF $1000. FOR 28 YEARS AT 9.00 PERCENT

MONTHLY PAYMENT :$ 8.163105

END OF YEAR	BALANCE DUE	INTEREST	MTGE. REDUCT.
1	991.7051	89.66234	8.294922
2	982.6316	88.88377	9.073486
3	972.707	88.0327	9.924561
4	961.8511	87.1013	10.85596
5	949.9773	86.08348	11.87378
6	936.9897	84.96971	12.98755
7	922.7837	83.75121	14.20605
8	907.2449	82.41844	15.53882
9	890.2483	80.96068	16.99658
10	871.6575	79.36644	18.59082

MORTGAGE OF $1000. FOR 28 YEARS AT 9.50 PERCENT

MONTHLY PAYMENT :$ 8.518889

END OF YEAR	BALANCE DUE	INTEREST	MTGE. REDUCT.
1	992.4487	94.6754	7.55127
2	984.1482	93.92613	8.300537
3	975.0237	93.10216	9.124512
4	964.9937	92.19664	10.030029
5	953.9678	91.20079	11.02588
6	941.8474	90.10631	12.12036
7	928.5249	88.90416	13.32251
8	913.8804	87.58214	14.64453
9	897.7822	86.12852	16.09814
10	880.0859	84.53038	17.69629

MORTGAGE OF $1000. FOR 28 YEARS AT 10.00 PERCENT

MONTHLY PAYMENT :$ 8.879651

END OF YEAR	BALANCE DUE	INTEREST	MTGE. REDUCT.
1	993.1335	99.68935	6.866455
2	985.5486	98.97084	7.584961
3	977.1692	98.17641	8.379395
4	967.9121	97.29872	9.25708
5	957.686	96.32973	10.226074
6	946.3894	95.25917	11.29663
7	933.9097	94.07607	12.47974
8	920.1228	92.76894	13.78687
9	904.8923	91.32533	15.23047
10	888.0667	89.73012	16.82568

MORTGAGE OF $1000. FOR   29 YEARS AT   6.00 PERCENT

MONTHLY PAYMENT :$ 6.070521

END OF YEAR	BALANCE DUE	INTEREST	MTGE. REDUCT.
1	986.793	59.63922	13.20703
2	972.7717	58.82501	14.02124
3	957.8853	57.95978	14.88647
4	942.0811	57.04205	15.8042
5	925.3025	56.06769	16.77856
6	907.4885	55.03229	17.81396
7	888.5757	53.93341	18.91284
8	868.4963	52.76691	20.07935
9	847.179	51.52887	21.31738
10	824.5466	50.21393	22.63232

MORTGAGE OF $1000.   FOR   29 YEARS AT   6.50 PERCENT

MONTHLY PAYMENT :$ 6.392507

END OF YEAR	BALANCE DUE	INTEREST	MTGE. REDUCT.
1	987.9333	64.64342	12.06665
2	975.0583	63.83507	12.875
3	961.3215	62.97325	13.73682
4	946.6641	62.0526	14.65747
5	931.0254	61.0714	15.63867
6	914.3391	60.02379	16.68628
7	896.5361	58.90709	17.80298
8	877.5405	57.71446	18.99561
9	857.2727	56.44225	20.26782
10	835.6472	55.08458	21.62549

MORTGAGE OF $1000.   FOR   .29 YEARS AT   7.00 PERCENT

MONTHLY PAYMENT :$ 6.721603

END OF YEAR	BALANCE DUE	INTEREST	MTGE. REDUCT.
1	988.991	69.65021	11.00903
2	977.1851	68.85333	11.80591
3	964.5266	68.00079	12.65845
4	950.9529	67.08551	13.57373
5	936.3975	66.10382	14.55542
6	920.7903	65.05206	15.60718
7	904.0544	63.9234	16.73584
8	886.1091	62.71393	17.94531
9	866.8667	61.41681	19.24243
10	846.2332	60.0257	20.63354

MORTGAGE OF $1000. FOR 29 YEARS AT   7.50 PERCENT

MONTHLY PAYMENT :$ 7.057441

END OF YEAR	BALANCE DUE	INTEREST	MTGE. REDUCT.
1	989.9695	74.65877	10.030518
2	979.1602	73.87996	10.80933
3	967.5115	73.0406	11.64868
4	954.9587	72.13655	12.55273
5	941.4309	71.16145	13.52783
6	926.8538	70.11214	14.57715
7	911.1445	68.98006	15.70923
8	894.2163	67.76106	16.92822
9	875.9731	66.44612	18.24316
10	856.3137	65.02986	19.65942

MORTGAGE OF $1000. FOR 29 YEARS AT   8.00 PERCENT

MONTHLY PAYMENT :$ 7.39964

END OF YEAR	BALANCE DUE	INTEREST	MTGE. REDUCT.
1	990.8728	79.66847	9.127197
2	980.9885	78.91139	9.884277
3	970.2834	78.09059	10.70508
4	958.6904	77.20265	11.59302
5	946.135	76.24025	12.55542
6	932.5371	75.19777	13.5979
7	917.811	74.0696	14.72607
8	901.863	72.84767	15.948
9	884.5906	71.52321	17.27246
10	865.8853	70.09035	18.70532

MORTGAGE OF $1000. FOR 29 YEARS AT   8.50 PERCENT

MONTHLY PAYMENT :$ 7.747838

END OF YEAR	BALANCE DUE	INTEREST	MTGE. REDUCT.
1	991.7065	84.68059	8.293457
2	982.6799	83.94743	9.026611
3	972.8552	83.14934	9.824707
4	962.1619	82.28069	10.69336
5	950.5242	81.33635	11.6377
6	937.8574	80.3073	12.66675
7	924.071	79.18767	13.78638
8	909.0664	77.96941	15.00464
9	892.7351	76.64275	16.3313
10	874.9607	75.19963	17.77441

MORTGAGE OF $1000. FOR 29 YEARS AT 9.00 PERCENT

MONTHLY PAYMENT :$ 8.101674

END OF YEAR	BALANCE DUE	INTEREST	MTGE. REDUCT.
1	992.4731	89.69322	7.526855
2	984.2402	88.98717	8.23291
3	975.2351	88.21495	9.005127
4	965.385	87.36998	9.850098
5	954.6108	86.44591	10.77417
6	942.8264	85.43565	11.78442
7	929.9363	84.32994	12.89014
8	915.8372	83.12096	14.09912
9	900.4153	81.7982	15.42188
10	883.5471	80.35191	16.86816

MORTGAGE OF $1000. FOR 29 YEARS AT 9.50 PERCENT

MONTHLY PAYMENT :$ 8.460783

END OF YEAR	BALANCE DUE	INTEREST	MTGE. REDUCT.
1	993.177	94.70639	6.822998
2	985.6775	94.02988	7.499512
3	977.4331	93.285	8.244385
4	968.3706	92.46689	9.0625
5	958.408	91.56674	9.962646
6	947.4575	90.57895	10.95044
7	935.4204	89.49228	12.03711
8	922.1882	88.29721	13.23218
9	907.6428	86.98398	14.54541
10	891.6543	85.54086	15.98853

MORTGAGE OF $1000. FOR 29 YEARS AT 10.00 PERCENT

MONTHLY PAYMENT :$ 8.824818

END OF YEAR	BALANCE DUE	INTEREST	MTGE. REDUCT.
1	993.8228	99.72057	6.177246
2	986.9985	99.07359	6.824219
3	979.4604	98.35973	7.538086
4	971.1326	97.56993	8.327881
5	961.9326	96.69786	9.199951
6	951.7693	95.73448	10.16333
7	940.5415	94.67003	11.22778
8	928.1377	93.494	12.40381
9	914.4355	92.19566	13.70215
10	899.2986	90.76085	15.13696

MORTGAGE OF $1000. FOR 30 YEARS AT 6.00 PERCENT

MONTHLY PAYMENT :$ 5.995955

END OF YEAR	BALANCE DUE	INTEREST	MTGE. REDUCT.
1	987.7129	59.66435	12.28711
2	974.668	58.90654	13.04492
3	960.8184	58.10185	13.84961
4	946.1145	57.2476	14.70386
5	930.5042	56.34111	15.61035
6	913.9307	55.37798	16.57349
7	896.3352	54.356	17.59546
8	877.6545	53.2708	18.68066
9	857.8213	52.11821	19.83325
10	836.7649	50.89507	21.0564

MORTGAGE OF $1000. FOR 30 YEARS AT 6.50 PERCENT

MONTHLY PAYMENT :$ 6.321038

END OF YEAR	BALANCE DUE	INTEREST	MTGE. REDUCT.
1	988.8169	64.66936	11.18311
2	976.8853	63.92082	11.93164
3	964.1538	63.12102	12.73145
4	950.5703	62.26897	13.5835
5	936.0771	61.3593	14.49316
6	920.613	60.38835	15.46411
7	904.1138	59.3532	16.49927
8	886.5088	58.24748	17.60498
9	867.7249	57.06853	18.78394
10	847.6831	55.81071	20.04175

MORTGAGE OF $1000. FOR 30 YEARS AT 7.00 PERCENT

MONTHLY PAYMENT :$ 6.653307

END OF YEAR	BALANCE DUE	INTEREST	MTGE. REDUCT.
1	989.8372	69.67683	10.162842
2	978.9395	68.94197	10.89771
3	967.2544	68.15462	11.68506
4	954.7241	67.3094	12.53027
5	941.2881	66.40364	13.43604
6	926.8804	65.43196	14.40771
7	911.4319	64.39119	15.44849
8	894.8665	63.27425	16.56543
9	877.1033	62.07649	17.76318
10	858.0566	60.79305	19.04663

MORTGAGE OF $1000. FOR 30 YEARS AT 7.50 PERCENT

MONTHLY PAYMENT :$ 6.992369

END OF YEAR	BALANCE DUE	INTEREST	MTGE. REDUCT.
1	990.7773	74.68576	9.222656
2	980.8391	73.97018	9.938232
3	970.1294	73.1987	10.70972
4	958.5876	72.36667	11.54175
5	946.1501	71.47092	12.4375
6	932.7471	70.50534	13.40308
7	918.3032	69.46457	14.44385
8	902.7383	68.34348	15.56494
9	885.9651	67.13522	16.77319
10	867.8899	65.83322	18.0752

MORTGAGE OF $1000. FOR 30 YEARS AT 8.00 PERCENT

MONTHLY PAYMENT :$ 7.337812

END OF YEAR	BALANCE DUE	INTEREST	MTGE. REDUCT.
1	991.6431	79.69681	8.356934
2	982.5923	79.00296	9.050781
3	972.7903	78.25174	9.802002
4	962.1748	77.43826	10.61548
5	950.6787	76.55765	11.49609
6	938.2275	75.60257	12.45117
7	924.7432	74.56937	13.48438
8	910.1394	73.44998	14.60376
9	894.324	72.23831	15.81543
10	877.196	70.92581	17.12793

MORTGAGE OF $1000. FOR 30 YEARS AT 8.50 PERCENT

MONTHLY PAYMENT :$ 7.68926

END OF YEAR	BALANCE DUE	INTEREST	MTGE. REDUCT.
1	992.4375	84.70862	7.5625
2	984.2061	84.03967	8.231445
3	975.2476	83.31262	8.958496
4	965.4973	82.52087	9.750244
5	954.885	81.65881	10.6123
6	943.3352	80.72131	11.5498
7	930.7637	79.69958	12.57153
8	917.0811	78.5885	13.68262
9	902.1885	77.37854	14.89258
10	885.9802	76.06287	16.20825

MORTGAGE OF $1000. FOR 30 YEARS AT 9.00 PERCENT

MONTHLY PAYMENT :$ 8.046316

END OF YEAR	BALANCE DUE	INTEREST	MTGE. REDUCT.
1	993.1655	89.72131	6.834473
2	985.6902	89.08044	7.475342
3	977.5129	88.37854	8.177246
4	968.5693	87.61218	8.943604
5	958.7861	86.77258	9.783203
6	948.0854	85.8551	10.70068
7	936.3809	84.8512	11.70459
8	923.5779	83.75281	12.80298
9	909.5745	82.55237	14.00342
10	894.2573	81.23865	15.31714

MORTGAGE OF $1000. FOR 30 YEARS AT 9.50 PERCENT

MONTHLY PAYMENT :$ 8.408607

END OF YEAR	BALANCE DUE	INTEREST	MTGE. REDUCT.
1	993.8315	94.73482	6.168457
2	987.051	94.12276	6.780518
3	979.5974	93.44966	7.453613
4	971.4036	92.70943	8.193848
5	962.397	91.89668	9.006592
6	952.4966	91.00288	9.900391
7	941.6133	90.01997	10.8833
8	929.6499	88.9399	11.96338
9	916.499	87.7524	13.15088
10	902.0435	86.44771	14.45557

MORTGAGE OF $1000. FOR 30 YEARS AT 10.00 PERCENT

MONTHLY PAYMENT :$ 8.775758

END OF YEAR	BALANCE DUE	INTEREST	MTGE. REDUCT.
1	994.4395	99.74854	5.560547
2	988.2964	99.16602	6.143066
3	981.5098	98.52246	6.786621
4	974.0129	97.81226	7.496826
5	965.731	97.0271	8.281982
6	956.5818	96.15991	9.14917
7	946.4741	95.20142	10.107666
8	935.3086	94.14355	11.16553
9	922.9739	92.97437	12.33472
10	909.3474	91.68262	13.62646

Table II   Payment Stipulated

Rates: 6% to 10%, ½% intervals

MORTGAGE OF $1000. AT   6.00 PERCENT

PAYMENT STIPULATED AT 1% OF LOAN.

MONTHLY PAYMENT :$ 10

END OF YEAR	BALANCE DUE	INTEREST	MTGE. REDUCT.
1	938.3208	58.3208	61.6792
2	872.8372	54.51636	65.48364
3	803.3147	50.47754	69.52246
4	729.5046	46.18994	73.81006
5	651.1418	41.63721	78.36279
6	567.9456	36.80371	83.19629
7	479.6179	31.67236	88.32764
8	385.843	26.2251	93.7749
9	286.2837	20.44067	99.55933
10	180.5851	14.30142	105.6986

MORTGAGE OF $1000. AT   6.50 PERCENT

PAYMENT STIPULATED AT 1% OF LOAN.

MONTHLY PAYMENT :$ 10

END OF YEAR	BALANCE DUE	INTEREST	MTGE. REDUCT.
1	943.3301	63.33008	56.66992
2	882.8647	59.53467	60.46533
3	818.3501	55.48535	64.51465
4	749.5146	51.16455	68.83545
5	676.0691	46.55444	73.44556
6	597.7051	41.63599	78.36401
7	514.093	36.38794	83.61206
8	424.8811	30.78809	89.21191
9	329.6943	24.81323	95.18677
10	228.1332	18.43887	101.56113

MORTGAGE OF $1000. AT   7.00 PERCENT

PAYMENT STIPULATED AT 1% OF LOAN.

MONTHLY PAYMENT :$ 10

END OF YEAR	BALANCE DUE	INTEREST	MTGE. REDUCT.
1	948.3628	68.36279	51.63721
2	892.9927	64.62988	55.37012
3	833.6204	60.62769	59.37231
4	769.9556	56.33521	63.66479
5	701.6887	51.73315	68.26685
6	628.4866	46.79785	73.20215
7	549.9929	41.50635	78.49365
8	465.8252	35.83228	84.16772
9	375.573	29.7478	90.2522
10	278.7959	23.2229	96.7771

MORTGAGE OF $1000. AT 7.50 PERCENT

PAYMENT STIPULATED AT 1% OF LOAN.

MONTHLY PAYMENT :$ 10

END OF YEAR	BALANCE DUE	INTEREST	MTGE. REDUCT.
1	953.4197	73.41968	46.58032
2	903.2227	69.80298	50.19702
3	849.1287	65.90601	54.09399
4	790.8352	61.70654	58.29346
5	728.0156	57.18042	62.81958
6	660.3198	52.3042	67.6958
7	587.3684	47.04858	72.95142
8	508.7539	41.3855	78.6145
9	424.0366	35.28271	84.71729
10	332.7422	28.70557	91.29443

MORTGAGE OF $1000. AT 8.00 PERCENT

PAYMENT STIPULATED AT 1% OF LOAN.

MONTHLY PAYMENT :$ 10

END OF YEAR	BALANCE DUE	INTEREST	MTGE. REDUCT.
1	958.4988	78.49878	41.50122
2	913.5532	75.05444	44.94556
3	864.8767	71.32349	48.67651
4	812.1604	67.28369	52.71631
5	755.0686	62.9082	57.0918
6	693.2378	58.16919	61.83081
7	626.2759	53.03809	66.96191
8	553.7559	47.47998	72.52002
9	475.217	41.46118	78.53882
10	390.1594	34.94238	85.05762

MORTGAGE OF $1000. AT 8.50 PERCENT

PAYMENT STIPULATED AT 1% OF LOAN.

MONTHLY PAYMENT :$ 10

END OF YEAR	BALANCE DUE	INTEREST	MTGE. REDUCT.
1	963.6023	83.60229	36.39771
2	923.9875	80.38525	39.61475
3	880.8708	76.8833	43.1167
4	833.9431	73.07227	46.92773
5	782.8674	68.92432	51.07568
6	727.2776	64.41016	55.58984
7	666.7739	59.49634	60.50366
8	600.9221	54.14819	65.85181
9	529.25	48.32788	71.67212
10	451.2424	41.99243	78.00757

MORTGAGE OF $1000. AT   9.00 PERCENT

PAYMENT STIPULATED AT 1% OF LOAN.

MONTHLY PAYMENT :$ 10

END OF YEAR	BALANCE DUE	INTEREST	MTGE. REDUCT.
1	968.7297	88.72974	31.27026
2	934.5259	85.79614	34.20386
3	897.1133	82.5874	37.4126
4	856.1912	79.07788	40.92212
5	811.4309	75.23975	44.76025
6	762.4712	71.04028	48.95972
7	708.9192	66.448	53.552
8	650.3438	61.42456	58.57544
9	586.2732	55.92944	64.07056
10	516.1926	49.91943	70.08057

MORTGAGE OF $1000. AT   9.50 PERCENT

PAYMENT STIPULATED AT 1% OF LOAN.

MONTHLY PAYMENT :$ 10

END OF YEAR	BALANCE DUE	INTEREST	MTGE. REDUCT.
1	973.8813	93.88135	26.11865
2	945.1699	91.28857	28.71143
3	913.6091	88.43921	31.56079
4	878.9163	85.30713	34.69287
5	840.7803	81.86401	38.13599
6	798.8586	78.07837	41.92163
7	752.7766	73.91797	46.08203
8	702.1213	69.34473	50.65527
9	646.4382	64.31689	55.68311
10	585.2288	58.79053	61.20947

MORTGAGE OF $1000. AT 10.00 PERCENT

PAYMENT STIPULATED AT 1% OF LOAN.

MONTHLY PAYMENT :$ 10

END OF YEAR	BALANCE DUE	INTEREST	MTGE. REDUCT.
1	979.0559	99.05591	20.94409
2	955.9185	96.86255	23.13745
3	930.3584	94.43994	25.56006
4	·902.1221	91.76367	28.23633
5	870.929	88.80688	31.19312
6	836.4692	85.54028	34.45972
7	798.4014	81.93213	38.06787
8	756.3474	77.94604	42.05396
9	709.8899	73.54248	46.45752
10	658.5674	68.67749	51.32251

Table III   Capital Appreciation Factors

For use in computing the appreciated value of an asset on a compound basis at rates from 1% to 10% per year for years held from 1 to 10.

ANNUAL COMPOUNDING AT   1.00   PERCENT

YEARS HELD	FACTOR
1	1.0099993
2	1.0200977
3	1.0302973
4	1.0405989
5	1.051003
6	1.061512
7	1.072125
8	1.082846
9	1.093673
10	1.104609

ANNUAL COMPOUNDING AT   2.00   PERCENT

YEARS HELD	FACTOR
1	1.0199995
2	1.0403986
3	1.061206
4	1.082429
5	1.104076
6	1.126157
7	1.148679
8	1.171651
9	1.195083
10	1.218984

ANNUAL COMPOUNDING AT   3.00   PERCENT

YEARS HELD	FACTOR
1	1.0299997
2	1.060899
3	1.092725
4	1.125505
5	1.15927
6	1.194048
7	1.229869
8	1.266764
9	1.304766
10	1.343908

ANNUAL COMPOUNDING AT   4.00   PERCENT

YEARS HELD	FACTOR
1	1.04
2	1.081599
3	1.124863
4	1.169857
5	1.216651
6	1.265316
7	1.315928
8	1.368565
9	1.423306
10	1.480238

ANNUAL COMPOUNDING AT   5.00   PERCENT

YEARS HELD	FACTOR
1	1.049999
2	1.102498
3	1.157621
4	1.215501
5	1.276275
6	1.340087
7	1.40709
8	1.477443
9	1.551313
10	1.628878

ANNUAL COMPOUNDING AT   6.00   PERCENT

YEARS HELD	FACTOR
1	1.059999
2	1.123598
3	1.191013
4	1.262473
5	1.338221
6	1.418512
7	1.503622
8	1.593838
9	1.689466
10	1.790833

ANNUAL COMPOUNDING AT   7.00   PERCENT

YEARS HELD	FACTOR
1	1.07
2	1.144898
3	1.22504
4	1.310792
5	1.402547
6	1.500724
7	1.605774
8	1.718177
9	1.838449
10	1.967139

ANNUAL COMPOUNDING AT   8.00   PERCENT

YEARS HELD	FACTOR
1	1.08
2	1.166399
3	1.25971
4	1.360487
5	1.469325
6	1.58687
7	1.71382
8	1.850924
9	1.998998
10	2.158916

ANNUAL COMPOUNDING AT   9.00   PERCENT

YEARS HELD	FACTOR
1	1.089999
2	1.188098
3	1.295025
4	1.411575
5	1.538615
6	1.677089
7	1.828025
8	1.992545
9	2.171872
10	2.367338

ANNUAL COMPOUNDING AT   10.00   PERCENT

YEARS HELD	FACTOR
1	1.099999
2	1.209998
3	1.330997
4	1.464095
5	1.610503
6	1.771552
7	1.948706
8	2.143575
9	2.35793
10	2.593721

Table IV   Compound Interest Factors

For use in calculating the ending balance of a savings account.

FOR 5 PERCENT COMPOUNDED DAILY

YEAR	FACTOR
1	1.051299
2	1.105229
3	1.161926
4	1.221532
5	1.284195
6	1.350073
7	1.41933
8	1.49214
9	1.568685
10	1.649157

FOR 6 PERCENT COMPOUNDED DAILY

YEAR	FACTOR
1	1.061799
2	1.127417
3	1.197089
4	1.271068
5	1.349618
6	1.433022
7	1.521582
8	1.615614
9	1.715457
10	1.82147

FOR 7 PERCENT COMPOUNDED DAILY

YEAR	FACTOR
1	1.072
2	1.149191
3	1.231955
4	1.320691
5	1.415833
6	1.517838
7	1.627212
8	1.744475
9	1.870204
10	2.005003

FOR 7.5 PERCENT COMPOUNDED DAILY

YEAR	FACTOR
1	1.07753
2	1.161084
3	1.251132
4	1.348177
5	1.452766
6	1.565482
7	1.686953
8	1.817862
9	1.958946
10	2.110998

Index